THE ČECHS
(BOHEMIANS)
IN AMERICA

AUGUSTINE HERRMAN
The first known Čech immigrant in America

THE ČECHS
(BOHEMIANS)
IN AMERICA

A STUDY OF THEIR NATIONAL, CULTURAL
POLITICAL, SOCIAL, ECONOMIC
AND RELIGIOUS LIFE

By THOMAS ČAPEK

AUTHOR OF BOHEMIAN (ČECH) BIBLIOGRAPHY, ETC.

Illustrated

GREENWOOD PRESS, PUBLISHERS
WESTPORT, CONNECTICUT

Originally published in 1920
by Houghton Mifflin Company, Boston and New York

First Greenwood Reprinting 1970

Library of Congress Catalogue Card Number 74-109745

SBN 8371-4205-9

Printed in the United States of America

INTRODUCTORY

THE subject of Germanic immigration has been treated in all its aspects, in German and in English alike. Literature relating to the settling of the Scandinavians, notably Swedes, is considerable. The achievements of the Irish, the English, and the Dutch have been recorded in detail by numerous writers. That the story of Spanish colonization is adequately described goes without saying, for the Spaniards, like the Dutch, the English, and in a lesser degree the French, were history-makers on a large scale. The large influx of Jews to the United States within the last three decades has stimulated scholars of the Hebrew race to study more intensively than ever before their past here.

What has been written on the theme of Čech immigration? In English very little. Emily Greene Balch's volume, *Our Slavic Fellow Citizens*, discusses not Čechs alone, but all the Slavs; besides, Miss Balch devotes the greater portion of her book to the consideration of her favorite subject, economy. My volume aims to throw light, not only on the economic condition of the Čech immigrant, but on his national, historic, religious, cultural, and social state as well.

Considerable has, of course, been written, here and abroad, on the various phases of what the

INTRODUCTORY

Čechs loosely call their "national life" in America, although a full, connected story of the transatlantic branch of the race is still unwritten even in the national tongue.

In 1908 the St. Louis *Hlas* published the *Dějiny Čechův Amerických* (History of the Čechs in America), by Dr. John Habenicht of Chicago. The volume is not sufficiently dispassionate to fall within the more rigid definition of historical writing. It is frankly propagandist literature and ardently partisan.

In compiling this work I have made generous use of the memoirs of pioneers in the Almanac *Amerikán*. Useful data are stored in the *Památníky* (Memorials) which various lodges publish from time to time to commemorate some noted event in their existence. Old newspaper files have yielded abundant, if not always authoritative, information. I have had access to the files of the *Slavie, Dennice Novověku, Pokrok Západu, Dělník Americký, New Yorské Listy,* and other papers. Of the greatest help to me were notes which I had collected for my work, *Padesát Let Českého Tisku v Americe* (Fifty Years of Bohemian Letters in America, published in 1911). This volume contains a complete list of books, brochures, and newspapers beginning with January 1, 1860, the day and year the first Čech language paper made its appearance on this continent. To Mr. Miloš Lier, of the University of Prague, I am indebted for valuable material which

INTRODUCTORY

he extracted from the files of Prague papers bearing on emigration between the years 1848–60.

Statistics are not always dependable. In five or ten years the figures here quoted will be out of date. America, which still feels the growing pains of national adolescence, has a way of confounding the statistician. When I finger the pages of Dr. John Palacký's book, *Spojené Státy Severoamerické* (United States of North America), I can hardly realize that the mass of figures contained in that volume relate to the land in which I live — so unlike is the America of 1919 and Palacký's America of 1876.

I do not describe Čech America as a tourist who passes hurriedly through a foreign country and records the impressions of the moment; I write as a close relative, a member of the family, who for thirty-nine years has lived uninterruptedly in Čech America or very close to its border. I know it in its holiday attire and in its working clothes. I know its faults, which are many, and its virtues, which, I like to think, outweigh them. A residence of seven years in Omaha, spent partly in a newspaper office, partly in a law office, gave me a rare opportunity to observe at close range the evolution of the virile settler of the Middle West, while life in large cities (in New York since 1894) has brought me in direct and daily contact with the men and women who live in those queer but cozy corners of America called, somewhat patronizingly, "foreign quarters."

INTRODUCTORY

The Čechs sent to America not adventurers, but *bona-fide* settlers almost synchronously with the Dutch and earlier than the Swedes. Driven from their native land in the first half of the seventeenth century, Čech Protestant exiles are known to have settled in New Amsterdam, the present New York, and among the English in Virginia. The real Čech immigration, however, dates from 1848, the year of revolutionary changes in Austria, and it is of that immigration that the volume, *The Čechs (Bohemians) in America*, chiefly treats.

Most of the men and women who have taken a leading part in the affairs of American Čechs I have known personally, many of them intimately. My list of friends and acquaintances has included Charles Jonáš, F. B. Zdrůbek, L. J. Palda, John Rosický, Bartoš Bittner, Josephine Humpal-Zeman, Frances Gregor, Vojta Mašek, John Borecký, John Karel, Paul Albieri, Edward Rosewater, Frank Škarda, John A. Oliverius, Václav Šnajdr. Of these Václav Šnajdr is the only one now living. I exchanged letters with Joseph Pastor and corresponded with the widow of Frank Mráček, latterly a resident of Odessa, Russia, and with the widow of Vojta Náprstek. I never had the good fortune to meet Ladimír Klácel, but heard sufficient concerning that unhappy philosopher from my brother to enable me to form a fairly accurate picture of the purely human side of the man. The younger men and women who now stand at the helm of affairs are known to me personally or through their work. Thirty-odd years ago Čech America was so Lilliputian that it was possible, without consulting *Who's Who*, for every one to know every one else. If a meeting of nationals was held, all the men of consequence could be crowded under a common roof, if not conveniently seated around one table. Those were the days when the newspaper editors were the sole intellectuals of the nation. The politicians, big and little, lawyers, teachers, physicians, merchants, and others who presently clamor for their share of sunshine and popularity, were yet unborn or were striplings, attending school, when the veteran journalists like Jonáš ruled Čech America.

As appears from the context, the volume discusses the Čech branch of the Čechoslovak nation only; the Slovaks are not included, for although the two race groups live side by side in several urban centers, each attends its own churches, patronizes its own club-houses, joins its own fraternal and other societies, lives its separate life. The Čech immigration was fully thirty years old when the Slovaks began coming in. Their habitats are not the same. The Slovaks, as is shown by statistics, are massed in Pennsylvania, where the Čech population is small by comparison.

Is the Čech an asset or a liability to his adopted country?

"Our nation," comments Charles Veleminský, a

pedagogue who traveled in the United States, "has ever been idealistic, sacrificing all for its ideals. Idealism is the most precious offering of the Čech immigrant to America. Without ideals even practical America is unthinkable." The Declaration of Independence of the Čechoslovak Nation pledges itself to uphold the ideals of modern democracy "as they have been the ideals of the Čechs for centuries." From Hus to Havlíček the Čech has waged a ceaseless, though at times a losing war against the sinister powers of reaction. In the course of the struggle and directly due to it, his native land lost political independence, but the conqueror could not stifle in him the lofty ideals he inherited from his Hussite forebears.

The Čech is self-reliant. Note the names of the deputies in the former Austrian Parliament, or those now guiding the affairs of the Republic: Dr. Rieger, Dr. Pacák, Dr. Kramář, Dr. Soukup, Mr. Klofáč — all commoners. On the other hand, observe, for the sake of comparison, who had been the spokesmen of the Magyars in the Hungarian Parliament: Count Károlyi, Count Andrássy, Count Batthyány, Count Tisza, Count Apponyi. The native Čech nobility practically disappeared in the seventeenth century. The aristocracy owning estates in Bohemia was, up to the time of the war, almost without exception Austrian in sentiment, ultramontane in politics, feudal in traditions. Stern necessity has taught the Čech commoner to rely on none save himself, to think and act for himself. It is astounding what progress in art, literature, commerce, and industry he has made within the last few decades of national revival unaided by aristocracy and hampered, if anything, by the Vienna Government.

He is intelligent. At Ellis Island he has established two records. Of all the races from the old Dual Empire, Germans and Magyars not excepted, the Čech was the lowest in the percentage of illiterates — one and one half per cent — and the highest in the percentage of skilled labor. If it is true, as their enemies contend, that the Slavs are as yet barbarians, the Čech, who in culture is foremost among the Slavs, can boast of being the first barbarian in Europe.

THOMAS ČAPEK

BEDFORD PARK, NEW YORK CITY
October, 1919

CONTENTS

CONTENTS

ILLUSTRATIONS

ILLUSTRATIONS

ILLUSTRATIONS

ILLUSTRATIONS

ILLUSTRATIONS

NOTE ON ČECH PRONUNCIATION

THE diacritic mark occurs on the following letters: á, é, ě, č, ď, í, ň, ř, š, ť, ú, ů, ý, ž. Ď and ó are seldom used. The mark tends alike to soften and shade the sound of the letter.

> á is pronounced long as in darling.
>
> é as a in care.
>
> ě as ye in yellow.
>
> č as ch in cherry.
>
> í and ý as ee in tree.
>
> ň as ñ in cañon.
>
> ř as rsh in Pershing.
>
> š as sh in shall.
>
> ú and ů long as in rule.
>
> ž as j in the French word jour.
>
> ch as in the Scottish loch.

THE ČECHS
(BOHEMIANS)
IN AMERICA

CHAPTER I
SEVENTEENTH-CENTURY IMMIGRATION

THE opening act of the drama of the Thirty
Years' War, which was essentially a struggle
for supremacy between Protestantism and Catholicism, was staged in Bohemia. The Bohemian Protestant Estates in 1619 deposed their ruler and
elected Frederick of the Palatinate, son-in-law of
James I of England, as King of Bohemia. One year
after the coronation ceremony, or to be exact,
November 8, 1620, the armies of the imperialists
engaged the Bohemian army in battle near Prague,
on what is called White Mountain, signally defeat-
ing it.

The Battle of White Mountain was destined to
become the most momentous event in the history of
Bohemia. It marked the downfall of the nation's
independence; it was directly responsible for the
collapse of Protestantism in Bohemia and in countries confederated therewith.

A number of the rebel chiefs fled from the country with Frederick; others soon followed the Winter
King, so that Liechtenstein, Lieutenant-Governor

I

of Bohemia, was able to report to his imperial master, on January 17, 1621, that the principal conspirators, to the number of sixty, were already beyond the border. Scores of suspects who could not get away in time or who, for some reason or other, scorned to save themselves by flight, were apprehended and tried for treason. On June 21, 1621, unforgettable as the "Bloody Day of Prague," twenty-seven of the rebels perished on the block. Still others were punished by the confiscation of their property, or by prison sentence.

Those condemned to suffer death were Count Joachym Andrew Šlik, Director under Frederick and Governor of Upper Lusatia; Václav Budovec of Budova, orator, traveler, and author; Christopher Harant of Polžic, a soldier and writer whose description of a journey to Egypt and Palestine is one of the ornaments of Čech literature of the seventeenth century; Count Caspar Kaplíř of Sulevic, an old man of eighty-six; Dr. John Jessenius of Jessen, a distinguished physician, rector of the University in Prague, writer and speaker. Jessenius was condemned to have his tongue cut out, to be beheaded, and to have his body quartered. The other victims who on that day gave their lives for their faith and country were: Prokop Dvořecký of Olbramovic, Frederick of Bílé, Henry Otto of Los, William Konec-Chlumský, Bohuslav of Michalovic, Diviš Černín of Chudenic, Valentin Kochan of Prachov, Tobias Šteffek of Koloděj,

SEVENTEENTH-CENTURY IMMIGRATION

Christopher Kobr, John Šultys, the mayor of Kutná Hora, Maximilian Hošťálek, the mayor of Žatec, Václav Jizbický, Henry Kozel, Andrew Kocour, Henry Řečický, Michael Vitman, Simon Vokáč, Leander Rüppel, and George Haunschild. The last two were Germans. Theodor Sixt of Ottersdorf was pardoned at the last moment on the scaffold. John Kutnaur, councilman of the Old Town of Prague, and his father-in-law, Simon Sušický, were hanged from a beam in the window of the Old Town Council Hall. Nathanael Vodňanský was hanged from a gibbet set up in the center of the Old Town Square. "On this day of grief and sorrow [1] it seemed that the victors were determined to put to the sword the whole of Bohemia and their pitiless revenge smote down all those who, by reason of their birth, their intellectual or moral attainments, their political services, their names, or their wealth, had raised themselves to the position of leaders among their people, guardians of the nation's traditions and defenders of its rights."

Count Slavata, a nobleman who himself played no inconsiderable part in the terrible drama of anti-reformation, and who, on account of his religious convictions, cannot be accused of bias, is authority for the statement that 36,000 Protestant families, including 185 houses of the nobility (some of these

[1] Ernest Denis: *Fin de l'Indépendance Bohême.* Paris, 1890. Translated into Čech by Henry Vančura. Prague, 1904; also, Antonín Gindely: *History of the Bohemian Rebellion in the Year 1618.* Prague, 1878.

3

houses numbered as many as fifty members each), spurning the Emperor's terms, went into exile.

Historians recognize three stages in the exodus of Protestants. The first emigration began in 1621 when the conqueror ordered the banishment of teachers and ministers of the gospel. By reason of this edict about a thousand members of these two professions were forced to leave the country.

Next, the wrath of the ruler turned against laymen. He caused their property to be confiscated. By the end of 1623 more than six hundred of the largest estates had been confiscated. On such a stupendous scale was the seizure of property carried out that but one fourth of the entire land in Bohemia remained undisturbed in the hands of the original owners. This brought about the second emigration.

Toward the close of 1626 Count Harrach, the Archbishop of Prague, submitted to the government a plan for the re-Catholization of Bohemia. As amended by the crown, the plan contemplated not conversion, but extirpation of the Protestants. The imperial patent of July, 1627, provided that non-Catholics should not be permitted henceforth to live in the country. Now ensued the third emigration, the most far-reaching of all.

The exiles at first sought refuge in the neighboring states of Saxony, Silesia, Hungary, and Poland. As their hopes of an early return to the native country waned, they migrated to more distant

4

lands: Transylvania, Russia, Sweden, Denmark, Hamburg, Holland, England, Brandenburg, Switzerland. Not a few of the bolder spirits sailed on Dutch and English ships to America.

In Saxony the refugees were numerous enough to people whole villages: Johanngeorgenstadt, Altgeorgfeld, Neugeorgfeld, Neusalz. Strong city colonies were formed in Schandau, Freiberg, Annaberg (at Annaberg and Freiberg were the centers of titled emigrants), Schneeberg, Zwickau, Chemnitz, and Dresden. Those professing the Lutheran faith favored Pirna and Zittau. In 1691 the Zittau community built a church, in which Čech services continued to be held till 1846. At Neusalz worship in the native language was maintained far into the second half of the eighteenth century. At Pirna the number of exiles reached 2710 by the end of 1628; in 1631 the colony counted 2256 members. By 1639 only 1700 persons remained. About fifty aristocratic families settled in Pirna. Dresden received the first contingent in 1622. Services in Čech were first permitted to be held in Dresden in 1650, and the congregation held together until 1845, when a German-speaking pastor took charge of the parish.

Bishop Komenský could truly say that his was a scattered flock. Statesmen, scholars, teachers, divines, soldiers, artisans, the flower of the nation, were forced "to eat the bitter bread of banishment."

Doctor Mathias Borbonius (Burda) of Borben-

5

hayn, Latin poet, and Paul Stránský of Zapská Stránka, author of the *Respublica Bohemiæ* (printed by the Elzevir Press in Leyden), sought asylum in the city of Thorn. George Holík, writer, resided in Germany, publishing at Wittenberg, in German, the *Blutige Thränen des hochbedrängten Böhmerlandes.*

Jacob Jacobeus of Kutná Hora, author of a short *Church History of Bohemia* (published in Amsterdam), retired to Holland.

Daniel Škréta, a Director of the Revolution, earned his living as City Clerk in Danzig.

John Raik became professor of medicine at Upsala, Sweden; Philemon taught history at Bremen. F. Natus, Orientalist, died in Braunschweig. Václav Clemens, humanist (from his birthplace also called Žebrácký, Zebracenus), dwelled from time to time in Holland, Danzig, and Sweden. He died in the last-named country, a pensioner of Chancellor Oxenstierna.

Bishop John Amos Komenský established himself in Holland. Other refugees of note who made Holland their home were Doctor Habervešl of Habernfeld, author of numerous works, one of which, *Bellum Bohemicum ab Anno 1617* was issued at Leyden; Daniel Kohout, Director of the Revolution; Paul Skála of Zhoř, author of *The Church History*, *Church Chronology*, and other learned books; Paul Ješín of Bezdědice, jurist and writer; Paul Kaplíř of Sulevic, one of the commanders of the

6

Bohemian Army; Václav William Roupovský of Roupov, jurist.

Ferdinand Charles Švihovský of Risenberg died in Amiens, Adam Lokšan of Lokšan, in Sedan.

The most famous exile who made his home in England was Václav Hollar of Prácheň, etcher. Some twenty-four hundred plates bear the name of Wenceslaus Hollar Bohemus, or Wenceslaus Hollar of Prague. Hollar died in 1677 in London. Another distinguished wanderer to England was Simon Partlic (Partlicius) of Špicberk, mathematician and author.

Samuel Martinius of Dražov, traveler, writer, theologian, leader of the Lutheran party among his countrymen, took up an abode in Germany.

Heník of Valdštein, a Director of the Revolution, died in Thorn.

Charles of Žerotín, author and statesman, served the King of Denmark in a high capacity at court.

Tobias Šteffek of Koloděj accepted service with the Prince of Anhalt.

Radslav Vchynský of Vchynic and Tetov (or Kinský, as the family name is now written), Director of the Revolution, died at Leyden. A poet of acknowledged ability, Vchynský is said to have been a master of eight languages.

The Saxon family, von Ronau, traces its ancestry to John Albrecht Křinecký of Ronov, a man of letters.

Von Treitschke, the German historian and publicist, also claims to be descended from a family of Čech exiles. So does General Woyrsch, who commanded a German army on the Polish front. Woyrsch's forebears were the Vojířs, an ancient and honorable family.

Thomas V. Bílek [1] enumerates fifty lords and knights who accepted commissions in the Swedish army alone.

Count Hendrich Mates of Thurn attained the rank of field marshal; four rose to the rank of general, Zdenko, Count of Hodic, Václav Ferdinand Sádovský of Sloupno, Wolf Colon of Fels, Frederick Sobětický of Sobětic. Colonels and lieutenant-colonels were: Jaroslav Count Kinský, Václav Čabelický of Soutic, Adam Berka of Dubé, Henry Frederick of Štampach, Mathias Jizbický, Václav Záborský of Brloh, Henry Pětipeský of Chyš, and Nicholas of Těchenic. Two were brevetted majors, eleven captains, mostly of cavalry, two quartermaster-generals, thirteen officers belonging to various lines of the service.

Exiles belonging to the military class joined as volunteers the armies of the state in which they happened to be living. Many enlisted in the Danish army; the greater part, however, made common cause with the Swedes, "shedding their blood," to quote the language of a historian, "for allies who afterward betrayed them."

---

[1] Thomas V. Bílek: *Reformace Katolická*, p. 176. Exile of non-Catholic nobility from the country. Prague, 1892.

SEVENTEENTH-CENTURY IMMIGRATION

The first known emigrant to America by way of a Dutch port was Augustine Herrman.[1] "Herrman came to New York in 1633, in the employment of the West India Company," says Charles Payson Mallery.[2] "Three years later he was appointed by the Director and Council of New Netherlands, one of the Nine Men, a body of citizens selected to assist the government by their counsel and advice." Mallery states that he was "a man of good education, a surveyor by profession, skilled in sketching and drawing, an adventurous and enterprising merchant, . . . the first beginner of the Virginia tobacco trade." Some time in 1660 he moved from New York, where he owned land along the present Pearl Street, to Bohemia Manor in Maryland. This manor consisted of some twenty thousand acres in Cecil and New Castle Counties and it was granted by Lord Baltimore in recognition of services rendered by Herrman in drawing the map of "Virginia and Maryland. As it is Planted and Inhabited this present Year 1670 Surveyed and Exactly Drawne by the Only Labour and Endeavour of Augustin Herrman, Bohemiensis."

Of Herrman's early life prior to his appearance in New Netherland, reports are conflicting. An American genealogist thinks he was born in Prague in

[1] Dutch chroniclers spell the name indifferently: Herman, Herrman, Harman, Heerman, Hermans.

[2] Charles Payson Mallery: *Ancient Families of Bohemia Manor; their Homes and their Graves.* 74 pp. The Historical Society of Delaware. Wilmington, 1888.

1605 and that his father's name was Augustine Ephraim. A Čech writer (Kořenský) has expressed the belief that Herrman might have been a scion of a noble family.

In the *Memorial Book of the Town of Mšeno* (Bohemia) Litt.D., p. 39, the following entry is recorded: "A.D. 1621, the Sunday before Christ's birth, on a cold day, our beloved pastor, Abraham Herzman, went into exile, with his family to the City of Žitava (Zittau). His noble-minded and pious wife did not live to see this humiliation, having died of grief one month before his departure. . . . Before the parish house waited a vehicle, in which sat the entire family, that is, son Augustine and three daughters. The pastor blessed his flock and followed the conveyance on foot, the people meanwhile chanting, 'From the depths of my sorrows, I appeal to Thee, Oh Lord,' and accompanying their minister to the village of Bezdědice." [1]

If the Augustine Herzman of Mšeno, disregarding the slight variation in the spelling of the surname, is not the Augustine Herrman of Bohemia Manor, it is, admittedly, a remarkable coincidence in date and name.

[1] Misled by Herrman's German-sounding name, German-American writers, notably Kapp, Faust, and Cronau, have appropriated Herrman as their own. This is an error which refutes itself. Tens of thousands of Čechs bear German names, just as there are tens of thousands of kern deutsch Germans, whose patronymics are unmistakably Slavic. Why should Herrman have signed himself on documents, as he did on his map of Virginia and Maryland, Bohemian, had he been a German? The inconsistency of this claim is obvious.

SEVENTEENTH-CENTURY IMMIGRATION

Herrman's fondness for the land of his nativity amounted to an obsession. In addition to his naming the first tract of land which he received from Lord Baltimore, Bohemia Manor, he named other land grants, Three Bohemia Sisters and Little Bohemia. The supposition is not unreasonable that Herrman contemplated founding in America a colony of compatriots. The Swedes in Delaware had established a New Sweden, the Dutch New Netherland, the Puritans New England, why not a New Bohemia? Herrman's Bohemia Manor contained sufficient elbow-room for a good-sized settlement. In a New York deed [1] he describes himself as Augustine Herrman of Nova Bohemia, in the Province of Maryland. To Herrman the misery of his co-religionists in Europe was well known, for he had been one of them. How successful he was with his colonization plan and how many, if any, Čech families found a home on his estate, local historians do not inform us.

By his will, executed in 1684 he directed that in the event of his family becoming extinct, a portion of Bohemia Manor should go to the State of Maryland for the purpose of founding a Protestant school, college and hospital, to be known by the name Augustine Bohemia.[2]

[1] Liber A, p. 145, July 9, 1672, New York City Register's Office.
[2] "Augustine Herrman, Bohemian, 1605–1686." A paper prepared by General James Grant Wilson, of New York, an honorary member of the New Jersey Hist. Soc. Read at a meeting of the Society, May 15, 1890. New Jersey Hist. Soc. *Proceedings*, v. 21, no. 2, pp. 21–34.

THE ČECHS IN AMERICA

Genealogists agree that Frederick Philipse, as the name was spelled at that period, or Vrederyck Felypsen, founder of the noted American family of that name, was a native of Bohemia. Hon. John Jay, diplomatist and jurist, has this to say of the Philipses: "The first ancestor of this family who settled in this country was Frederick Flypsen, a native of Bohemia, where his family, being Protestants, were persecuted. His mother, becoming a widow, was constrained to quit Bohemia with him and her other children. She fled to Holland with what little she could save from the wreck of their estate. The amount of that little not admitting her to provide better for Frederick, she bound him to a carpenter, and he became an excellent workman. He emigrated to New York, which was then under the Dutch Government, but in what year I am not informed." According to another source [1] Philipse's father "was the honorable Viscount Felyps of Bohemia, who sprang from the ancient viscounts of that name and country." Again: "Besides their high rank as nobles, they appear to have held the office of grand veneurs or keepers of the deer forests in Bohemia, as there is still preserved in the family the color and badge of office, consisting of a gold chain set with amethysts, diamonds, rubies and emeralds to which was suspended a deer beautifully chased in gold."

[1] Robert Bolton: *History of the County of Westchester, from its First Settlement*, p. 508. New York, 1848.

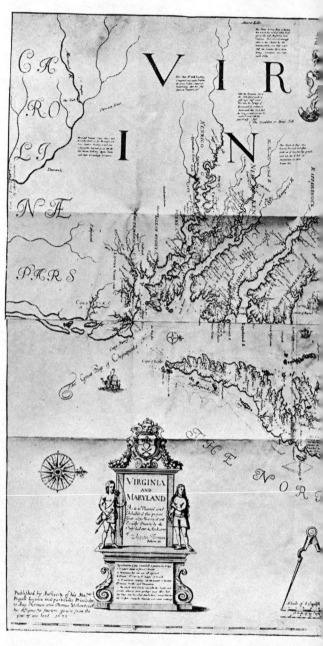

MAP OF VIRGINIA AND

AUGUSTINE HERRMAN

Singularly enough, the register of Bohemian nobility of the seventeenth century does not contain the name Philipse or Felypsen. Neither does anyone bearing that name appear to have suffered through confiscation of property. Thomas V. Bílek's *History of Bohemian Confiscation after the year 1618*, sets forth the name of every landowner whose property had been confiscated, but Philipses are not among them. Then, too, the rank of viscount was all but unknown in Bohemia. A more likely explanation is — providing, of course, that Philipses belonged to the nobility — that they had discarded their Čech name, difficult to pronounce by foreigners, assuming instead their given name, Philip. "The surname Felypsen," remarks Bolton, "is a patronymic from Philip, hence the English substitute Frederick Philipse, which at an early period became the adopted name of the family" (page 319).

Chroniclers refer to Philipse as "Bohemian merchant prince." He was one of the wealthiest men of his day in the American colonies. The Manor Hall in Yonkers, still standing, was one of the residences of the family; another seat, at Philipsburg, bore the name "Castle Philips." The story is told that George Washington fell in love with pretty Mary Philipse, a descendant of this illustrious family.

According to one version, Philipse traveled to America in 1647, on the same ship with Stuyvesant. It is certain that in 1653 the family was already in

New Amsterdam, for in that year Philipse is mentioned as one of the appraisers of the property of Augustine Herrman. This, by the way, would indicate that Herrman and Philipse knew each other.

Records prove that other natives of Bohemia lived in New Amsterdam besides Herrman and Philipse.[1]

In the Reformed Church was married, December 10, 1651, Herrman to Johanna Varlet. Another record of marriage of a Bohemian or rather a Moravian, which is one and the same, reads: "1645. 26 Febr. Jeúrian Fradell, j. m. Uyt Moravian en Tryn Herkser." Who would suspect a Bohemian under the name of Fradell?

A few years later, another Fradell, Jeúraen Simon Fradell, weduwanaer (widower), was married in the same church. From the records it is not clear whether the entry refers to Jeúrian Fradell, who had become a widower, or to another Fradell, Jeúrian Simon.

An entry in the Dutch Church notes the marriage of a girl by the name of Hollar. This might have been a relative of Wenceslaus Hollar, the etcher. Adam Unkelba, who was married in the church on September 12, 1660, was, without doubt, a Čech. Styntje Hermans, who contracted wedlock in the Dutch Church, May 14, 1655, with Cornelis Hendrickszen, may have been Herrman's sister, for

---

[1] Berthold Fernow, editor: *Marriages from 1639 to 1801 in the Reformed Dutch Church; records of New Amsterdam from 1653 to 1674.* Published by the City of New York.

the *Memorial Book of Mšeno* mentions him as having sisters. What about John Kostlo, a resident of New Amsterdam? This name is neither Dutch nor English. [1]

The Dutch Government commissioned one Loketka to go overseas and report on the condition of New Netherland. Loketka, presumably a Čech, sent an exhaustive report to his home government. Whether Loketka subsequently settled here or returned to Holland is not known.

It is more than probable that William Paca, one of the signers of the Declaration of Independence for Maryland, was of Čech extraction. Genealogists are inclined to believe that Paca is of Italian or Portuguese origin; yet if they have no other proof for their belief save the supposedly Latin structure of the name, they will be surprised to learn that the cognomen Paca, root and termination, is Čech. Pacov is the name of a town in Bohemia; Paca, Pacák, Pacovský, Pacalt, are family names common in Bohemia. Might not William Paca have been a descendant of a family which settled on Herrman's Bohemian Manor in Maryland? [2]

That Čechs settled in Virginia is attested by ship manifests. These immigrants sailing for Virginia were beyond doubt Čech: Christopher Donak, who

[1] *New Eng. Hist. and Gen. Reg.*, v. 11, p. 123.

[2] In the *Památky Českých Emigrantů v Americe*, the present author expressed the belief that Paca might be of Čech origin. J. V. Nigrin, writing to the Chicago daily *Svornost*, under date July 4, 1914, shares the belief.

15

purchased land in 1655 in Northampton County; John Doza, a fellow passenger of the Donaks, who settled in the same county; Anna Dubes, who had taken land in 1652 in Lancaster County. Other immigrants were John Duch, settling in 1650 in Northumberland County, and Anna Simco, in 1653, in the same county.[1] It is a gross exaggeration, however, to say that "between 1650–80 several thousand Čechs came to America, settling in the penal colonies of Georgia and Virginia. . . ." [2] The Čechs could not have settled in Georgia between 1650–80 for the very good reason that Georgia was first settled by a colony of one hundred and twenty whites in 1733.

That stragglers might have made their way with the Puritans to Massachusetts is more than likely; the Bohemian Church observed many of the stern concepts of religious duties which distinguished the Puritans. Matthew Cenig (Čeněk) died in Massachusetts in 1654.[3]

If the names of Elizabeth Baysa, Mary Bunc, and Loues (Louis) Standla are Čech, as they seem to be, it would go to prove that Čech exiles settled in Connecticut.[4]

[1] George Cabell Greer (clerk, Virginia State Land Office): *1623–66. Early Virginia Immigrants*. Richmond, 1912.

[2] *Památník Slovanských Baptistů v Americe*, p. 8. Chicago, 1909.

[3] *Early Records of Boston;* also, *New. Eng. Hist. and Gen. Reg.*, v. 10, p. 219.

[4] *Births, Marriage and Deaths. Original Distribution of the Town of Hartford, Connecticut, among the Settlers;* also, *New. Eng. Hist. and Gen. Reg.*, v. 12, p. 173.

SEVENTEENTH-CENTURY IMMIGRATION

Samuel Barta,[1] bearer of a typically Čech name, signed a petition dated April 22, 1755, in which settlers living along the Kennebec River in Massachusetts appealed for protection to Governor Shirley. On the obverse of the petition, the name is spelled correctly Barta; on the reverse, however, the petitioner is already transformed by the chronicler into Barter. Alexander Barta, evidently a relative of Samuel, is on the roster of prisoners who were captured by the British in 1777. Alexander, too, is spelled carelessly Barta and Barter. John Spital, in some documents assumes the anglicized name John Spittle.[2]

It is possible that individual exiles had joined the Swedes who, under Governor Prins, founded a settlement on the Delaware River (1638), naming the country New Sweden. Soldiers of Čech nationality served in the army of Gustavus Adolphus. Always friendly, the relations between the Swedes and Protestant Čechs were notably close about this time.[3]

Unerring traces of Čech exiles lead to one of the Barbados, the group of West India Islands which the British occupied in 1625. Augustine Herrman, it is known, had extensive business interests on the

---

[1] *New York Hist. and Gen. Reg.*, v. 44, pp. 203–04.

[2] *Ibid.*, v. 19, p. 136.

[3] "When the Thirty Years' War was brought to a close, Sweden, anxious to gain the friendship of all nations, sent Mathias Palbitsky to congratulate the King of Spain on the conclusion of peace." (Amandus Johnson: *The Swedes in America, 1638–1900*, v. 1, p. 164.)

island; so did his fellow countryman Frederick Philipse. The ship Expedition, bound in September, 1635, for the Barbados, had aboard one Edward Benes, a name peculiarly Čech. In the "True and Perfect List of all ye Names of ye Inhabitants in ye Parrish of Christ Church, with an Exact accompt of all ye Land, white Servants; and Neg's [negroes] within ye Said Parrish Taken this 22th Decemb 1679," we find three other Čech names: John Hudlice, tailor, who shipped from Southampton on the Virginia, Captain John Weare, bound for the Barbadoes; Edward Marsan "has 10 acres and 6 negroes," and Anthony Slany "has 2 negroes."

CHAPTER II

THE resolve of the Moravian Church to found colonies overseas marks a distinct epoch in the history of Čech emigration in the eighteenth century. These emigrants came with the Germans at the time or times when religious ferment had made people restless in Central Europe. While the seventeenth-century arrivals had been assimilated by the English or the Dutch, according to where they happened to settle, the eighteenth-century immigrants to Pennsylvania merged into the larger Teutonic immigration.

As told in detail in the preceding chapter, Protestantism in Bohemia and Moravia had been crushed in the first quarter of the seventeenth century; yet what theological writers describe as "the hidden seed" was never wholly destroyed. Here and there survived individuals and groups of individuals (in Bohemia, particularly in the Litomyšl district) who, notwithstanding stern repression, clung in secret to the proscribed faith. To be sure, open adherence thereto was out of the question; there were no houses of worship in the land and none were allowed to be built. Yet what the followers of Hus were forbidden to do publicly they could not be stopped from practicing clandestinely. Devotional literature, which partisans contrived to smuggle into the country from across the Saxon border, was found to be the most efficacious means of keeping together the faithful. The city of Zittau, in Saxony, became the recognized book mart of the Čech Protestants. There Wenzel Kleych (1678–1737) set up a printing shop, and manuals and prayer books printed in Kleych's establishment were distributed in Bohemia despite the watchfulness of the Austrian authorities. Kleych's most indefatigable assistant in this missionary activity was Adolph Christian Pescheck, himself a descendant of a family of exiles who had settled in Germany. Another name inseparably associated with Kleych's publishing house was that of John Liberda (1701–42), a schoolmaster and a pamphleteer, later a pastor of a Čech congregation in the suburb of Berlin.

The Moravians never quite forgot that Bishop Komenský had been at one time a minister of a church in Fulnek, Moravia. In 1724 a number of families, tiring of endless molestation, decided to emigrate from Moravia to Saxony. Herrnhut was the name these emigrants gave to a settlement they founded on the estate of Count Zinzendorf.

The families and individuals more or less prominent among these emigrants from Moravia were: Melchior Kunz, Andrew Beyer, Matthew Stach, John and David Zeisberger, all of Zauchtenthal; the Jaeschke and Neisser families of Sehlen; the

EIGHTEENTH-CENTURY IMMIGRATION

Grasman family of Senftleben and the Nitschmann family of Kunwald.[1]

Though they had come from German-speaking towns and villages of Moravia and bore German names, it should not be believed that all were German. There were among them co-religionists of Čech birth or ancestry as is proved by a list of them prepared by George Neisser.[2]

In border lands where the Slavs and the Teutons live side by side mixing more or less freely, the patronymic is not an unerring index to the ancestry. All are not Slavs who bear Slavic names; conversely, all are not Germans who have German names. For what they are worth, we extract from Neisser's list those patronymics which by sound or structure appear to be Čech-Slavic:

Anna Neisser, maiden name Anna Holaschek (p. 41), Catherine Riedel, maiden name Zudolska (p. 43), Thomas Procop, married Anna Neisser (p. 51), Friedrich Boenisch, married Anna Stach (p. 54), Matthew Stach (p. 55), Rosina Stach, his wife (p. 55), Melchior Kunz, married Judith Holaschek (p. 56), George Schmidt, married Maria Wachofsky (p. 55), Matthew Miksch and Martha Miksch (p.

[1] Edmund de Schweinitz: *The History of the Church known as the Unitas Fratrum.* 641 pp.

[2] George Neisser: *A List of the Bohemian and Moravian Emigrants to Saxony.* Collected from various sources in print and manuscript; begun and compiled at New York from June 2 to July 20, 1772. Translated and edited by Albert G. Rau. Transactions of the Moravian Historical Society, v. IX, parts 1 and 2. Printed for the Society. Bethlehem, Pa., 1911. Times Publishing Company.

57), Thomas Stach (p. 58), Michael Schukal and —— Schukal, his wife (p. 60), Paul Jersabeck (p. 61), Christian Stach, brother or cousin of Matthew Stach (p. 61), —— Hukuff, wife of Zacharias Hukuff (p. 64), Anna Maria Lawatsch (p. 71), Andrias Anton Lawatsch (p. 71), Joseph Bullitschek (p. 75), Wenzel Procop (p. 76), Wenzel Till (p. 76), Anna Watscheck (p. 77), Zacharias Hirschel, Čech name Gecinek, pastor in Berlin (p. 77), Balthasar Dworzinsky (p. 78), Lucas Paresch (p. 78), John Kopatschek (p. 78), —— Neskunda (p. 78), Susanna Peiter, daughter of Christopher Fakesch (p. 78), George Wenzel Golkowsky (p. 79), Susannah Helena Golkowsky (p. 80), Rosina Kisselova (p. 80), Johann Czerny (p. 80), Rosina Stuschike (p. 81), Franz Herodicz (p. 81), Anna Kreitsche, maiden name Boschena (p. 81), Dorothea Pospischill (p. 81), Carl Urban (p. 81), Matthew Pochobratsky (p. 82), John Kaplan (p. 82), Catherine Weiprachtitzke (p. 82), Eva Brachatshin (p. 82), Wenzel Slatnik (p. 83), Anna Kissela (p. 83), Wenzel Bonar (p. 83), Matthew Prokopek (p. 83), John Prokopek (p. 83), Elisabeth Keetschar, married Kowarsch (p. 83), Magdalena Fihol (p. 83), Marie Kubasek (p. 83), Andreas Broksch (p. 83), Martin Powalka (p. 83), Judith Shukal (p. 84), Jacob Swihola (p. 84), Joh. Jacob Swihola, Jr. (p. 84), Andreas Budemansky (p. 84), John Gilek (p. 84), John Matema (p. 84), Wenzel Oudrzik (p. 84), George Pakosta (p. 84), Anna Swoboda (p. 84), Carl Matschek (p. 84),

EIGHTEENTH-CENTURY IMMIGRATION

Thomas Juren (p. 85), Augustin Witthofsky (p. 85), John Holeschofsky (p. 85).

Some of the emigrants we find later among settlers in Pennsylvania. In Egle's catalogue we meet with Michael Miksch (p. 167), Catherine Butmansky (p. 168), Andrew Broksch (p. 170), Thomas Stach (p. 209), Andrew Anton Lawatsch (p. 210), George Wenceslaus Golkowsky (p. 302), Joseph Bullitschek (p. 303), Ulrick Pitcha, Anna Maria Masin, etc.[1] In another register we note these Čech surnames: Martin Blisky, John Ludwig Buda, Mathias Hora, Gabriel Gascha, Johann Seirutschek.

Without doubt a descendant of a Čech family which settled in Pennsylvania in the eighteenth century was John W. Kittera, a member of Congress from 1791 to 1801. At the completion of his congressional terms he was appointed United States District Attorney for the Eastern District of Pennsylvania and removed to Philadelphia, where he died. He was the son of Thomas Kittera of East Earl Township, Lancaster County.

The first attempt at missions by Moravians under British auspices was undertaken in Georgia. Toeltschig was one of nine missionaries sent to Georgia in 1734. Toeltschig died in Dublin in April,

[1] William Henry Egle, editor: *Notes and Queries: Historical, Biographical and Genealogical*. Relating chiefly to interior Pennyslvania. Fourth series, v. I. Also, *Names of Foreigners who took the Oath of Allegiance to the Province and State of Pennsylvania 1727-75*. With the foreign arrivals, 1786-1808. Harrisburg, Pa., 1892.

1764.[1] The second colony was founded in Pennsylvania, where the Moravians purchased a tract of five hundred acres in Bucks County in the spring of 1741, and a second tract of five thousand acres at Nazareth. To Pennsylvania now set in a steady inflow of Moravians and it is reckoned that between 1741 and 1762 upwards of seven hundred men and women, most of them members of congregations on the Continent and in Great Britain, crossed the seas and settled in Pennsylvania.[2]

[1] Abraham Reincke: *A Register of Members of the Moravian Church between 1727 and 1754.*

[2] W. C. Reichel: *A Register of the Members of the Moravian Church.* With historical annotations; also, I. Daniel Rupp: *A Collection of upwards of 30,000 Names of German, Swiss, Dutch, French and other Immigrants in Pennsylvania, from 1727–76.*

CHAPTER III

NINETEENTH-CENTURY IMMIGRATION AND AFTER

PRIOR to 1840 no one in Bohemia thought of emigrating, says a contemporary. In the first place, Bohemia experienced a wave of prosperity after the Napoleonic wars. Everything was cheap and there was plenty of work. In 1840, however, blighting droughts visited the country [1] and there was a failure of the potato crop. Suffering actual want, the Čech people at that time began to think of migrating to America. The first to leave Kutná Hora, as the gubernatorial passport of 1845 proves, was innkeeper Pospíšil, the second, cabinet-maker Fürst. The passport cost fifty florins in silver. Without it not even a mouse could slip across the border which was carefully patrolled by the grenzjägers. One incurred the risk of being shot if one attempted to cross without a passport.

In 1847, thirty-nine men of the Thirty-fifth Pilsen Regiment (Khevenhüller) escaped to America from the Mainz fortress, Tůma, the orderly of General Uhlmann, of the artillery,[2] among them. Following Tůma, these soldiers deserted: Stropek, Skála, Zajíček, Lexa, Cukr, Osoba. In 1849 the

[1] The *Pokrok Západu.* 1888. Reminiscences of Anton Kocián (Kotzian) of Břeclava.

[2] In New York Tůma bore the by-name of Čech Columbus, a jocular allusion to his early landing.

military accountant Toužimský ran away to America, having embezzled the regimental funds. The latter's successful flight gave courage to other soldiers. "I planned with twenty-one other men to get away, too," relates Anton Kocián, "inasmuch as Tůma had written us that he owned in New York a Čech Casino and that the Čechs in that city had organized a club. At times as many as 700 emigrants, chiefly from the Slané, Beroun and Kouřim district (Čech — Kraj, German — Kreis) concentrated at Mainz.[1] There they waited for the ship to sail and if not accommodated in taverns, they were given shelter in the military barracks. I am certain some of the oldest deserters will recall the circumstances well. Stropek, Zajíček, Toužimský, my school mates, were from Kutná Hora. Tůma, Lexa, Skála and Cukr belonged by domicil to Kouřim and Tábor. Where these men settled I do not know. I lost sight of the nineteen save one who, under the assumed name of Senna (Senner) worked in a brickyard in Brooklyn. Tůma was the first correspondent from America to newspapers in Bohemia. He contributed to Charles Havlíček's paper. My brother-in-law wrote me when I served in the army, that an ex-soldier, Tůma by name, from time to time wrote for the papers." [2]

[1] Emigrants traveled from Bohemia *via* Bavaria to Mainz through the traveling agency of Karl Rabe who had an emigration bureau in Rheinstrasse.

[2] If it is true, as Kocián says, that Tůma contributed to Prague papers, his letters were not published under his signature, for an

Robert H. Vickers
Author of "History of Bohemia"

Will S. Monroe
Author of "Bohemia and the Čechs"

TWO AMERICAN ČECHOPHILES

NINETEENTH-CENTURY IMMIGRATION

Until 1884 the authorities kept a record of emigration in the *Emigration Tabellen*. These tables registered annually persons who left the empire and "emigrated to foreign lands with the intention of not returning." They noted the age, sex, and property interests of the emigrant. After 1867 the authorities began to lose control of the movement, and in 1884 the central bureau of statistics in Vienna abandoned this tabulation as unsatisfactory. Instead it began to publish in the *Statistische Monatschrift* data bearing on the transoceanic emigration only, based on figures collected by Austrian consuls at the principal seaports of the world.[1]

In the sixties of the last century the Frenchman Alfred Legoyt [2] could say truthfully that the people of Austria showed no inclination to emigrate. With apparent satisfaction he noted that there were several factors which militated against emigration on a larger scale. Among other considerations there were the great distances to seaports, strict, almost prohibitive regulations by the state, prosperity among the small farmers, large areas of undeveloped land awaiting skilled cultivators, and so forth. Yet, before long, economists were amazed to wit-

examination of the files of Havlíček's journals has failed to bring out Tůma's name.

[1] Dr. J. Buzek: *Das Auswanderungs-problem und die Regelung des Auswanderungswesens in Oesterreich*, v. x, pp. 441, 553. *Zeitschrift für Volkswirtschaft, Socialpolitik und Verwaltung*. Wien und Leipzig, 1901.

[2] Alfred Legoyt (1815–85): *L'Émigration Européenne*. Paris, 1861.

ness an almost revolutionary change in this respect.

From Bohemia there were two distinct kinds of emigration: the political one which had its origin in the revolutionary disturbances of 1848; the other emigration, due to economic causes.

The wonderful stories of the discovery of gold in California excited the Čechs no less than they agitated other Europeans. Newspapers published highly colored articles about the rich California gold fields, while emigration agents, plying their trade surreptitiously, magnified what was already exaggerated by the press. Warning by the authorities against emigration had little or no effect; in a like manner admonitions by the church proved futile. It is probably true that the gold craze affected Bohemia more generally than it agitated other Austrian states. In 1853, 1311 people emigrated from Plzeň district, 1009 from Budějovice district. The year following witnessed the departure from the first-named district of 1946, from the second 1386, and from Pardubice district 1068. In 1855, Tábor district lost by emigration 649, Chrudim 499, Eger (Cheb) and Plzeň 426 each. A falling-off occurred in 1859, when only 842 left Bohemia. Non-official statisticians estimate, however, that the figures here given are by far too low and that we should strike the mark by doubling them. All told, the number of emigrants from the empire to the United States during the California gold fever excitement amounted to about 25,000.

It will be noticed in the following table that from the outset Bohemia and Moravia sent out an almost even ratio of males and females. Tabulated according to age, a majority of the emigrants were between seventeen and forty, which years, experience has demonstrated, represent a period of the highest physical productivity. In the adult male wage-earner it is a time when ambition impels him to most intensive effort and action.

EMIGRATION ACCORDING TO SEX AND AGE BETWEEN 1850–60 [1]

1850

Land	Sex		Up to 7 years	7–17 years	17–40 years	40–50 years	Past 50	Total
	Males	Females						
Bohemia	87	79	15	22	103	23	3	166
Moravia	9	4	1	5	5	2	–	13
Silesia	42	66	2	16	77	12	1	108

1851

Land	Sex		Up to 7 years	7–17 years	17–40 years	40–50 years	Past 50	Total
	Males	Females						
Bohemia	187	154	58	43	193	23	24	341
Moravia	3	8	3	1	5	1	1	11
Silesia	21	28	7	3	31	7	1	49

1852

Land	Sex		Up to 7 years	7–17 years	17–40 years	40–50 years	Past 50	Total
	Males	Females						
Bohemia	229	198	89	79	188	43	28	427
Moravia	18	19	5	12	14	6	–	37
Silesia	47	38	14	10	53	7	1	85

[1] *Mittheilungen aus dem Gebiete der Statistik*, v. XVII, part 3, p. 89. Herausgegeben von der K. K. Central = Commission. Wien, 1870.

THE ČECHS IN AMERICA

1853

Bohemia	1730	1689	300	1235	1284	480	120	3419
Moravia	140	132	69	80	93	23	5	272
Silesia	124	100	55	49	99	16	5	224

1854

Bohemia	3149	2979	1495	1315	2309	708	301	6128
Moravia	150	148	82	55	115	36	10	298
Silesia	73	74	32	31	63	14	7	147

1855

Bohemia	1507	1514	714	706	1109	324	168	3021
Moravia	252	250	123	108	200	57	14	502
Silesia	18	14	4	6	19	3	–	32

1856

Bohemia	1054	1034	480	483	790	219	116	2088
Moravia	96	89	49	49	63	19	5	185
Silesia	–	–	–	–	–	–	–	–

1857

Bohemia	1102	1065	527	460	858	219	103	2167
Moravia	29	22	8	12	22	5	4	51
Silesia	42	31	9	13	42	9	–	73

1858

Bohemia	678	663	284	300	346	141	70	1341
Moravia	49	26	6	16	39	9	5	75
Silesia	30	23	4	7	30	10	2	53

1859

Bohemia	432	410	171	176	335	112	48	842
Moravia	32	33	11	12	33	7	2	65
Silesia	23	20	3	7	32	1	–	43

1860

Bohemia	685	617	269	294	556	126	57	1302
Moravia	138	120	60	66	100	26	6	258
Silesia	31	19	5	11	29	4	1	50

30

NINETEENTH-CENTURY IMMIGRATION

During the eight years between 1860 and 1868 the emigration from Bohemia, Moravia, and Silesia was, respectively:

Year	Bohemia	Moravia	Silesia
1861	1927	88	64
1862	1246	55	25
1863	1124	52	29
1864	1950	8	57
1865	2417	38	59
1866	3089	158	66
1867	7430	371	126
1868	3220	71	64

The total number of emigrants from Austria between 1850–68 was 57,726; of this no less than 43,645 is Bohemia's share. The backward districts of the southern part of the country furnished by far the heaviest quota.

Emigration to Russia from Bohemia began to assume at this time marked proportions. Thousands were lured thither by the prospect of high wages — high, compared to wages paid in Austria — and by land grants offered to settlers by the Russian Government. After the Austro-Prussian War in 1866, the flow of surplus population toward America again increased; in fact, the Austro-Prussian War, synchronous as it was with the end of the Civil War, marked an epoch in emigration which from that year on mounted steadily and rapidly.

After 1880 the character of the emigration is seen to change noticeably. The Čechs and Germans who had been supplying the bulk of the arrivals from Austria, gradually begin to give room to a new ethnic element, the Hungarians.

Later the Jugo-Slavs follow the Hungarians and in the overshadowing figures that result, the Čech portion becomes, by comparison, negligible.

Notwithstanding strict police regulations, advertisements, though veiled, appear here and there telling of the great opportunities in America, giving instructions how to travel and other advice. *Die Constitutionelle Allgemeine Zeitung von Böhmen* (September 22, 1848) contains the advertisement of the firm of Knorr & Janssen, of Hamburg. The representative of the firm in Bohemia is Ed. Zenk of Liebenau.

Another advertisement is that of Postschiff Verbindung London-New York. Passagiere und Auswanderer aus oest. Staate. The agent is G. H. Paulsen.

The same newspaper recommends to readers in its issue of April 15, 1849, to purchase a book on America, bearing the title, *Auf, nach Amerika*, by Fr. Jäger.

An announcement, printed May 31, 1849, assures the public that despite the Danish War, emigration to America *via* Bremen proceeds uninterruptedly.

The *Pražský Večerní List* lends space (in 1849) to the following advertisements:

"May 22. Travelers to America are conveyed by

vessels on the 15th of every month by S. H. P. Schröder in Bremen. Agent C. Poppe, Prague, Koňský Trh, No. 833."

"June 30. Announcement to Travelers to America. The firm of Lüdering & Co., in Bremen, ships emigrants on the 1st and 15th of every month by fast going vessels. Agent, F. A. Dattelzweig, Klatovy (Klattau)."

The *Pražské Noviny* of September 16, 1847, edited by Karel Havlíček, admonishes the readers not to emigrate. The article is obviously a reprint from the German. If the Čechs, the writer argues, who contemplate going to America, work as hard at home as Americans are known to toil, they will be surprised to find America at their own threshold. The *Politické wesnické nowiny z Čech* of September 11, 1849, pleads with the readers that love of the fatherland, if nothing else, should deter Čechs from emigrating. Who but adventurers dare the trip to America, anyway? Yet it is futile to try to divert the thoughts of the poor and the resolute from America.

"Reports continue to arrive from California concerning the large quantities of gold unearthed there," says the *Noviny Lípy Slovanské* of February 14, 1849. "Nuggets of gold ore weighing as much as a pound, in some cases two, have been found. There are instances on record of emigrants making in gold digging and in trading with the Indians as much as $30,000. The average earnings of a person per day amount to $100. Fever is prevalent among the inhabitants but it is not fatal. Clothing, food and domestic labor are very high; shirts sell at $10 each, beef from $1 to $2 a pound, laundering a dozen shirts costs $6. A merchant's clerk commands $3,000 a year."

Writing from New York to the Prague *Národní Noviny*, April 3, 1849, J. Č.[1] harps on the same favorite theme, California and its fabulous riches.

Emigrants traveled to the United States by the four ports of Hamburg, Havre, Antwerp and Bremen. As late as 1849 not a mile of railroad existed in Wisconsin, Iowa, Missouri, Arkansas, Tennessee, or Texas.[2] Up to 1850–55 but a small percentage of emigrants went west by railroad. They chose their homes in lake or river cities which had been benefited by canal and railroad construction. Buffalo, on Lake Erie, was of small importance until 1825 when by the opening of the Erie Canal, it became the gateway from the great valley to the Atlantic States. Cleveland in the same way benefited by the opening of the Erie Canal, as did Detroit, the oldest of the Western cities. Steamboats plied regularly between Milwaukee and Buffalo in the season of lake navigation. As a general rule the French and English clung to the seacoast, while the German, Scandinavian, and Čech pushed into agricultural

---

[1] "J. Č." is conceivably Joseph Čilinský, a jeweler from Prague, and an early resident of New York.

[2] McMaster's *History of the United States*, v. VIII, p. 88.

THE ČECHOSLOVAK LEGATION IN WASHINGTON
Charles Pergler (second from left) and part of his Staff

States. Before an all-rail connection had been established between New York and Chicago, Buffalo was a kind of Mecca, where immigrants, journeying westward, assembled. The city presented a sight not to be seen elsewhere on this continent. Endless caravans of coaches, of lumbering moving vans, of country wagons, the latter loaded with household furniture, agricultural implements, boxes, trunks, moved through the principal thoroughfares. Immigrants, with packs and baskets strapped to their backs, lounged on the sidewalks or crowded in front of lodging-houses. In 1845, says a chronicler, 96,000 Europeans passed through the city. Boats which maintained communication with points west of Buffalo seemed to do no other business, except the transport of immigrants and their luggage. The decks of these boats were provided with stalls for domestic animals. In appearance, they suggested nothing so much as Noah's Ark. Their decks were loaded with passengers, horses, horned cattle, vehicles, and household belongings. Ordinarily, travelers journeyed from New York to Albany by water, from Albany to Buffalo by rail, from Buffalo to Detroit by a lake boat. From the latter-named city to Chicago, again by boat, the journey lasted from five to six days. The *Missouri Republican* of July 20, 1849, advertises the trip from St. Louis to LaSalle, a distance of 281 miles for $5. From LaSalle to Chicago, 100 miles, $4. From Chicago to Buffalo *via* Buffalo and Detroit, from $5 to $8.

From Buffalo to Albany by rail, $9.75. From Albany to New York by boat, 50 cents. Owing to the popular clamor that transportation companies overcharged immigrants, a committee was appointed in New York to investigate the alleged charges of extortion. It was claimed that immigrants were treated brutally by agents and runners, particularly those who were unable to speak English. Buffalo never appealed to Čechs. Borecký mentions by name about ten families who lived there in the mid-fifties. Even these few moved to other parts, eventually, save the Myškas or Mischkas, as the name came to be spelled later.[1]

In the following seacoast, river, and lake cities the nuclei of settlements began forming in or after the fifties: New York, Baltimore, New Orleans, Buffalo, St. Louis, Dubuque, Cincinnati, Milwaukee, Detroit, Cleveland, Chicago, Racine, Manitowoc, and Kewaunee. Always small, the settlements in New Orleans, Buffalo, and Dubuque soon disappeared, owing partly to removal, partly to assimilation.

The first farming communities sprang up in Wisconsin. This State possessed advantages over others which strongly appealed to the Central European. The climate, though severe with long winters, was salubrious and singularly free from those frequent and unhealthy changes which prevail farther south.

[1] John Borecký: *Chapters on the History of Čech-Moravians in America*, p. 9.

NINETEENTH-CENTURY IMMIGRATION

The soil was adaptable to the raising of maize, rye, wheat, oats, and vegetables, all products with which the Čech husbandman was familiar. Moreover, there was no fear of the humiliating competition with negro labor. Wisconsin's attractions were widely advertised in German and Austrian newspapers. In the aggregate, it had the largest proportion of foreign citizens. Out of a population of 305,391 in 1850, there were 106,691, or more than one out of three, born abroad. Of that number nearly 40,000 were Germans. "The state [Wisconsin] commended itself to settlers in other ways. Taxes were low; one could become a citizen within one year. Good land could be bought at $1.25 an acre and the ground of poorer quality for less price than that. The state maintained in New York City a salaried official, so called Immigration Commissioner, whose duty it was to seek to divert the flow of newcomers thither. This commissioner advertised extensively in the foreign language press, mainly German, sending besides, generous quantities of printed matter to points in Germany, Austria, Switzerland." [1]

One of the pamphlets read: "Come! In Wisconsin all men are free and equal before the law. . . . Religious freedom is absolute and there is not the slightest connection between church and state. . . . In Wisconsin no religious qualification is necessary for

[1] Albert B. Faust: *The German Element in the United States*, v. 1, p. 477.

office or to constitute a voter; all that is required is for the man to be 21 years old and to have lived in the state one year." [1]

Wisconsin, for a long time, stood at the front of Čech effort in the United States. The weekly *Slavie* made familiar in every household the names of Milwaukee, Racine, Caledonia, Manitowoc, and Kewaunee. The Germans called Milwaukee the German Athens, the Čechs baptized Racine, where stood the cradle of the *Slowan Amerikánský* and later *Slavie*, the Čech Bethlehem.

At one time or another, Wisconsin was the home of Vojta Náprstek, John Heřman, Frank Kořízek, J. B. Letovský, Václav Šimonek, Vojta Mašek, Charles Jonáš, Ladimír Klácel, Franta Mráček, John Borecký, John Karel. Here were projected and came into existence, at the promptings of the *Slavie* the first Čech language schools; here, too, were organized the Slovanská Lípa chain of societies. When the newer States, Nebraska and Kansas, had been thrown open to settlers, it was the hardy Wisconsin pioneer who was ready to advise his less experienced countrymen in those States.

"The Čech community of Milwaukee is one of the oldest in America; it is older than either the one in Chicago or Cleveland, for the Čechs were permanently settled in Milwaukee the first half of the

[1] John G. Gregory: *Foreign Immigration to Wisconsin*. Address delivered before the Wisconsin State Historical Convention at Milwaukee, October 11, 1911.

RACINE ("ČECH BETHLEHEM") IN 1850

INVITATION TO A BESEDA, RACINE, OCTOBER, 1861

nineteenth century.... In 1848 Vojta Náprstek came. It was he, who here had sown the seed of national life; he was the founder of the local Čech library; from him came the incentive to publish a Čech newspaper.... Synchronously with him arrived in Milwaukee Hans Balatka of Moravia...."
"In no other state of northern America are so many Čechs settled as in Wisconsin. Admittedly, the first stopping point of our countrymen was Milwaukee, where now live between two and three hundred families; by far the largest numbers are found in the city and county of Manitowoc...." "Many large Čech settlements may be found especially in the counties of Manitowoc, Kewaunee, Oconto, La Crosse, Adams, and Marathon."[1]

Vojta Mašek (Mashek, 1839–1903), a well-to-do merchant, tells in his reminiscences [2] that when he

[1] F. K.: "The Cradle of Bohemian National Life in Milwaukee," The *Květy Americké*, December 22, 1886. — "The Bohemian Opera House in Manitowoc," The *Květy Americké*, April 13, 1887. — Václav Čížek: "Reminiscences of the Old Settlers." The Almanac *Amerikán*, 1897. — J. J. Vlach: (e) "Our Bohemian Population." *Proceedings* of the State Hist. Soc. of Wisconsin. Madison, 1902. — Nan Mashek. (e) "Bohemian Farmers in Wisconsin," *Charities*, New York, December 3, 1904. — Anton Novák: "Brief Account of the Bohemian Community in Milwaukee, in *Memorial* published on the occasion of the fourteenth convention of the Č.S.P.S., held in Milwaukee, 1909.

[2] The *Květy Americké*, January 5, 1887, biography and portrait; the Almanac *Amerikán*, 1891; the Almanac *Amerikán*, 1901, memoirs and portrait. A lifelong friend of Jonáš and his schoolmate from Prague, Mašek, gave up journalism (Jonáš took over the *Slavie* from him) because "it did not offer enough opportunity to an ambitious man."

came to Racine in 1861 the farmers, unable to make a living out of the few acres of soil which they had under cultivation, sought employment in the lumber industry, laboring in the saw mills in towns, cutting and rolling logs in camps. Many of them worked as shingle cutters. Often the only domestic animal owned by the farmer was a cow or a calf. All around the country was thickly wooded; beautiful maples, cherry trees and birches were cut and stumps burned to clear the land for cultivation. Unfortunately, beauty was the only asset of these trees. Market value they had none. Stumps were left in the ground until they rotted or were burned; in the patches, which by the way, widened year by year, the farmer planted his potatoes and his corn.

Of the seacoast cities New York was the only one to attract Čechs in greater numbers. For a good many years New York served merely as a jumping-off place, a point of distribution, from which immigrants scattered to inland places. Although tens of thousands had passed through its gates on their journey westward, Joseph Pastor, in a communication to the *Slavie*, estimated in 1867 their strength there at 1500. The New Yorkers hired rooms in the poorest quarter of the city. The furniture consisted of only the necessary pieces; chairs, tables and beds. Cases were by no means uncommon where two related families shared the same diminutive apartment. On the lower east side, in Essex, Division, Houston, Delancy, and Rivington Streets, which is the habitat of the poor from southeastern Europe, still may be seen many of the old-time ramshackle structures in which they lived. Worse yet was the back-yard tenement; shut off from light and air, the tenant and his children enjoyed within them about as much comfort as an inmate of a jail.[1]

No rural community in New York State of any consequence took root except one. That is situated at Bohemia, on Long Island, about fifty miles from New York City. John Vávra, John Koula, and John Kratochvil are the reputed founders of it in 1855. A local historian says that eleven families settled in Bohemia Village in 1859.[2]

St. Louis bid fair at one time to become a Čech metropolis. There the first Catholic church was erected in 1854; there the Č.S.P.S. benevolent brotherhood was organized in 1854. And had not Racine deprived it of the honor by a close margin of

[1] Jacob Riis: (e) *How the Other Half Lives* (studies among the tenements of New York), pp. 136–47. New York, 1891. — Jane E. Robbins: (e) "The Bohemian Women in New York and their Work as Cigarmakers," *Charities*, New York, December 3, 1904. — *Memorial* issued on the occasion of the twenty-fifth anniversary of the existence of the New York Supreme Lodge, Č.S.P.S., and of lodges subordinated thereto. 148 pp. January 16, 1904. — John V. Čapek: *The History of the Čech Community in New York and the Národní Jednota* (Society of National Union) *of American Čechs*. 48 pp. New York, 1904. — *The Almanac of the Čech-Slavic People in New York*, v. 1. 164 pp. New York, 1904. — J. E. S. Vojan: "The Čech Quarter of New York," pp. 176–84, in *Greater New York*, 1908.

[2] Joseph F. Thuma: "History of Bohemia Village," The Almanac *Amerikán*, 1896. "Reminiscences of John Koula," The Almanac *Amerikán*, 1903.

twenty days, St. Louis might have been the birth-place of the Čech press in America.

St. Louis attracted European settlers because it was the terminus of boats sailing up the Mississippi from New Orleans. Passenger and freight carrying lines navigating the Mississippi, Missouri, Illinois, and Ohio Rivers made regular stops there. Settlers bound for points west of the Mississippi River pre-ferred St. Louis to Chicago. It had four times as many inhabitants as Chicago; in 1845 two German dailies were published there. When in 1853 Chicago was connected with the east by rail and travelers found it more convenient and cheaper to reach the northwest by way of New York and Chicago rather than enter it *via* New Orleans and the Missis-sippi River, the claim of St. Louis to the title of Čech metropolis was irretrievably lost. Chicago ultimately wrested the scepter from its old rival.[1]

In Cleveland the Čechs began concentrating in larger numbers about the same time, that is, after 1852.[2] The story is told that sixteen families who

[1] The Almanac *Amerikán*, 1901. Václav Jirouch believes that no more than thirty Čech families lived in St. Louis in 1852. The growth of the St. Louis center suffered a setback during the Civil War; the tide of immigration turned, Jirouch thinks, to Cleveland, Chicago and to eastern cities generally. — *The Memorial* of the Fiftieth Jubi-lee of Č.S.P.S. 1854–1904, published on the occasion of the Thir-teenth Convention of the Č.S.P.S. Brotherhood, August 1, 1904, at St. Louis.

[2] *The Čech Community of Cleveland and the Social Life thereof.* 192 pp. Published the year of the Ethnographic Exhibition in Prague, 1895. Substantially the same story by Hugo Chotek, though concise, is reprinted in the Almanac *Amerikán*, 1895, pp. 201–11.

arrived that year found temporary shelter in the home of a kind-hearted Bohemian Jew by the name of Levy. The fact should be noted that the Israelites in many instances preceded others from Bohemia. "When we reached Cleveland in 1853," says Mrs. Novák, "Indian tents were pitched beyond Newburgh. We settled in Brooklyn (suburb of Cleveland), where we found many of our countrymen. I recall the following names of old settlers: F. Zíka, V. Benda, J. Kaiser, old man Kocian, Bláha, Zeman, Hladík, Stein, Bauer, Ptáček, Marek, etc."[1]

Land prices in Cleveland, according to Novák, who came in 1853, were ridiculously low. All the pioneers could have become rich had they been foresighted. Any kind of work was welcome in the start, as long as it assured existence to the immigrant.

A private census taken of the Cleveland community in 1869[2] lists 696 families, numbering a total of 3252 persons. Of these 1749 were men, 1503 women. The occupations of the men, the census gives as follows: 346 laborers, 76 masons, 72 joiners, 56 tailors, 44 shoemakers, 39 coopers, 25 locksmiths and machinists, 13 musicians, 11 smelters,

More trustworthy data on the Cleveland community than Chotek's story are contained in the narratives of Francis Sýkora (arrived in 1853), Joseph Kříž (1853), Martin Krejčí (1854), Francis Sprostý (1866), Francis Payer (1868), Joseph V. Sýkora (1863), in the Almanac *Amerikán*, 1895. — Magdalena Kučera: (e) "The Slavic Races in Cleveland," *Charities*, January, 1905.

[1] *The Čech Community of Cleveland*, etc., p. 17.
[2] *The Slavie*, February 17, 1869.

12 butchers, 9 saddlers, 9 weavers, 8 stone cutters, 7 wheelwrights, 6 furriers, 6 tinsmiths, 5 bakers, 5 tanners, 5 dyers, 4 cutlers, 2 builders, 2 bookbinders, 1 printer, 1 watchmaker, 1 sanitary inspector, 1 policeman, 1 brewer, 1 lithographer, 1 priest, 22 saloonkeepers. The census gatherer (Payer? Erhart?) records 396 owners of cottages.

Into Chicago, the first groups began filtering in 1852–53. The Chicago pioneers squatted on the outskirts of the city, on land that is now a part of Lincoln Park. There they lived until 1855 in shacks when the owner of the land drove the squatters off. The men earned their living by loading and unloading lumber on the river front. The women and children did the customary chores around the house. On market days, the women went to market to buy groceries and to the abattoirs for cheap meats (haslet, tripe, kidneys, brains, etc.). Often the purchases were made on the coöperative plan.[1]

[1] F. B. Zdrůbek: "History of Chicago and of its Čech Residents, pp. 139–71 — in the Almanac, *Amerikán*, 1884. — Charles Jonáš: (e) "The Bohemians in Chicago" *Chicago Sunday Times*, January 24, 1892. — St. J. Halík and J. R.: "Hall of the T. J. Sokol in Chicago," the *Květy Americké*, March 16, 1887. — *The Directory of American Čechs*, published to commemorate the Čech Slavic Ethnographic Exhibition in Prague, in 1895. 320 pp. — Josephine H. Zeman: (e) *The Bohemian People in Chicago*. The Hull House Papers, pp. 115–28. 1895. — Dr. John Habenicht: *Reminiscences of a Čech Physician.* A contribution to the history of Čech Americans. 89 pp. Chicago, 1897. — Dr. John Habenicht and Anton Pregler: *Memorial of old Čech Settlers of Chicago*, published in commemoration of the second anniversary of the society, held August 20, 1899. 51 pp. — Paul Albieri: "The Čech Element in Chicago," pp. 5–40, in *The Directory of Bohemian Merchants, Tradesmen and Societies*. Chicago, 1900. — Frank

ČECH RESIDENTIAL SECTION, CHICAGO

Millard Avenue, looking north from Ogden Avenue

ČECH BUSINESS QUARTER, CHICAGO

Blue Island Avenue, looking south from Eighteenth Street

NINETEENTH-CENTURY IMMIGRATION

Minnesota boasted, in 1850, of 6077 white inhabitants. Settlers, chiefly of Scandinavian ancestry, poured in so fast that ten years later the population had already mounted to 172,023. Though the Germans constituted a goodly percentage, yet their numbers in Minnesota never even approximated the grand total of Germandom in Wisconsin and it was far behind the figure made up by the combined populations of Swedes and Norwegians. In 1900 the census reported 211,769 settlers of Swedish and 224,892 of Norwegian ancestry. Of the Germanic race the census enumerator found in the State that year 289,822 people. New Prague greeted the first Čechs in 1856. "The fine stretch of land comprising LeSueur, Rice and Scott counties, peopled chiefly by our Čech countrymen and which we may truly call Little Bohemia was, fifty years ago, the stamping ground of droves of deer, roebuck and other beasts of the field." [1]

B. Zdrůbek: *The History of the Čech National Cemetery in Chicago*, from 1877, the year of its foundation, to the twenty-fifth year of its existence in 1902. 144 pp. Chicago, 1902. — *Memorial of Ludvík's Theatrical Troupe*. Published to commemorate the tenth anniversary of a permanent Čech playhouse in Chicago. 52 pp. Chicago, 1893–1903. — Alice G. Masaryk: (e) "The Bohemians in Chicago," *Charities*, December 3, 1904. — *The History of Ten Years Duration of the Society of Old Čech Settlers of Chicago*. 86 pp. Chicago, 1908. — J. E. S. Vojan: "Čech Chicago, its Beginnings and Present Development," pp. 29–68, in *Directory and Almanac of the Čech Population of Chicago*.

[1] Rev. John Rynda: *Guide to the Čech Catholic Congregations in the Archdiocese of St. Paul*. 233 pp. Published by the League of Čech priests of that diocese. 1910.

THE ČECHS IN AMERICA

John Kašpar, who emigrated as a lad of fourteen, tells how the Kašpar, Malý, and Navrátil families journeyed from Racine (Wisconsin) to McLeod County in Minnesota. Each family provided itself for the long trek with an ox-team and a prairie schooner, in which were piled featherbeds, kitchen utensils, clothing, provisions. The caravan started from Racine on April 1, reaching its objective in McLeod County after untold hardships, on July 6.[1]

Iowa received the Čechs somewhat later than Wisconsin. A local annalist counted 139 Čechs in Cedar Rapids in 1856.[2] Václav Drbohlav is known to have lived in Cedar Rapids in 1850; Vít Fibikar and Václav Rigl settled there either in 1851 or 1852. The arrivals of 1854 were John Bárta Letovský, Anton Sulek, F. Kubias, Joseph Vaňous (Wallace), John Witoušek, Joseph Woytišek, John Černin, Joseph and F. Renčin, Jacob Polák.[3]

"The first permanent settlement was made in the northern part of Johnson County, in Jefferson township and College township in Linn County. The majority of the older settlers in this section

[1] The Almanac *Amerikán*, 1891.

[2] Joseph E. Marcombe: (e) *The History of Linn County.*

[3] *Memorial of the Čech American Day during the Golden Jubilee of Cedar Rapids,* June 14, 1906, p. 42. — L. J. P. (alda): "Hall of the Reading Club in Cedar Rapids," the *Květy Americké*, February 16, 1887. — Šárka B. Hrbkova: (e) "Bohemians have done much for Cedar Rapids," *The Cedar Rapids Republican*, June 10, 1906. — J. R. Jičínský: (e) *Bohemians in Linn County.* Linn County Atlas. Davenport, 1907.

came in the years 1854 to 1856, but stragglers followed for many years later." [1]

Members of the Pecinovský family were pioneers in Dubuque and Davenport.[2] The settling of Spillville and vicinity took place later when railroads made traveling more convenient. M. B. Vosoba, Václav Jílek and Anton Šimerda bought land in Jones County in 1855.[3]

Home-builders began arriving in Nebraska in noticeable numbers after 1863, following the passage of the Homestead Law. Saline County, and especially the stretch of land lying between the towns of Crete and Wilber, welcomed the vanguard of the strangers, all or nearly all of whom had come from Wisconsin. Some, it is said, were discontented with the climate, others with the soil of Wisconsin.[4] A. L. Schlesinger [5] (1806–93), who died in Denver at a ripe old age, was the first-known settler there. Schlesinger had been a deputy to the Bohemian Diet. Dissatisfied with political conditions he emigrated in 1856. After various unsuccessful attempts to gain a footing elsewhere, he landed in Washington County, Nebraska, in 1857. For a number of years

[1] B. Šimek: (e) *The Bohemians in Johnson County.* (Ia.) p. 1.

[2] The Almanac *Amerikán*, 1891.   [3] *Ibid.*, 1896.

[4] Rev. John Stephen Brož: *History of the St. Václav Bohemian Catholic Congregation in Dodge.* 73 pp. — Jubilee edition of *Osvěta Americká*, June 15, 1904. — (e) *History of the Bohemians in Nebraska.* Published by the Nebraska State Historical Society, 1914. — Otto Kotouč: (e) "The Bohemian Settlement at Humboldt," in *History of Richardson County.*

[5] The *Květy Americké*, January 6, 1886. Biography and portrait.

Schlesinger made his living as a teamster, hauling food-stuffs and goods over the trackless plains between Omaha and Denver.

Another old settler was Edward Rosewater (originally Rosenwasser), the founder of the *Omaha Bee* and of the *Pokrok Západu*. Indisputably, Rosewater was the most distinguished Bohemian Jew in the State.

John Heřman who, like most Nebraskans, had first tried Wisconsin, is said to have brought with him more cash money to America than any other pioneer; according to John Rosický, a Nebraska newspaper editor, some 80,000 florins. Like Schlesinger, Heřman had taken an active part in the national movement in Bohemia; like Schlesinger, he too was elected to the Diet. Emanuel Arnold and Charles Havlíček, patriots and revivalists, were his personal friends. Both, when danger threatened, found succor under Heřman's hospitable roof. Police terrorism forced him to sell his property and emigrate in 1856. Due to unfortunate investments first in St. Francis, then in Manitowoc in Wisconsin, Heřman lost his fortune and settled as a poor man in Saline County.[1]

Why the Čechs from Moravia have shown pref-

---

[1] The *Květy Americké*, March 30, 1887. — Biography and portrait, Jubilee edition of the *Osvěta Americká*, June 15, 1904. Heřman was one of the striking figures among the pathfinders. Not without reason co-nationals looked up to him as a leader. The author served a term in the Nebraska Legislature with Heřman's oldest son, Stephen.

48

VÁCLAV POHL

JOHN HEŘMAN

FRANCIS KORBEL

JOHN BORECKÝ

erence for Texas [1] to the exclusion of other Southern States, is explained in another chapter. Dr. Habenicht, who practiced his profession there, is authority for the statement that the men who were instrumental in diverting the initial migration to that State were Pastors Bergman of Zapudov (Moravia) and Joseph J. Zvolánek of Liptál and Vsetín (Moravia). Letters written by them to members of their former congregations induced many Protestants from Moravia and Bohemia to migrate there. Catspring in Austin County, all accounts agree, formed the base and concentration point of the newcomers. Here they rested, took counsel, and bought supplies for the fatiguing journey inland. Čech Texas still recalls the old families of Joseph Lešikar, Joseph Šiller, John Reymershoffer, Joseph Mašík. Lešikar, his biographer records, reached Catspring in 1853. An admirer of Havlíček, he did his bit in preparing the ground for Čech journalism in the United States. As agent in Texas of the St. Louis *Národní Noviny*, an outspoken Unionist paper, Lešikar was threatened with death by Confederate neighbors unless he gave up the agency of this mischief-making publication. One of the Šiller family studied law and was either the first or one of the first Čechs in the United States to devote himself to the practice of that profession. The Reymershoffers passed through Catspring in 1855.

[1] Kenneth D. Miller: (e) "Bohemians in Texas," *The Bohemian Review*, May, 1917.

Drifting to Galveston, they became prominent in business and politics there. John Reymershoffer, a son of the pioneer, acted as Austrian Consul. By Joseph Mašík is claimed the distinction of having been the first teacher of his nationality in Texas. In company with fifteen other families, Mašík landed in Galveston in 1855; thence the travelers proceeded by boat to Houston and from Houston in prairie schooners to Catspring.[1] Substantially the same story is reported by Antonín Štrupl, a photographer, having a studio in Industry.[2]

A prominent figure in Texas is August Haidušek of La Grange, proprietor of the journal *Svoboda*, jurist and banker. Haidušek migrated to Texas as a lad before the Civil War. He served in the Confederate army. He thinks he was the first lawyer of Čech birth in this country, having been admitted to the Texas bar in 1870.[3]

In Kansas, the oldest settlement took root ten years after the Civil War. "Meandering southwest, we entered Kansas at the corner of Washington and Republic Counties going through Republic, Jewell, Mitchell, and Lincoln Counties into Wilson township, Ellsworth County. . . . The founding of the settlement in Palacky Township occurred in June, 1876. . . . The largest party of Bohemian home-seekers came September 1, 1876, from Chicago. It was one of the organized clubs or colonization socie-

[1] The Almanac *Amerikán*, 1887.
[2] *Ibid.*, 1892.   [3] *Ibid.*, 1901.

ties (p. 477)." The newcomers spread over the counties of Osborne, Mitchell, Lincoln, Russell, Ellsworth, Barton. The locust pest, which ruined crops in Saline County, was the direct cause of many Nebraskans emigrating to Kansas.[1]

Settlements in North and South Dakota were founded, not by professional farmers arriving direct from Bohemia, as was the case with the farming settlements in Wisconsin, Nebraska, and Iowa, but by proletarians from large cities, such as Chicago. The longing to get away from the grinding misery in the shop and factory impelled New Yorkers, within the last fifteen or twenty years, to buy farms in Connecticut.

A few wayfarers went to Pennsylvania (Allegheny) before the Civil War, but the main influx did not set in there until the seventies. The character of the Pennsylvania immigration is essentially different; not farmers, but millworkers and miners migrated there.

An attempt at farming on the coöperative plan was made by a number of families from Chicago at Vontay, in Virginia. The community, however, dissolved in 1900, after an existence of less than three years. Another settlement centering about Petersburg, near Richmond, has been, on the other hand, highly successful.

The agricultural contingents in Oregon and

[1] Francis J. Swehla: (e) "The Bohemians in Central Kansas." *Collections of the Kansas State Historical Society.* Topeka, 1915.

Washington are not only small, but necessarily recent. This is also true of Oklahoma.

The farmer constructed his dwelling as necessity dictated. If he chose his future home in prairie States such as Nebraska, Kansas, Iowa, where timber was scarce, he built a sod house; if his preference was for a woodland country, like Wisconsin, he constructed a log cabin. F. J. Sadílek, Register of Saline County in Nebraska, narrates how on a dark night he once rode with his horse and wagon right over a dugout, realizing his blunder only when he heard the terrified shrieks of the inmates. The sod houses were mere burrows in the ground. Where a stream ran through the land, the settler usually dug himself into the slope of it.[1]

Farmer Joseph Klíma, who settled in 1854 near Prairie du Chien, Wisconsin, describes how members of his family, harnessing themselves, pulled logs to the site chosen for the cabin. Corn bread and "coffee," the latter ground from roasted corn, was the daily if not the sole food of the family. At times even that gave out. By dint of hard labor and self-denial, Klima saved enough to buy a team of oxen, a wagon, and a plow. After that, the progress of breaking up the ground went on more quickly than when the sole farming implement was a pick and a shovel.

"I dragged on my back feather beds tied in a bundle and some kitchen utensils. My wife carried

[1] F. J. Sadílek: *My Reminiscences.* 60 pp. Omaha, 1914.

A. L. Šlesinger

Joseph Křikava

Joseph L. Lešikar

The Hubáček Brothers

THE PATHFINDERS

cooking-pots and our nine-year daughter had in her arms a kitten. Thus equipped we started house-keeping in Wisconsin. Upon a closer examination of the land we had picked out, we espied on it some deserted log cabins, or rather the odds and ends of cabins, for everything but the walls was gone. With another family we put up in one of the cabins; our pallets consisted of a few logs on which we strewed brushwood to make them softer." [1]

"With hoes we raked a patch of ground to plant potatoes. Our house was a very simple affair. We dug a hole in the ground, lining it with sod. Then we threw a top over it, overlaid that with brush-wood and thatch and our dwelling was complete." [2]

To get a true perspective on the old immigrations something should be known of the social and political conditions as they existed in Bohemia about 1848. First of all let it be borne in mind that it was the agricultural and domestic labor from the provinces which supplied the major part of the new-comers. Secondly, the peasantry had just emerged from a condition resembling semi-slavery, the law which abolished forced labor having been passed in 1849. The elementary school taught little more than reading, spelling, and arithmetic. The sovereign desired not educated citizens, but loyal and obedient subjects. For centuries the ruling class drummed into the head of the peasant its specious

---

[1] The Almanac *Amerikán*, 1903. Narrative of Frank Hrbek.
[2] *Ibid.*, 1891. Narrative of Joseph Pecinovský.

theories: obey the Church, obey the Government, obey the lords. The archbishop claimed a prior lien on the peasant's soul; the emperor held a chattel mortgage on his body; the lord usurped the fruits of his labor. To the peasant little was left that was free and unencumbered.

Regimented from childhood up to obey and never to command; knowing little or nothing of constitutional liberty, was it any wonder that, if compared to an Englishman, a Swede, or a German, the old-time Čech immigrant appeared backward and servile and sheepish? The fault, of course, was not his; the blame rested on the shoulders of those who for centuries held captive his intellect, who sought to retain their hold on him by the pernicious teaching that dumb obedience and unreasoning faith were his only hope of salvation.

"When I came to St. Louis in May, 1857," says John Borecký,[1] "I found in that city a strong Čech community. They had a Catholic Church, and a Č.S.P.S. fraternal lodge. Yet the genuine Čech spirit somehow or other was lacking. Among so many of my countrymen I found no books except prayer books."

When the author last visited his native land he was importuned with all sorts of questions concerning the Americans. "Tell us how our country-

[1] Lecture delivered by John Borecký on the occasion of the fiftieth anniversary of the Slovanská Lípa Society. *St. Louiské Listy*, January, 1909.

men are doing in America. — Do you know my cousin, a manufacturer in Chicago? — Have you heard of my uncle, Mr. X? He is said to be doing excellently. — What do you hear about Mr. N., a wealthy notary in Chicago?" Everywhere the author met people who had or claimed to have uncles, cousins, brothers-in-law, grandfathers, who were manufacturers, wholesale merchants, superintendents, and foremen. In every instance the relative held some commanding position; that all were wealthy was self-understood, for can one imagine an American uncle who is poor?

A Prussian captain of industry has said that America was a land of unlimited possibilities. Yet despite all these possibilities we know that the process of transforming a peasant into a great merchant and a mechanic into a manufacturer is not as rapid as some would wish and others want to believe. Every Čech community, of course, has its superintendents, foremen, and merchants, but these men, without an exception, have worked themselves up only after a hard and long-drawn-out struggle. Dollars and gray hair invariably come to the successful man together.

A young Prague machinist remarked to the author: "I shall go to America next spring. I shall remain there three or five years, no longer, until I have saved some money, then I shall return to Prague." That in America one gets rich quickly or easily is another illusion. Čech immigration is more than seventy years old, and yet how many wealthy men are there of that nationality? They can be counted on the fingers of two hands. But what immigrant has amassed a fortune overnight? Not one. Five years are spent in preparatory work; another five or ten years elapse before our Central European disappears in the melting-pot. Then there is the English language, the knowledge of which is useful to the mechanic and small business man and indispensable to the professional. Without it the newcomer is much in the same predicament as the handsome prince in the fable whom the sorceress had lured into the bewitched circle: he was powerless to extricate himself from his position and none could reach him from without. To master English is in itself a problem. In three, five years, few succeed in accomplishing the task; those who shut themselves within the narrow confines of their own communities seldom learn it except in a perfunctory fashion.

In the beginning they held their social functions in halls owned by Germans. The reason was obvious. Next to the mother tongue, they were proficient in German. English sounded unfamiliar to them. The community grew socially and economically, and churches and lodge-halls were built. These structures were modest, and judged by present-day standards, unsightly. They answered the purpose, however, and satisfied the taste of the time. The material used in every instance was

SOKOL SLOVANSKÁ LÍPA HALL
CHICAGO

Č.S.P.S. HALL, CHICAGO

ČECH-AMERICAN HALL, MILWAUKEE

PLZEŇSKÝ SOKOL GYMNASTIC ASSO-
CIATION HALL, CHICAGO

wood. The Catholics in St. Louis built in 1854 a frame chapel (St. John Nepomuk); their Chicago co-religionists built in 1864 a frame chapel (St. Václav). The Sokol Slovanská Lípa erected a frame hall on Taylor Street in Chicago in 1869. The Perun Hall, the social center of the Cleveland community, originating in 1871, is, however, constructed of brick. The Č.S.P.S. Hall on Eighteenth Street, Chicago, which for many years housed a language school, is of the same material, brick. It dates to 1871. From wood to brick — a step forward. Years pass by, the old country sends annually a contingent of from 5000 to 10,000 future citizens; the fresh arrivals augment the strength of those already here. Gradually the more enterprising shop-workers branch out as master mechanics; others leave factories to go into small business as bakers, grocers, butchers. The more Americanized settlers begin to buy real estate, at first for home purposes, later for speculation. Real estate rises in price, property interests multiply, the well-to-do middle class, appreciating the value of higher school education, gives the children the benefit of high school or college training. In time the sons and daughters of butchers, grocers, saloon-keepers, and farmers graduate as school-teachers, lawyers, doctors, pharmacists, dentists. These American-born and American-bred children, if they decide to live for professional or other reasons in or near the settlement, make its inner life not only more complex, but also more refined. They refuse to live in the dark flats and ugly tenements which had housed their parents for years. As individuals prosper, their social and economic requirements correspondingly increase.

A prompt decentralization of races, composing the old Dual Monarchy, a separation from bed and board, an alignment according to language and race ensues: a Pole to Pole, no matter whether in the old country your John Lubomirski owed allegiance to Austria, Prussia, or Russia; a Čech to Čech; the Magyar to his own; the Austro-German to the Germans from the Fatherland. The State idea to which Austro-Hungarian statesmen have clung as tenaciously as the dervish holds fast to his fetich, is that moment proved an illusion, or rather a delusion: political boundaries that had separated people of the same race are seen to disappear as a rainbow fades. Only two binding ties survive: race and language.

CHAPTER IV

THE DISTRIBUTION OF THE STOCK

THE Thirteenth (1910) Census found 539,392 foreign-born persons of Bohemian (and Moravian) stock. Of this number 237,283 were of the same mother tongue, 8199 of mixed mother tongue; 41,724 were of foreign-born father, 23,448 of foreign-born mother.[1]

DISTRIBUTION ACCORDING TO COUNTRIES OF ORIGIN IN DETAIL [2]

	Foreign-born 1910	Total foreign 1910
Bohemia (and Moravia)...............	228,738	539,392
Austria	219,214	515,183
Germany...........................	6,263	17,382
Hungary...........................	1,755	2,868
Russia.............................	1,898	1,694
Europe, not specified.................	148	405
Canada............................	118	236
At sea.............................	102	173
England...........................	30	67
Roumania..........................	27	38
Belgium	26	59
France............................	22	33
Turkey in Europe....................	18	20
Switzerland........................	16	34
Greece............................	11	18
Turkey in Asia......................	8	13
Denmark..........................	7	13
South America......................	7	8
Australia..........................	5	43
Serbia.............................	5	7

[1] *Thirteenth Census of the U.S. 1910:* Mother Tongue of the Foreign White Stock. Table 2, p. 963.

[2] *Ibid.,* Table 22, pp. 995–96.

THE ČECHS IN AMERICA

Norway	4	16
Montenegro	4	4
India	4	4
Netherlands	3	17
Africa	3	10
Ireland	3	7
Luxemburg	3	3
Sweden	2	13
Bulgaria	2	3
Scotland	1	9
Italy	1	7
Asia, not specified	1	6
Finland	1	5
Central America	1	1
China	1	1
Spain		2
Country not specified	24	41
Mixed foreign		949

DISTRIBUTION OF STOCK ACCORDING TO STATES [1]

Illinois	124,225	California	3,707
Nebraska	50,680	Massachusetts	3,010
Ohio	50,004	Washington	2,984
New York	47,400	Colorado	2,903
Wisconsin	45,336	Connecticut	2,693
Texas	41,080	Indiana	2,126
Minnesota	33,247	Oregon	1,709
Iowa	32,050	Montana	1,653
Pennsylvania	13,945	Virginia	1,059
Missouri	13,928	Arkansas	778
Kansas	11,603	Wyoming	671
Michigan	10,130	Idaho	663
So. Dakota	9,943	West Virginia	535
Maryland	9,199	Rhode Island	346
No. Dakota	7,287	Kentucky	305
New Jersey	6,656	Utah	268
Oklahoma	5,633	Alabama	184
Tennessee	176	Florida	92

[1] *Thirteenth Census of the U.S. 1910:* Mother Tongue of the Foreign White Stock. Table 17, pp. 985–86.

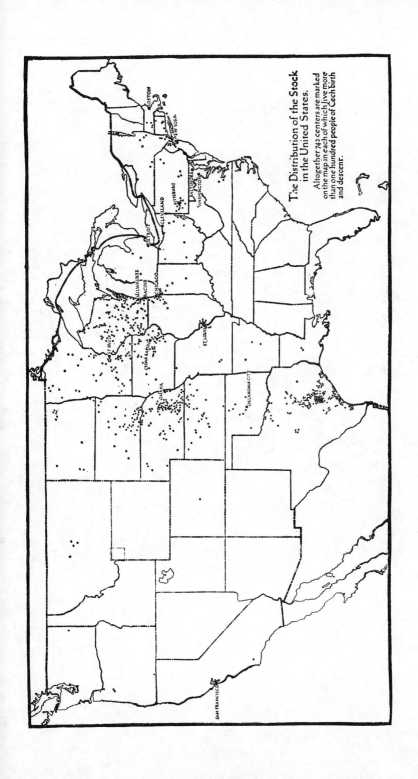

The Distribution of the Stock in the United States.

Altogether 741 centers are marked on the map in each of which live more than one hundred people of Čech birth and descent.

New Mexico	175	Nevada	84
Louisiana	173	So. Carolina	71
District of Columbia	135	Mississippi	61
Georgia	127	New Hampshire	44
Delaware	121	Maine	41
Arizona	97	No. Carolina	16

It will be seen that the stock is bulked in the Middle West. South of the Mason and Dixon line, Texas comes first with considerable Čech population, and Oklahoma next.

DISTRIBUTION IN CITIES HAVING 100,000 OR MORE INHABITANTS [1]

	Total foreign white stock 1910	Foreign-born	Native of foreign or mixed parentage
Albany, N.Y.	91	56	35
Atlanta, Ga.	25	9	16
Baltimore, Md.	7,750	3,354	4,396
Birmingham, Ala.	17	7	10
Boston, Mass.	551	233	318
Bridgeport, Conn.	559	295	264
Buffalo, N.Y.	271	152	119
Cambridge, Mass.	24	13	11
Chicago, Ill.	110,736	50,063	60,673
Cincinnati, O.	368	170	198
Cleveland, O.	39,296	17,134	22,162
Columbus, O.	172	106	66
Dayton, O.	147	78	69
Denver, Colo.	607	248	359
Detroit, Mich.	2,641	1,133	1,508
Fall River, Mass.	5	5	
Grand Rapids, Mich.	177	71	106
Indianapolis, Ind.	104	38	66
Jersey City, N.J.	222	120	102
Kansas City, Mo.	171	72	99
Los Angeles, Cal.	564	272	292
Louisville, Ky.	56	24	32

[1] *Thirteenth Census of the U.S. 1910:* Mother Tongue of the Foreign White Stock. Table 24, p. 1012.

Lowell, Mass................	6	3	3
Memphis, Tenn..............	30	16	14
Milwaukee, Wis.............	6,370	2,785	3,585
Minneapolis, Minn..........	1,649	684	965
Nashville, Tenn..............	37	15	22
New Haven, Conn...........	109	43	66
New Orleans, La............	98	43	55
(New York, N.Y..............	40,988	21,078	19,910)
" " Manhattan Boro .	31,167	16,506	14,661
" " Bronx " .	3,206	1,498	1,708
" " Brooklyn " .	1,615	857	758
" " Queens " .	4,851	2,129	2,722
" " Richmond " .	149	88	61
Newark, N.J................	1,150	582	568
Oakland, Cal................	229	99	130
Omaha, Neb................	5,414	2,622	2,792
Paterson, N.J...............	87	43	44
Philadelphia, Pa.............	1,652	778	874
Pittsburgh, Pa...............	3,453	1,907	1,546
Portland, Oreg..............	354	178	176
Providence, R.I..............	95	63	32
Richmond, Va...............	47	24	23
Rochester, N.Y..............	86	33	53
St. Louis, Mo................	10,282	4,118	6,164
St. Paul, Minn...............	4,140	1,621	2,519
San Francisco, Cal...........	960	489	471
Scranton, Pa................	134	69	65
Seattle, Wash................	402	239	163
Spokane, Wash..............	174	77	97
Syracuse, N.Y...............	83	38	45
Toledo, O...................	393	262	131
Washington, D.C............	135	59	76
Worcester, Mass.............	42	19	23

DISTRIBUTION IN TEN SELECTED CITIES [1]

Chicago..............	110,736	Milwaukee............	6,370
New York............	40,988	Omaha................	5,414
Cleveland............	39,296	St. Paul..............	4,140
St. Louis............	10,282	Pittsburgh............	3,453
Baltimore...........	7,750	Detroit...............	2,641

---

[1] The *Slavie* of November 3, 1864, estimates the Čech urban popu-

THE DISTRIBUTION OF THE STOCK

Immigration of Bohemian and Moravian stock from 1882 (in which year Bohemia first appeared independently in the census) to date, the figures since 1910 being those of the Commissioner-General of Immigration: [1]

1882	6,602	1900	3,060
1883	5,462	1901	3,766
1884	8,239	1902	5,590
1885	6,352	1903	9,577
1886	4,314	1904	11,838
1887	4,579	1905	11,757
1888	4,127	1906	12,958
1889	3,085	1907	13,554
1890	4,505	1908	10,164
1891	11,758	1909	6,850
1892	8,535	1910	8,462
1893	5,548	1911	9,223
1894	2,536	1912	8,439
1895	1,607	1913	11,091
1896	2,709	1914	9,928
1897	1,954	1915	1,651
1898	2,478	1916	642
1899	2,526	1917	327

lation as follows: St. Louis, 7000; Chicago, 2500; New York, 1500; Milwaukee, 1200; Cleveland, 800; Detroit, 300. The same paper, dated August 15, 1865, overstates when it asserts that there were (in 1865) 120,000 people of Čech stock in America. The tendency among immigrants is to overestimate their number, so that if official figures are inaccurate, private estimates are in most instances worthless.

According to the census of 1870 there were little over 36,000 Čechs in the country. The *Slavie* of May 3, 1872, thinks that if to this number were added those who, through ignorance, had been tabulated as Austrians, we should get a total of 42,000 born in Bohemia. The city population was: Chicago, 6277; St. Louis, 2652; New York, 1487; Milwaukee, 1435; Detroit, 537; Allegheny, 324; Pittsburgh, 49.

[1] *Annual Report* of the Commissioner-General of Immigration to the Secretary of Labor, pp. 74–75. Washington, 1917.

THE ČECHS IN AMERICA

Communities having more than 100 People of Čech Stock [1]

Alabama: Silverhill.
Arkansas: Hazen, Dardanelle, Pine Bluff.
California: Los Angeles, Oakland, San Francisco.
Colorado: Denver.
Connecticut: Bridgeport, East Haddam, New Haven, Chester, Stamford, West Willington.
District of Columbia: Washington.
Illinois: Antioch, Algonquin, Belleville, Berwyn, Braidwood, Cary Station, Chicago, Cicero, Coal City, Collinsville, East St. Louis, Edwardsville, Granite City, Lockport, Lyons, Madison, Oak Park, Pullman, Pullman Junction, Streator, Wilmington.

---

[1] The list of communities is based on the United States official census and on private estimates, furnished by persons who, by reason of their social or business standing or length of residence, are qualified to speak with authority for their respective States. The following collaborated on the list:

Alabama, Anton Svoboda, farmer, Silverhill. *Arkansas,* John Kocourek, merchant, Hazen. *California,* Dr. Clara V. Winlow, social worker, writer, Los Angeles. *Connecticut,* L. C. Frank, former manager of the *New Yorské Listy,* New York. *Illinois and Indiana,* the late L. J. Tupý, publisher of the *Slavie;* J. V. Nigrin, secretary of the Bohemian Literary Society, and Vladimír A. Geringer, publisher of the *Svornost,* all of Chicago. *Iowa,* Professor Bohumil Shimek, Iowa City. *Kansas,* Dr. Joseph F. Pecival, Chicago (former practitioner in Kansas), and W. F. Sekavec, County Clerk, Ellsworth. *Maryland,* V. Miniberger, editor of the *Čecho-Američan,* Baltimore. *Massachusetts,* Joseph Kovář, South Boston. *Michigan,* John Bedrych, Č.S.P.S. official, Detroit. *Minnesota,* F. B. Matlach, real-estate broker, St. Paul, and Rev. Joseph Břeň, Hopkins. *Missouri,* Hynek Dostal, editor of the *Hlas,* and A. J. Čejka, Č.S.P.S. official, both of St. Louis. *Montana,* V. Simáček, farmer, Kolin. *Nebraska,* Rose Rosický, Secretary of the National Printing Company, Omaha. *New Jersey,* Rev. Norbert F. Čapek, Newark. *New York,* the author. *North Dakota,* Rev. V. F. Mikolášek, Lankin. *Ohio,* F. J. Svoboda, publisher of the *Američan,* Cleveland. *Oklahoma,* J. Hruška, Prague. *Oregon,* Adolph Groulik, farmer, Crabtree. *Pennsylvania,* Fred. Kalina, merchant, Pittsburgh, and Rev. Václav Losa, editor of the *Křeslanské Listy,* Coraopolis. *South Dakota,* Monsignor E. A. Bouška, Tabor. *Texas,* Rev. J. W. Dobiáš, Houston. *Washington,* James Tyra, Spokane, and John Nedělka, Seattle. *Wisconsin,* Caroline Jonáš-Salák (daughter of Charles Jonáš), Racine, and the late Anton Novák, publisher of the *Domácnost,* Milwaukee.

THE DISTRIBUTION OF THE STOCK

Indiana: Crown Point, Gary, Hammond, Indiana Harbor, Indianapolis, Lockport, North Judson, Whiting.

Iowa: Belle Plaine, Britt (or Duncan), Calmar (with surrounding country), Cedar Rapids, Center Point (with surrounding country), Chelsea, Clutier, Cou Falls, Cresco (with surrounding country), Davenport, Elberon, Ely, Fairfax (with surrounding country), Fort Atkinson, Fort Dodge (with surrounding country), Iowa City, Irving, Lone Tree (with surrounding country), Manly, Marion, Marshalltown (or Marshall Quarry, with surrounding country), Mason City, Morse, Mount Vernon, North Liberty, Oxford, Oxford Junction, Plymouth, Pocahontas, Prairieburg, Protivin, Richmond, Riverside, St. Ansgar, Shueyville, Sioux City (with surrounding country), Solon, Spillville, Swisher, Tama, Toledo, Turkey River, Vail, Vining, Walker, Walford, Wakish.

Kansas: Ada, Atwood, Belleville, Black Wolf, Caldwell, Clebourne, Cuba, Ellsworth, Esbon, Everest, Glasco, Hanover, Hollyrood, Irving, Jennings, Kanopolis, Lucas, Marysville, Munden, Narka, New Tabor, Ogallah, Olmitz, Palacky, Pilsen, Plainville, Rosseville, Timken, Washington, Wilson, Zurich.

Louisiana: New Orleans, Libuse, Kolin.

Maryland: Baltimore, Curtis Bay.

Massachusetts: Boston, New Bedford, Springfield, Three Rivers, Turners Falls, Westfield.

Michigan: Detroit, East Saginaw, Grand Rapids, Iron Mountain, Ludington, Owosso, Traverse City.

Minnesota: Alexandria, Austin, Badger, Bass Lake, Bear Creek, Bechyn, Beroun, Biscay, Blooming Prairie, Breckenridge, Brookpark, Browerville, Canby, Cromwell, Denham, Eden Prairie, Foley, Glencoe, Glenville, Greenbush, Heidelberg, Hill City (doubtful), Homolka, Hopkins, Hutchinson, Jackson, Jordan, LeSueur Center, Lonsdale, Lucan, Mahnomen, Maple Lake, Meadowlands (doubtful), Melrose (doubtful), Minneapolis, Minnetonka, Montgomery, Myrtle, New Prague, Olivia, Owatonna, Pine City, St. Louis Park, St. Paul, Sauk Center, Seaforth, Silver Lake, Stewart, Tabor, Taunton, Thief River Falls, Ulen, Veseli, Virginia, Vlasaty, Willow River, Winona.

Missouri: Bolivar (and Karlin), Cainesville, Fenton, High Ridge, Kansas City, Mashek, Rock Creek, St. Charles, St. Joseph, St. Louis.

Montana: Coffee Creek, Denton, Great Falls, Kolin.

Nebraska: Abie, Atkinson, Barnston, Bee, Beemer, Brainard, Bris-

65

tow, Bruno, Burwell, Clarkson, Colon, Comstock, Crete, David City, Deweese, De Witt, Diller, Dodge, Dorchester, Du Bois, Dwight, Elyria, Exeter, Farwell, Friend, Galena, Garrison, Geneva, Geranium, Hallam, Hay Springs, Hemingford, Heun, Howell, Humboldt, Kramer, Lawrence, Leigh, Lewiston, Linwood, Lindsay, Lincoln, Lodgepole, Loma, Lynch, Madison, Milligan, Morse Bluff, Niobrara, North Bend, Odell, Ohiowa, Omaha, Ord, Osmond, Pierce, Pishelville, Plainview, Plasi, Plattsmouth, Pleasant Hill, Prague, Praha, Ravenna, Richland, Rogers, Rushville, St. Paul, Sargent, Schuyler, South Omaha, Spencer, Spring Ranch, Swanton, Stuart, Table Rock, Tate, Thurston, Tobias, Touhy, Ulysses, Valparaiso, Verdigre, Virginia, Wahoo, Western, Weston, West Point, Wilber, Wilson, Wymore.

New Jersey: Bayonne, Boundbrook, Elizabeth, Garfield, Hoboken, Jersey City, Little Ferry, Newark, Passaic, Paterson, Trenton, Union Hill, West Hoboken, West New York.

New York: Albany, Bay Shore, Bay Side, Binghamton, Bohemia, Buffalo, East Islip, Gloversville, Haverstraw, Herkimer, Newfield, New York, Poughkeepsie, Riverhead, Rochester, Rockland Lake, Sayville, Schenectady, Yonkers.

North Dakota: Bechyn, Conway, Dickinson, Lankin, Lawton, Lidgerwood, Mandan, New Hradec, Pisek, Praha, Ross, Veseleyville, Wahpeton.

Ohio: Akron, Bellaire, Bridgeport, Canton, Cincinnati, Claysville, Cleveland, Columbus, Dayton, Defiance, Dillonvale, Drill, Lorain, Maynard, Mingo Junction, Mt. Carmel, Tcledo.

Oklahoma: Canute, Garber, Hennessey, Kingfisher, Medford, Oklahoma City, Perry, Prague, Yukon.

Oregon: Crabtree (and Scio), Malin, Portland, Scappoose.

Pennsylvania: Allegheny (and Millvale), Bowerton, Coraopolis, Dauphin, East Pittsburg (and Turtle Creek), Irwin (and Jeannette Manor), Loyalhanna (and Latrobe), McKees Rocks, Monaca, Mt. Pleasant, North Braddock, Philadelphia, Russellton, Scranton, Steelton (and Harrisburg), Uniontown, Verona, Wilkes-Barre.

South Dakota: Academy, Armour, Bendon, Bijou Hills, Chamberlain, Crow Lake, Dante, Dixon, Eagle, Butte, Fairfax, Gannvalley, Geddes, Gettysburg, Gregory, Herrick, Houghton, Ipswich, Kadoka, Lake Andes, Lakeport, Lesterville, Letcher, Okaton, Platte, Ree Heights, Redfield, Red Lake, Roscoe, Scotland, Sisseton, Tabor, Tripp, Tyndall, Utica, Veblen, Vienna, Vodnany, Wagner, Winner, Yankton.

Pisek, North Dakota

A street in Protivin, Iowa

TWO TOWNS WITH ČECH NAMES AND ČECH INHABITANTS

THE DISTRIBUTION OF THE STOCK

Texas: Abbot, Alma, Ammansville, Ballinger, Barclay, Bartlett, Beasley, Beeville, Bleiberville, Bluff, Bomarton, Brenham, Breslau, Bryan, Buckholts, Burlington, Caldwell, Cameron, Catsspring, Chriesman, Cistern, Corpus Christi, Coupland, Crisp, Crosby, Cyclone, Dacosta, Dallas, Deanville, Dillworth, Dime Box, Dubina, East Bernard, El Campo, Elgin, Ellinger, Engle, Ennis, Eola, Fairchilds, Falls City, Fayetteville, Flatonia, Floresville, Fort Worth, Frelsburg, Frenstat, Frydek, Gainesville, Galveston, Glenflora, Gonzales, Granger, Guadelupe, Gus, Guy, Hackberry, Hallettsville, Harrold, Haskell, Henkhaus, Hillje, Hobson, Holik, Holland, Holliday, Holman, Houston, Houston Heights, Hubbard, Hungerford, Industry, Inez, Jarrell, Karnes City, Kaufman, Kendleton, Koerth, La Grange, Laneport, Louise, Lovelady, Lyra, Marak, Megargel, Merle, Miles, Moravia, Moulton, Mt. Calm, Nada, Needville, Nelsonville, Ocker, Oldenburg, Olmus, Penelope, Pierce, Pisek, Placedo, Plum, Port Lavaca, Poth, Praha, Primm, Rabb, Rices Crossing, Robstown, Rockdale, Rogers, Rosebud, Rosenberg, Rosprimm, Rowena, Roznov, Runge, St. John, Schulenburg, Sealy, Seymour, Shimek, Shiner, Skidmore, Smetana, Smithville, Snook, Strawn, Sublime, Sugarland, Sunnyside, Sweet Home, Taiton, Taylor, Telico, Temple, Terrell, Thrall, Thurber, Tours, Tunis, Vernon, Victoria, Waco, Waller, Wallis, Waterloo, Weimar, Wesley, West, Wheelock, Wichita Falls, Wied, Yoakum, Yorktown.

Virginia: Churchland, Disputanta, New Bohemia, Petersburg, Vontay.

Washington: Seattle, Spokane, Tacoma.

West Virginia: Wheeling.

Wisconsin: Adams, Alaska, Algoma, Alma, Antigo, Appleton, Ashland, Baraboo, Barron, Bayfield, Beaver, Belle Plaine, Belleville, Birchlake, Birchwood, Black River Falls, Blue River, Boscobel, Branch, Bridgeport, Brill, Brodhead, Bryant, Butternut, Cadott, Caledonia, Campbellsport, Carlton, Carolville, Casco, Cato, Cazenovia, Chelsea, Chetek, Chilton, Chippewa Falls, Clay, Cobb, Coleman, Cornell, Cudahy, Dane, Denmark, Deerbrook, Dilly, Dodge, Eastman, Eau Claire, Fairchild, Fennimore, Fifield, Flambeau, Fond du Lac, Fort Atkinson, Forestville, Francis Creek, Friendship, Grand Rapids, Green Bay, Grimms, Haugen, Hazelhurst, Hillsboro, Holy Cross, Hudson, Hurley, Janesville, Jefferson, Kaukauna, Kellnersville, Kenosha, Kewaunee, Kewaskum, Krok, Krakow, La Crosse, Ladysmith, Langlade, Lancaster,

THE ČECHS IN AMERICA

Lena, Lodi, Luxembourg, Manitowoc, Marathon, Marek, Maribel, Marion, Marinette, Marshall, Mauston, Medford, Mellen, Menasha, Menomonie, Merrill, Middleridge, Milladore, Milwaukee, Mishicot, Montfort, Mosinee, Muscoda, Necedah, Neva, New Auburn, North Milwaukee, Oconto, Odanah, Ogema, Oshkosh, Park Falls, Phillips, Pilot Knob, Pilsen, Plover, Prairie du Chien, Prescott, Prentice, Racine, Reedsville, Rib Lake, River Falls, Rochester, Shawano, Sheboygan, Sister Bay, Slovan, South Milwaukee, Spencer, Stangelville, Sturgeon Bay, Tisch Mills, Two Rivers, Union Center, Viola, Waterloo, Waukesha, Wausaukee, Wauseka, West Allis, Westboro, West Bend, Woodlawn, Yuba.

CHAPTER V

TRADES, BUSINESS, PROFESSIONS

THE Twelfth Census figures on occupations showed 71,389 Bohemian male breadwinners of the first generation and 32,707 of the second engaged in gainful occupations. Of this number, 32 per cent of the first and 43 per cent of the second generation were engaged in agriculture. These percentages are large and bear witness to the distinctively agricultural character of the Bohemian population; taken together, more than 35 per cent of all breadwinners of Bohemian origin were agriculturists in 1900. The concentration of Bohemian farmers in Wisconsin, Minnesota, Iowa, Nebraska, and Texas is very evident, not far from four fifths of the 18,094 farmers of the first generation in the United States being found in those States. Nebraska leads with one fifth of all Bohemian farmers of the first generation, Texas follows with one sixth.[1]

All in all few rural colonies were visited (by the Immigration Commission) where members appeared more intelligent or more prosperous than some of the Bohemian communities in Texas. In the Middle West — Wisconsin, for instance — Bohemians are reputed to be on a par with the average

[1] *Reports of the Immigration Commission*, v. II, part 24, pp. 375–481.

farmers of any race of the same generation farming under similar conditions. The old settlements in Wisconsin have attained a high state of prosperity.

The Commission investigated farming conditions in Texas, where it examined thirty colonies or settlements; one small group in Missouri was studied; in Connecticut about 60 farming families consisting of 320 persons were visited. No attempt was made to investigate the very prosperous communities in Wisconsin, Iowa, Nebraska, Minnesota, Kansas, etc.[1]

To sum up, 32 per cent of the first and 43 per cent of the second generation are engaged in farming; the balance are massed in towns, working at various trades. Retail merchants thrive everywhere and their number is steadily on the increase. Seldom one finds Čechs doing unskilled outdoor labor, blasting, tunneling, road-building; they prefer indoor jobs in the factory and the shop. Mining, likewise, does not seem to attract them; at least they are less in evidence than other Slavs in the Pennsylvania coal mines, coke regions, and steel mills. Musicians, professional and amateur, are numerous.

A rather large proportion are employed as tailors — 6.9 per cent of the male breadwinners in the first generation and 3.7 per cent of those in the second. The corresponding percentage for the Russians are, respectively, 18 per cent and 5.5 per cent and for

[1] *Reports of the Immigration Commission*, v. I, part 24, p. 9.

the Austrians 7.9 per cent and 1.9 per cent. No other nationalities have as high percentages in this occupation.[1] In general intelligence the tailors rank high; many of them have learned the trade in large European cities, Prague, Vienna, Paris.

A distinctive feature of the occupational distribution of immigrants is the comparatively large percentage (3.2) employed as tobacco operatives. This exceeds the corresponding percentage reported for any other of the seventeen classes of immigrants for which the occupation statistics have been computed, the next highest percentage being that for the Russians (2.1). Of the 2266 Bohemian male immigrants reported in this occupation, 1738, or more than three fourths, were in the State of New York, constituting more than one fourth (26.1 per cent) of the total number of Bohemian immigrant breadwinners in that State. In the second generation the percentage of tobacco and cigar factory operatives declines to 7.7 per cent in the State of New York and to 1.3 per cent in the United States.[2]

Why the old immigration went into cigarmaking is not an uninteresting story. In the town of Sedlec, in Bohemia, the former Austrian Government operated a large cigar factory employing over two

[1] *Reports of the Immigration Commission.* Occupations of the first and second generations of immigrants in the United States, Senate Doc. 282, p. 117.
[2] *Ibid.*, p. 117.

thousand men and women. The tobacco industry in Austria was a government monopoly. In the sixties a few of the Sedlec cigarmakers emigrated to New York. The newcomers earned good wages, they wrote to their friends, and presently more cigarmakers arrived. Eventually workmen from other trades, unable to find employment in their own particular lines, mainly owing to their ignorance of English, drifted into the tobacco shops, and soon butchers, blacksmiths, students, tailors, musicians, men, women, and children toiled at tobacco — some in the shops, others, usually families, at "housework." Editor Palda estimated that when he visited New York in 1873, fully 95 per cent of his countrymen were earning their living at this sort of work.

The system remembered in New York with horror as "housework" was abolished by act of the legislature in 1888. Theodore Roosevelt, by the way, was very active in the passage at Albany of this law. No greater menace to the public health ever existed than housework cigarmaking. The ban put on it liberated from the tobacco bondage thousands of women and children. Even the male workman profited thereby; for unable to find a job in the shops, which became congested in consequence, he was forced to look around for other work. In time he managed to get back to the trade to which he had been apprenticed in the old country. In the end the saying, "Every Čech a cigarmaker," ceased to be true. It is estimated that less than 15 per cent of Čechs are now attached to this industry directly or indirectly in New York City.

A New Yorker, well qualified to speak on the subject by reason of his long residence and his close intimacy with the home life of his nationals adduces these reasons why the second generation has given up cigarmaking and is going into other employments: "The young folks will not learn it and follow it as a trade. While it may have been good enough for their parents, they reason, it is not good enough for them. A girl who has graduated from a public school will not think of going to the tobacco factory, there to work side by side with Italian, Russian, and Greek girls freshly landed. The department store, the office, win them because they offer greater opportunities than work in cigar shops."

Fifty years of cigarmaking are back of the New York community, yet how many manufacturers of Čech nationality are there? Wertheimer, Bondy, Lederer, Krebs — not one Čech among them.

The percentage of clerks, copyists, and salesmen among Bohemian male breadwinners advances from 1.6 per cent in the first generation to 5.6 per cent in the second. These figures are for the United States. In the State of New York the percentage is 1.2 in the first generation and advances to 5.8 in the second.[1]

[1] *Reports of the Immigration Commission*, Senate Doc. 282, p. 118.

73

THE ČECHS IN AMERICA

In the first generation the leading occupation is that of farmer; in the second generation that of agricultural laborer. In each generation the four leading occupations are the same — farmers, general laborers, tailors, and agricultural laborers.[1] Four occupations — tobacco and cigar factory operatives, carpenters, miners, and butchers — appear in the list of the first ten for the first generation, but not in that for the second. In the second generation these places are taken by the clerks and copyists, the salesmen, the machinists, and the draymen, hackmen, and teamsters.[2]

Some thirty years ago a number of skilled pearl button makers came to the United States from Žirovnice, a provincial Bohemian town, known far and wide for its highly specialized pearl button industry. The Žirovnice workers introduced the craft here, and to-day there are some fifty pearl button shops owned by Čechs, employing in normal times from 1250 to 1300 operatives. This represents a total of 75 per cent of the industry in the East. The shops are in Manhattan, Astoria, and Winfield, in New York; Staffordville, West Willington, Higganum, Connecticut; Carlstadt, New Durham, Hoboken, Little Ferry, Cliffside, Newark, and Union Hill, New Jersey. The Mother

[1] By the caption "agricultural laborers" is not meant seasonal labor on the farm only; it includes the sons of farmers, who live on the place with their parents.

[2] *Reports of the Immigration Commission*, Senate Doc. 282, p. 118.

74

of Pearl Industry Association uses none other save ocean pearl.[1] A Žirovnice man is said to own in Chicago the largest shop of its kind in the United States. A machinist in New York who is interested in one of the local shops has invented a labor-saving machine which, by way of compliment, he exports to Žirovnice.

Land-ownership, more than any other agency, has contributed to the wealth of Čechs in America. All prospered who invested in land, the farmer in a higher degree than the city man. One can easily figure out how much the farmer has added to his competence when one remembers that fifty or sixty years ago he bought his land for a trifle of $5 or $10 an acre and now he values the same land at from $75 to $300 and even more an acre. If the buyer of city lots had the good fortune of getting in the pathway of the building wave, he was able to dispose of his property quickly and advantageously; a less astute or lucky buyer had to bide his time. Building lots were contracted for on the installment plan — one or two hundred dollars sufficed to bind the purchase. Early recognizing the value of self-help, they joined savings, loan, and building associations. With the aid of these associations thousands were enabled to build and own cottages in cities. In 1916 a Cleveland building association, the Mravenec (Ant), applied to the State authorities for permission to

[1] Figures furnished by William Lomnický, Secretary of the Mother of Pearl Industry Association, New York.

increase its shares from $3,500,000 to $5,000,000. Commenting on the application, newspapers stated that this made the Mravenec the second strongest savings and loan association in Ohio. According to the report of the Auditor of Public Accounts submitted to the Governor of Illinois showing the condition in that State of building, loan, and homestead associations as of December 1, 1910, 94 out of a total of 197 associations located in Chicago were Čech; of a total of $17,000,000 assets, the share of these Čech associations was $8,785,917, or more than 50 per cent of the whole.[1]

If one strolls along Broadway, New York's main business artery, one notices scores of business signs bearing Slavic names: Zemanski, Pulaski, Chuknin, Malowicz, Verbelovsky, are some of the patronymics that beam at one in gold letters. If one peeks over the window shutter, however, one finds no Slavs there. The truth is that the Slav, inclining by temperament to husbandry, is a novice, a newcomer in business; he began late and with the small capital which he commands he must court luck in less aristocratic business thoroughfares than Broadway. The Jews are almost the sole carriers of Slavic names in big business. To this state of things the Čechs are no exception, though some of them have demonstrated their ability to grapple with the more intricate commer-

[1] J. E. Salaba Vojan: *Čech American Epistles*, pp. 126–29. Chicago, 1911.

cial and industrial problems. The saloon-keeper no doubt preceded all others as a business man. To open a saloon required less preliminary training than almost any other business undertaking; the little capital that he needed for the start the brewer furnished, and if the beginner established himself in a foreign quarter, among the people of his own race, he could get on tolerably well with only the rudiments of English.

To deny the great influence of the saloon and the saloon-keeper on the immigrant would be disputing the obvious. Most, if not all, the lodges and clubs which honeycomb the so-called foreign quarters have had their birth under the saloon roof. When in 1873 the New York cigarmakers undertook to organize against the rapacity of the bosses, eight relief societies sprang into existence in eight different saloons. What old settler does not recall the saloons kept by Mottl in St. Louis, Slavík in Chicago, Hubáček in New York? To have traveled through New York and not to have stopped at August Hubáček's tavern on the East Side would have been tantamount to a gross betrayal of the national cause. The fame of Hubáček's name rang from one corner of Čech America to another. John Slavík's place on Clark Street before the sixties was a recognized rendezvous of Chicagoans. In Jacob Mottl's saloon and boarding-house in St. Louis, the Č.S.P.S. benevolent brotherhood experienced some of its initial triumphs. A liberal spender and a good fellow, the saloon-keeper, let it be admitted, was not always a liability. If he chose, or if he was the right sort of man, he could be a valuable asset. Of late years, however, the saloon-keeper's power has rapidly declined. His former prestige is now but a tradition and a tradition, by the way, which is utterly incomprehensible to the latter-day immigrant. The National Halls, which are now found in every community of any consequence, have dealt him the severest blow. Then there are the public reading-rooms and libraries, with their foreign departments; these take away from the saloon-keeper many a prospective patron. A formidable foe of the saloon are the Settlement and Neighborhood Houses with their manifold attractions for young people: gymnastic clubs and summer camps for the boys and girls. Last, but not least, is the influence of the school, which teaches the young to abhor the liquor traffic as something disreputable.

An examination of the advertising columns of the *Slavie* [1] at the time of the Civil War gives us a pretty good idea of the kind and magnitude of business. Of a total of eight pages, which the *Slavie* then printed, the advertisements take up less than two pages, and judging by their names, but five of the advertisers are of Čech nationality. Dr. Joseph Částka, physician and surgeon, occupying offices at 113 West Madison Street, Chicago, offers his

[1] The *Slavie*, June 25, 1862.

skilled services to his countrymen; F. A. Klimt informs the public that he has opened a saloon near the corner of Van Buren and Market Streets, Chicago; Joseph Novák operates a hardware store at 143 Milwaukee Avenue, and John Raisler, a carpenter shop in the same city. Frank Přibyl keeps a grocery in Racine, Charles Roth a saloon and boarding-house in St. Louis. Dr. J. R. Veeter admonishes the St. Louisians to patronize him, because "he has studied in Prague and his extensive practice embraces every known disease." Hynek & Kříž manufacture cigars on the corner of Chestnut Street, in Milwaukee, while J. Beck, near Union Hall, in Racine, "expects that all Čechs will purchase unstintingly of his large stock of boots and shoes." If, beside these, we take into account a few small advertisements, such as Wanted, and Take Notice, the sum is complete.

By 1865 the roster of advertisers has grown perceptibly, but the saloon-keeper leads. From Chicago Franta Bém sends gladsome news to his friends that he takes orders for crayon portraits, and sells pictures and books at reasonable prices.[1] John Borecký wishes all Chicago Slavonians to take notice that he has opened a New Čech Tavern at 239 Canal Street; Anna Brabenec, a midwife graduated with honors from the Prague Clinic of Midwifery, offers to women, at 153 East Sixth Street, New York, the benefit of her ten years'

---

[1] The *Slavie*, March 14, 1865.

experience. August Hubáček is owner of a Čech Saloon at 235 East Fifth Street, New York. Joseph Vozáb heralds to the Čech-Slavs the joyful tiding that he has fitted up the White Inn at 133 Essex Street, New York, "where Čech musicians give a concert every Sunday; dancing every Monday!" B. Chládek, dealer in household furniture, mirrors, and curtains, recommends his goods to the esteemed public, at 36 West Randolph Street, Chicago; Joseph Bureš & A. Matuška are proprietors of a Čech carpenter-shop in Chicago. "It is situated in Canal Street, No. 237, fifth house from the corner of Van Buren, next to the New Čech Tavern of J. Borecký." Fišer & Kubeš are the owners of a saloon at 160 Van Buren Street, next to the Rock Island Railroad Depot. Franta Seyk, tailor of Kewaunee, Wisconsin, has in stock hats, caps, shawls, gloves, shirts, clothing, and woolen goods for men. Frank Pivrnec, also of Kewaunee, manufactures all kinds of wagons, sleighs, plows, and cutters. Mašek & Stránský, of Kewaunee, sell patent medicines, oils, paints, and supplies for painters, dry goods, spices, coffee, sugar, hardware, farmers' implements, the best quality of boots and slippers made to order, farm and garden seeds, school supplies and clocks, jewelry, hats and caps, lamps and oil, wall-paper, glaziers' supplies, writing-paper, penholders, perfumery, shoemakers' supplies. J. Vancl & J. Králíček, in Cedar Rapids, Iowa, deal in sugar,

Male Breadwinners of Bohemian Parentage (Parents born in Bohemia), First and Second Generations, Classified by Occupations, with per cent Distribution, 1900 [1]

Occupation	First generation (born abroad)		Second generation (born in United States)	
	Number	Per cent distribution	Number	Per cent distribution
All occupations................	71,389	100.0	32,707	100.0
Agents	395	.6	151	.5
Agricultural pursuits...........	22,857	32.0	13,997	42.8
Agricultural laborers..........	4,428	6.2	8,928	27.3
Farmers, planters.............	18,094	25.3	4,961	15.2
All others in this class........	335	.5	108	.3
Blacksmiths...................	864	1.2	325	1.0
Boot and shoe makers..........	1,041	1.5	214	.7
Bookkeeper and accountants.....	144	.2	249	.9
Building trades................	3,749	5.3	1,321	4.0
Carpenters and joiners........	1,947	2.7	521	1.6
Masons.....................	703	1.0	92	.3
Painters.....................	792	1.1	434	1.3
Plumbers....................	159	.2	196	.6
Other building trades.........	82	.1	64	.2
Clerks and copyists............	509	.7	929	2.8
Draymen, teamsters............	863	1.2	591	1.8
Iron and steel workers..........	1,672	2.3	605	1.8
Hucksters and peddlers.........	194	.3	60	.2
Laborers not specified..........	9,996	14.0	2,659	8.1
Machinists....................	926	1.3	643	2.0
Manufacturers and officials	498	.7	140	.4
Messengers and errand boys......	86	.1	393	1.2
Merchants and dealers	2,130	3.0	759	2.3
Miners and quarrymen..........	1,567	2.2	254	.8
Printers, lithographers..........	417	.6	438	1.3
Professional service	979	1.4	653	2.0
Salesmen	649	.9	930	2.8
Saloon-keepers and bartenders....	1,064	1.5	305	.9
Saw and planing mills employees..	720	1.0	169	.5
Servants and waiters...........	230	.3	114	.3
Steam railroad employees........	847	1.2	300	.9
Tailors.......................	4,931	6.9	1,198	3.7
Textile mill operatives..........	375	.5	57	.2
Cotton mill operatives.........	48	.1	5	
Hosiery.....................	5		5	
Silk mill....................	38	.1	9	
Woolen mill.................	61	.1	9	
Other textile mills	223	.3	29	.1
Tobacco and cigar factory	2,266	3.2	420	1.3
All other	11,420	16.0	4,788	14.6

[1] *Reports of the Immigration Commission*, Senate Doc. 282, p. 120.

coffee, tea, chicory, spices, chocolate, almonds, raisins, dates, nuts, dry prunes, pears, and dried apples, rice, pearl barley, millet; buy and sell produce and pay to farmers the highest cash prices; keep in stock patent medicines of all the firms of repute, lamps, oils and purest kerosene; excellent Limburger and Swiss cheeses, cigars of every brand, and particularly a large stock of old wines and best beers. J. Gerhardy & Frank Novák, of 100 Milwaukee Avenue, Chicago, "hereby announce that, as heretofore, they have on hand a varied assortment of iron and tinware and other goods, stoves included; they also deal in Austrian scythes, the latter being the make of the most renowned Bohemian and Styrian factories." Frank Malý gives notice to all Čech-Slavs that he has opened the first tavern, "U Sokola," between Fifth and Sixth Streets, New York. Incidentally he expresses the hope "that all patriots will patronize him."

The New York City Directory for 1850–51 registers the name of John Kubin, jeweler, 357 Houston Street; Christopher J. Kuchar, bookkeeper, 27 Bowery; the Directory for 1852–53, Joseph Hubatchek, capmaker, 19 Avenue A.; Andrew Hubaczek, engraver, 86 East Broadway; the Directory for 1851–52, Wenzel Twrdy (spelled by descendants Twidey), tailor, 91 Willet Street. The Directory for 1859, Anthony Pokorny, capmaker, 213 Avenue A.; Francis Pokorny, saloon-keeper,

294½ Grand Street; Gabriel Pokorny, turner, 70 Willet Street; Louis Pokorny, tailor, 213 Clinton Street.[1]

Francis Vlasák or Francis W. Lasak (*alias* Lassak, as the name looked after it had been becomingly trimmed by the owner), who started as furrier at 376 Broome Street, was one of the first merchants of Čech nationality in the United States.[2] From that street Lassak removed to 19 John Street, where he remained for years. The story is that Lasak owed his start in the fur business to John Jacob Astor. The Lassaks intermarried with well-to-do New York families and acquired considerable wealth. Another pioneer merchant was John Konvalinka, likewise a furrier. Konvalinka began cutting furs at his home, 11 Division Street, moving later to 36 Maiden Lane.[3] The name Konvalinka is still seen above a fur shop in Maiden Lane. He died in June, 1896, at the age of seventy-five years, leaving four children.

The Mathushek Piano (now a corporation) derives its name from Fred Mathuscheck,[4] who began after the fifties as a piano-maker on a small scale at 34 Third Avenue. Another Čech piano-maker was J. Laukota, who, in partnership with

---

[1] *Trows' New York City Directory.* 1859.

[2] Thomas Longworthy: *New York Register and City Directory for the Sixty-fourth Year of American Independence.* New York, 1839.

[3] Henry Wilson: *The Directory of the City of New York for 1852–53.*

[4] According to Čech orthography, Matoušek. In the 1852 New York City Directory Mathuscheck is put down as a wood-carver.

one Marschall, conducted a business at 5 Mercer Street.[1]

The following table, extracted from the *Directory of Bohemian Merchants*,[2] throws an illuminative sidelight on the business life of the community in Chicago. The table, of course, does not include all the merchants and traders of that nationality, rather only those in business there whose card is inserted in the Directory. Twenty-six different occupations are classified.

Contracting tailors	322	Barbers	43
Saloon-keepers	321	Lawyers	43
Grocers	266	Custom tailors	40
Butchers	147	Bakers	39
Boots and shoes	107	Builders	38
Milkmen	97	Druggists	27
Confectioners and stationers	84	House-painters	26
Insurance and real estate brokers	60	Masons	25
Midwives	60	Undertakers	22
Dressmakers	58	Music conservatories	22
Wood and coal	51	Bandmasters	19
Cigar manufacturers	51	Plumbers	19
Physicians	45	Blacksmiths	19

Lawyers, physicians, and dentists are multiplying so fast of late that warnings have been sounded of "overproduction of the learned proletariat." Chicago alone supported, in 1917, 46 male and 22 female medical practitioners and 78 lawyers.[3] *The*

[1] Henry Wilson: *The Directory of the City of New York for 1851-52.*
[2] *Directory of Bohemian Merchants, Traders, and Societies.* Chicago, 1900.
[3] For the information on medical practitioners the author is indebted to Dr. L. J. Fisher; for the figures on lawyers, to Joseph A. Holpuch.

Joseph Sosel

J. W. Sýkora

John Karel

August Haidušek

THE FIRST LAWYERS

TRADES, BUSINESS, PROFESSIONS

Directory and Almanac of 1915[1] prints (p. 241) the cards of 36 male and (p. 245) 19 female physicians.

In the number of their *inteligence* the Čechs far surpass all other American Slavs. The great majority of the professionals are, of course, Americans by birth or education. Physicians graduated from Prague or Vienna are comparatively few, the glamour of their foreign diplomas being no longer as overpowering as it was in the past.

Who came first, the physician or the lawyer? Obviously the physician, since a diploma from a European medical school entitled him to practice medicine without an admission examination. Not so with the lawyer, in whose case the knowledge of English and also of American law was indispensable. And who but a native or a long-time resident possessed that knowledge in a sufficient degree to enable him to plead cases in court? Joseph W. Sýkora[2] of Cleveland believed he was entitled to wear the toga of the first Čech Blackstone. Frederick Jonáš, however, disputes Sýkora's contention. According to him, Joseph Sosel of Cedar Rapids was undoubtedly the first. F. Koláčník is reported to have been a practitioner in Chicago in 1862. F. Partl, who did a law business in Chicago at the

---

[1] *Directory and Almanac of the Bohemian Population of Chicago.* 1915.

[2] J. W. Sýkora came to Cleveland in 1863 as a student of the Latin School at Písek. In the early years he took a conspicuous part in the social life of his countrymen of that city. At Písek, Sýkora was a classmate of John V. Čapek.

85

close of the sixties, was an old settler.[1] Very likely
Partl was a type one encounters in the doorways
leading to piepoudre courts — a go-between and,
on occasion, interpreter. Joseph Šiller of Texas is
said to have had a law office at Eagle Lake, Colorado, at the close of the Civil War. In New York
there was Konvalinka, son of the furrier of that
name, and John E. Brodský; on the paternal side
both were of Čech origin. "From this it would
appear," comments Frederick Jonáš, "that Sýkora
was not the first but probably the third among
pioneer lawyers."

August Haidušek, a newspaperman, jurist, and
banker at La Grange, was admitted to the bar in
Texas in 1870. He also advances his claim to priority
as a valid one.[2] Dr. Francis A. Valenta, a Čech by
name, if not by affiliation, commenced practicing in Chicago in 1851. Valenta is said to have
early reëmigrated to Europe. Dr. de Lewandowski,
a "Bohemian" physician, enjoyed an extensive
practice in New York City in the seventies. Doctors of the stamp of de Lewandowski, who were
ready to pose — on the office door-plate or in
newspaper puffs — as a Bohemian for Bohemians, as a Pole for Poles, as a German for Germans,
were by no means uncommon. Older readers of the

---

[1] Dr. John Habenicht and Antonín Pregler: *Memorial of Old
Čech Settlers in Chicago*, p. 15. 1899. Reference to Koláčník and
Partl.

[2] The Almanac *Amerikán*, 1901.

86

A. M. Dignowity, San Antonio

Adolph Chládek, Chicago

John Habenicht, Chicago

Edward J. Schevcik, New York

PIONEER PHYSICIANS

foreign-language press recall with a shudder the glaring advertisements of the "Eminent European Specialists." Whether any of the practitioners of long ago became rich from the proceeds of their practice is extremely doubtful. From what Dr. John Habenicht has to tell us of conditions in Chicago, it may be believed they did not. In the first place, people were too ignorant or faint-hearted to go to the doctor save in desperate cases, when, as the Čech saying goes, "the patient's soul is on the tip of his tongue." Obstetrical cases were then wholly monopolized by the ubiquitous and complaisant midwife, "graduated with honors from the Prague clinic of midwifery." Then there was the proprietary medicine man to contend with — the greatest foe of the legitimate practitioner of foreign nationality. Forty or fifty years ago competition against him must have been discouraging, indeed. Nowhere was the humbug of his miracle-working liniments, pain-expellers, pulmonary teas (*brust thee*), cough syrups, blood-purifiers, more obstrusive and offending than in the foreign-language press.

Dr. Habenicht asserts that "at that time [1866] there were only two Čech physicians in Chicago, Dr. Adolph Chládek and myself."[1] Dr. Habenicht should not be understood as claiming that before his time there were no doctors outside of Chicago. There was, to mention one instance, Dr. Anthony

[1] Dr. John Habenicht: *Memoirs of a Čech Physician*, p.44. Chicago, 1897.

THE ČECHS IN AMERICA

M. Dignowity in Texas. Having landed in New York in 1832, Dignowity, after a somewhat adventurous career — he had been a manufacturer, real-estate speculator, inventor, saloon-keeper, abolitionist agitator, mine-owner, author, and physician — moved to San Antonio, Texas, where he died in 1875.[1]

Aldermen and councilmen, school trustees, assessors, justices of the peace, legislators, county and town treasurers, registers and town clerks of Čech nationality have increased so prodigiously of late that the chronicler cannot count them all. Twenty, thirty years ago the newspaper editor introduced a column with the caption "Čechs in America," and in this column he noted the elevation to public office of every co-national. In those strenuous days even constables and justices of the peace came in for a generous share of newspaper applause. The editor recorded triumphantly the name of every village statesman rising to fame, every school-teacher, every pupil graduating with honors or without them, from a high or normal school. No one was too small to be overlooked.

"The Cleveland people have no reason to complain that Čechs are unrepresented in the police and fire departments of that city. According to the latest official bulletin, A. B. Sprostý is chief of police; A Čadek, F. Sprostý and F. Hoenig are

---

[1] Anthony M. Dignowity: Autobiography. *Bohemia under Austrian Despotism.* New York, 1859.

Thomas F. Konop   Anthony Michálek

John J. Babka   Adolph J. Sabath

CONGRESSMEN OF ČECH NATIONALITY

captains; there are two lieutenants and 98 police-
men. In the fire department O. Čermák is captain;
J. Pecka lieutenant and there are 43 firemen of our
nationality." [1]

If not the first, Edward Rosewater, who was
sent from Omaha to the Nebraska State Legislature in 1870–71, was one of the pioneer lawmakers
of Čech nationality. [2] In Iowa, M. B. Letovský of
Iowa City, son of John Bárta Letovský, paved the
way for other legislators. Charles Jonáš served in
the lower house of Wisconsin, while John Karel,
merchant, lawyer, and country banker, was elected
from Kewaunee, in the same State. Among the
other early Solons was John E. Brodský of New
York and Leo Meilbek of Illinois. Meilbek attained
the further fame of having been a pioneer among
socialist legislators.

Lawmakers of Čech nationality in Nebraska,
Iowa, Minnesota, Kansas, Dakota, Wisconsin are
no longer rare. More than half a dozen of them
help to make and unmake laws in Nebraska alone.

The old-timers thought that Jonáš was the only
man fit to represent his countrymen in Congress.
Imagine, therefore, the surprise of all when in
1904 a young man, Anton Michálek, unknown
even by name outside of the city where he lived,
was elected to Congress by the Republicans of a
Chicago district. Soon thereafter came Adolph J.

---

[1] The *Květy Americké*, August, 1918.
[2] The *Pokrok Západu*, September 25, 1889.

Sabath, likewise from Chicago. A third repre-
sentative got in from Wisconsin — Thomas Konop.
Yet a fourth Congressman of Čech ancestry, John
J. Babka of Cleveland, was elected in the fall of
1918. Priority, however, belongs to Michálek. No
Čech has yet succeeded in being elected to the
Senate, though the late Edward Rosewater was
prominently mentioned as a candidate.

More numerous than either the doctors or
lawyers are the school-teachers. A recent estimate
put the number of teachers of Čech descent in
Nebraska alone at 290. Frederick Jonáš believes
that the daughters of J. B. Seykora of Iowa preceded all others as teachers. The two Landa sisters of Cleveland taught public school in the mid-
seventies. The elder of the sisters, Anna, married
Frank Škarda, publisher of the New York *Délnické
Listy*. After her marriage Anna Škarda assisted
her husband in newspaper work. Later she was
associate editor of a Texas weekly. The younger
sister, Catherine M. Čapek, taught in Cleveland
from 1874 to 1918.

Anna Nedobyty of St. Paul, Minnesota, Clara
Vostrovský Winlow of San José, California, and
Frances Gregor lead their sex as college graduates.

In recent years young men are forging ahead to
more responsible positions — as members of faculty staffs of colleges and universities. Several of
them are scholars of national reputation.

All students of chemistry know the name of

Dr. Paul J. Hanzlik

Dr. John Zelený

Dr. F. G. Nový

Dr. Alois F. Kovářík

TYPES OF AMERICAN SCHOLARS OF ČECH PARENTAGE

TRADES, BUSINESS, PROFESSIONS

F. G. Nový, of the University of Michigan. Born in 1864 in Chicago, Nový graduated from the school in which he has been for many years a professor. Then he took post-graduate courses in Europe; among others he attended the University of Prague. Dr. Nový discovered a compound claimed to be a preventive for intestinal diseases such as Asiatic cholera and typhoid fever. In 1901 he was appointed member of the United States Commission to investigate the bubonic plague in the Orient.

Dr. Robert Joseph Kerner, born in Chicago, is the author of *Slavic Europe* (a selected bibliography in the western European languages), published by the Harvard University Press in 1918. For this volume the author gathered material both here and in Europe for a number of years — practically since he graduated from Harvard University. To the Anglo-Saxon scholar *Slavic Europe* is an indispensable aid. When the war broke out, Kerner severed temporarily his connection with the University of Missouri and accepted employment with the Government. Because of his profound knowledge of the history, ethnology, and politics of the Slavic nations inhabiting central and southeastern Europe, Kerner's advice was sought by war experts both here and abroad whenever questions affecting the Slavs came up for discussion. Kerner's father is one of the publishers of the Chicago *Denní Hlasatel*.

On the staff of Yale University are two professors with excellent records: Dr. John Zelený, born (1872) in Wisconsin, one-time acting dean of the graduate school of the University of Minnesota. Dr. Zelený is Professor of Physics at Yale. He received degrees from the University of Minnesota, from Cambridge in England, and from Yale. His older brother, Dr. Anthony Zelený, is Professor of Physics at the University of Minnesota, and still another brother, Dr. Charles Zelený, is Professor of Zoölogy at the University of Illinois.

Dr. Alois F. Kovářík, an Iowan by birth, was formerly connected with the University of Minnesota; now he is attached to the Sloane Laboratory at Yale. The Victoria University of Manchester, in England, conferred upon Kovářík the degree of Sc.D., in recognition of researches in physics.

Professors and students of the Prague University were genuinely surprised when Bohumil Šimek, Professor of Botany in the State University of Iowa, delivered in 1914 lectures in impeccable Čech on the plant life of the United States. They were amazed upon being told that the learned botanist had never attended any but English language schools; that up to that time he had not been in Europe; that all the Čech he knew he had learned in Iowa City, his native town, by self-tuition.

Šimek occupies a unique position among university professors of Čech descent. He was never content to act the rôle of a mere onlooker or a critic. He felt he was a blood relative and that he must

DR. ROBERT J. KERNER

collaborate, not criticize. Therefore he joined the societies of his racial kinsmen; read Čech books and newspapers — for a time he edited the organ of the Č.S.P.S. Society; he interested himself in most of their cultural problems. Many a youth is indebted for his college education to the Matice Society, of which the professor is a co-founder.

Of his father, "a heretic and rebel" (as Austrian reactionaries used to call the Čech nationalists of 1848), Šimek is justly proud. The elder Šimek was a pioneer settler in that part of Iowa where the son was born in 1861. For his work as a scientist the Prague University recently made Šimek Sc.D.

Dr. Paul J. Hanzlik, Assistant Professor of Pharmacology, Western Reserve University, was born in Iowa (1885), studied in the Universities of Iowa and Illinois, and in 1914 was a research student in the Pharmacological Institute of the University of Vienna. He has published important papers dealing with subjects in biological chemistry, pharmacology, and therapeutics.

The first professor of Čech nationality was M. Charles Hrubý, who came in 1834. He taught German language and literature in an Ohio College.

CHAPTER VI

THE IMMIGRANT AS A LIABILITY

OF the police reports obtained from the principal cities of the United States, only those of Chicago contained records of arrests admitting of statistical analysis of the relations of immigrants to crime. The reports of the Chicago Police Department for the four years from 1905 to 1908 contained tabular statements of arrests by crime and nationality. The records for these four years were therefore combined and retabulated. These figures form the material on which this chapter is based.[1]

Figures show that offenses of personal violence are relatively most frequent among the crimes of the immigrants coming from eastern and southern Europe — the Lithuanians, Slavs, Italians, Poles, Greeks, Čechs, and Austrians. The largest proportion is found in the Lithuanian group, of whose total crimes those of personal violence form 12.1 per cent.[2]

The relatively large proportion of burglaries among the crimes of Čechs (1.7 per cent) is noticeable, though ten other nationalities have larger percentages of the total gainful offenses. The Bohemian percentage of burglary is the same as the

---

[1] *Police Arrests in the City of Chicago*, chap. IX, p. 133, Senate Doc., v. 18. Washington, 1911.

[2] *Ibid.*, p. 136.

THE IMMIGRANT AS A LIABILITY

Canadian and the German, but both of these latter nationalities have higher percentages of the total gainful offenses and of the specific crimes of forgery and fraud and of larceny and receiving stolen property.[1]

Among eight nationalities — Bohemian, Chinese, Danish, French, Irish, Norwegian, Slavonian, and Scotch — no arrests for abduction and kidnaping were made.[2]

The nationalities having the six highest percentages for simple assault are the Lithuanians, Slavs, Bohemians, Greeks, Poles, and Russians.[3]

Of the nationalities from the south and east of Europe only the Bohemians and the Russians have smaller percentages of homicide than any nationality from northern and western Europe.[4]

The Polish, Bohemian, Slavonian, Canadian, Danish, German, Lithuanian, and Austrian all exceed the American white group in percentage for arrests for disorderly conduct.[5]

The record of the immigrant as a charity-seeker and pauper,[6] as a dynamic force in industry,[7] as a social problem in large cities,[8] is adequately considered in the Senate Documents herein referred to.

[1] *Police Arrests in the City of Chicago*, chap. IX, p. 140, Senate Doc., v. 18. Washington, 1911.

[2] *Ibid.*, p. 143. [3] *Ibid.*, p. 143.

[4] *Ibid.*, p. 144. [5] *Ibid.*, p. 147.

[6] *Immigrants as Charity Seekers*, Senate Doc., v. 10.

[7] *Immigrants in Industries*, Senate Doc., vs. 68, 69, 70.

[8] *Immigrants in Cities*. Senate Doc., vs. 66, 67.

CHAPTER VII

THROUGH INTERMARRIAGE INTO THE MELTING-POT

WHILE, as a rule, the young folks choose life partners from among their own race, it will be noted from the figures given below that mixed marriages are increasingly popular. As a matter of fact there are not many Čech families unrelated, through one branch or another, to non-Čechs. Unions with mid-European races, particularly the Teutonic, have been most popular in the past. With Latin nations, Italians or French, or with the far Northern races (Scandinavians), Čechs rarely concluded marital relations. Comparatively few are the cases of Čechs mating with other Slavs: Poles, Russians, South Slavs (Jugo-Slavs). That the Teutons have supplied more marrying partners than all the other nationalities put together, may dismay the idealist and the Slavophil, but it does not surprise one who is familiar with pre-war conditions in Central Europe. Love not only laughs at locksmiths, but it scorns to be made a party to a race feud. A vital link is the ability to speak the language of the other race; and much as the Slavophil may deplore it, there still are more Čechs who know German than there are Čechs who speak Russian, Polish, or Serbo-Croatian.

The 1910 census made no investigation concern-

DR. BOHUMIL ŠIMEK

ing mixed marriages and hence it is impossible to give later official statistics than those of 1900.[1]

Father born in	Mother born in	
Bohemia	Austria	1676
Bohemia	Canada (English)	154
Bohemia	Canada (French)	33
Bohemia	Denmark	22
Bohemia	England	89
Bohemia	France	68
Bohemia	Germany	4024
Bohemia	Hungary	455
Bohemia	Ireland	132
Bohemia	Italy	11
Bohemia	Norway	22
Bohemia	Poland	294
Bohemia	Russia	166
Bohemia	Sweden	35
Bohemia	Switzerland	103
Bohemia	Other countries	223

Mother born in	Father born in	
Bohemia	Austria	1741
Bohemia	Canada (English)	357
Bohemia	Canada (French)	92
Bohemia	Denmark	91
Bohemia	England	241
Bohemia	France	171
Bohemia	Germany	7143
Bohemia	Hungary	728
Bohemia	Ireland	203
Bohemia	Italy	85
Bohemia	Norway	72
Bohemia	Poland	771
Bohemia	Russia	191
Bohemia	Scotland	61
Bohemia	Sweden	98
Bohemia	Switzerland	240
Bohemia	Wales	20
Bohemia	Other countries	274

[1] *Twelfth Census (1900) of the United States Population*, Part I, p. 850, Table 56. Total persons of mixed foreign parentage.

Is there any particular factor that enters into these mixed marriages? Sometimes it is the occupational contact — employment in the same shop or factory — which brings two young people together. Common faith, if not a determining, is yet an influencing, factor. Years ago when New York Čechs were largely employed at cigarmaking, several Cubans, specializing at what cigarmakers call "Spanish work," married Čech girls working in the tobacco industry. The author has been told that in and near Humboldt, Nebraska, Swiss and Čech farmers, being neighbors, have intermarried freely. The Chicago paper *Svornost* has recorded the case of the Mayor of Traverse City, Michigan, who boasted of German-Čech-French blood.

Cases of curious marital snarls and tangles inevitably occur in mixed marriages. The divorce calendar of the District Court of Douglas County, Nebraska, contains the case of Gaydou *vs*. Gaydou. The plaintiff was a Čech woman who knew her mother tongue and no other language; the defendant was a French-Canadian who could stammer, besides his native French, only a few words in English. And yet these two, blissfully ignorant of each other's language, managed to live together happily for three whole months. An Italian cobbler in New York, curly-haired and swarthy of skin, swore to love and cherish a flaxen-haired Čech lass from near Kutná Hora. When these two started out on their marital life journey, their lingual attainments were so rudimentary that they had to resort to the expedient of the sign language. It makes one realize the truth of the saying that, after all, the whole world is kin, when one reads among lodge notices in the *New Yorské Listy* a call for a meeting of the "Union of Čech Women," signed by Ludmila Cassidy, secretary, and Josefina O'Connell, treasurer. In this instance the Hibernian and the Čech hearts and hands have joined.

Are mixed marriages happy? Mrs. de C., having as a widow married a Belgian, does not advise Čech girls to enter into wedlock with partners not of their own blood. "Usually such marriages end unhappily," is her warning. Mr. —ský of Brooklyn, however, holds an opposite view. His two daughters have made ideal alliances with German-Americans, while his son married a Yankee girl. "What difference does it make," argues Mr. —ský, "whom my girls marry? They are born here, and are therefore Americans, like their husbands, who are also of the same (American) nation."

CHAPTER VIII

ALL BORN IN AMERICA BELONG TO AMERICA

A NOTED violinist came to New York. The local Čech community, proud of its renowned countryman, gave an evening in his honor. If not contrary to the terms of his contract with the manager, the violinist consented to play.

On the great day the Bohemian Hall was crowded with people eager to do homage to the artist who contributed to the fame of his country's music. Every one was pleasurably expectant when the artist arrived in company with his manager, carrying the magic violin under his arm. The violinist played a bar or two of the national anthem *Kde domov můj*, putting into the simple air all the feeling of which a Čech musician away from home is capable. At that moment, tense with emotion, women were seen to press handkerchiefs to their eyes. But it was interesting to note the unequal effect of the anthem on the hearers. While the old folks were visibly moved by the appealing tones that reminded them of the Fatherland, the young people listened coldly, critically.

In the orchestra sat an elderly man, a staid citizen, father of several children, all of whom had been born in the metropolis. As the violinist struck the first bar of the *Kde domov můj*, the old gentleman's powerful frame was seen to shake and his eyes grow moist. His son of about sixteen, who sat next to him, was also aroused by the music, but in a different way. He turned to his father and remonstrated: "Father, why do you weep? Why do you make such a show of yourself?"

Are Čech children not interested in the birthland of their parents? Or, to state the case more pointedly, are they indifferent about their ancestry? The answer is simple: the American Čech youth — American not only by cold statistics, but by sympathy as well, for all that is born in America belongs to America — are neither better nor worse than the children of Swedish, French, or Irish parentage. Their schooling is American, their mother tongue English. The spirit of the Anglo-Saxon race, happily blended with distinctive Slavic traits, is their spirit.

When Frances Gregor's English version of Božena Němcová's masterpiece *Babička* (Grandmother) came off the press, the Čech papers in the United States were deeply chagrined that the book, notwithstanding flattering newspaper notices, did not appeal more strongly to the younger generation. "We are keenly disappointed that our American-born children feel so little interested in the work of our authoress," commented one newspaper. "If *Babička* had been published here in Čech we should have condoned the apathy of our young folk, but Miss Gregor's *Babička* they should all be able to understand." Yet is it reasonable to expect from our American children and grandchildren, reasoned the same journal, whose heads are full of fractions and algebra, to love our adorable *Babička*, to listen patiently to her artless tales of rustic life, to evince curiosity about the contents of that wondrous, decorated dowry chest of hers?

The process of Americanization of children begins in the primary grades of the public school and is made complete in practical life. Often foreign-born parents are heard complaining of the rapid denationalization of their offspring. It is by no means unusual for such parents, in order to give to children a working foundation in their vernacular, to make it a practice to converse with them at home in the native tongue, to the exclusion of English. School-teachers are often incredulous that this or that child has been born in America, so elementary is the knowledge of English it brings to the schoolroom. The author has in mind the case of a boy, who, though born in New York, knew but a few words of English, and those he pronounced like a foreigner. At home, for his sake, English conversation was eschewed. Having been taken on a visit to his grandparents in San José, California, where there were no Čechs, the boy one day came running in to tell his grandfather how stupid his playmates were: they could not speak Čech! Yet all these expedients and precautions avail nothing. The moment the child crosses the threshold of the schoolhouse, the question of his future fealty is settled. With his grandmother, or other members of the family, he will talk Čech, because he has found out that grandmother knows no other language. Let the child, however, sense a speaking knowledge of English in any one, relative or neighbor, that person will ever afterward be addressed by him in English only. The oddity has been noticed among the children of foreign-born parents, that while the first born speaks the mother tongue of the parents passably well, the youngest offspring speaks it poorly or not at all. The explanation is simple enough. When the first child came, the parents in all probability were still monolingual, knowing no other except their own tongue. Meantime, as the other children began arriving, the parents already had acquired a speaking knowledge of English; that is to say, they had become bilingual. In consequence, the later-born children, no longer needing the "other language" in their intercourse with parents or older kin, never learned it.

You may persist in telling your child of the glory of Bohemia's past; that the land of your birth had an old and honorable record long before the Pilgrim Fathers landed on the Massachusetts coast. The child will answer: But how small *your* country is compared to *ours!* You realize how futile it is to argue with a youthful head to which nothing appeals more convincingly than physical greatness. The tallest mountain — Mount Whitney; the longest river — Missouri; two oceans; New York now estimated to be the largest city in the world; a republic of more than one hundred million inhabitants — is it possible to play a bigger trump-card in order to convince youthful minds? Prague, too, is a city of respectable size? Why, we have a dozen towns larger than Prague. Two of our smaller States, New Jersey and Maryland, will counter-pane the whole of Bohemia with a few hundred miles to spare! The area of a single American State is larger than the whole of the Čechoslovak Republic.

CHAPTER IX

NEW BOHEMIA IN AMERICA

TWO and a half centuries ago, Augustine Herrman, lord of Bohemia Manor, visualized a New Bohemia which should shelter exiles of his faith and race, as New England, New Sweden, New Holland, and New France had been planned to serve as a haven of refuge to men from England, Sweden, Holland, and France. Pathfinders like Náprstek and Oliverius fancied that a Čech community was realizable; the perplexing question was how and where to establish it. Klácel, to the end of his days, was obsessed with a like notion. He dreamt of Svojanovs, compact groups conducted somewhat on the pattern of Brook Farm. In the seventies Joseph W. Sýkora, a member of the Cleveland bar, drew an alluring picture in the *Slavie* of a New Bohemia. Unfortunately, Sýkora's Čech fairy tale was just what its name said — a fairy tale and nothing more. On December 31, 1865, and January 1 and 2, 1866, the so-called Slavic Congress met in Chicago to discuss the ways and means for the organization of a Čech-Slavic community. Charles Jonáš was elected chairman, Adolph B. Chládek, secretary. It was planned to send a delegation (Charles Jonáš and J. B. Erben) to Washington to petition the Government for a grant of land. But a public subscription which had been ordered to that end did not bring funds enough to defray the traveling expenses of the delegates to the capital, much less to lay a foundation for the proposed community.

John A. Oliverius urged his countrymen to migrate *en masse* to Oregon, and seek in that State, protected as it is on one side by the sea, the consummation of the long-cherished dream. The scheme was promptly voted down by Charles Jonáš, who always looked upon Oliverius as a harmless fanatic. The projected migration of American Čechs to Russia that had been advocated by J. B. Letovský, F. Mráček, and others at the beginning of the Civil War, was another manifestation of their yearning to live apart in settlements made up of their own people.

Experience has shown that the settlements thrived best in which the home-seekers were free to select their acres and choose their neighbors. Where land agents or leaders of colonizing expeditions did the choosing for the farmers, there was discontent, resulting in failure.

One of the earliest fruitful attempts at colonization originated in Chicago. Under the leadership of Franta Bém and Franta Janoušek, a company of agriculturists started in the seventies from Chicago for Knox County, Nebraska. On the way, so the story goes, the two leaders disagreed as to the merits of the land, with the result that the expedi-

A ČECH ALLEY IN CHICAGO

Walker Court, near Eighteenth and Throop Streets

tion split into two parties: a number of the settlers took land in Knox County,[1] near the present towns of Verdigre and Niobrara, while the other faction, led by Bém, crossed the Missouri River into the neighboring State of South Dakota and located in Bon Homme County. In 1874 a Chicago organization, styling itself *Slovanská Osada* (Slavic Colony) proposed to take workmen from congested centers and settle them in Nebraska or Kansas. About the same time some Omaha people organized the *Slavonia* club with the object of forming settlements in Nebraska.

The *Česká Osada* (Čech Colony) in Chicago, another organization, issued this appeal in 1876 to prospective land-tillers! "The idea of freeing one's self from the yoke of capital and building one's own existence in the country is excellent. We recognize it to be the only feasible and practicable solution of the so-called workingmen's problems. The fertile soil of the West is capable of giving sustenance and independence to millions of home-builders and we cannot do otherwise than approve of the plans of the society." The *Česká Osada* also favored settlements in a warmer climate. Onward to Texas, Arizona, and California, read their address; let the Čechs feel the joy of resting in the shade of orange trees after their daily toil! A com-

[1] The *Pokrok Západu* of August 3, 1900, contains an account of the thirtieth anniversary of the Knox County settlement. — The Almanac *Pionýr* for 1919: "What the first settlers in Nebraska endured." By one of them (Šedivý).

mittee of this organization was sent to Shasta County, California, to report on conditions there; a minority opposed the coast State because, in its opinion, the price of the land was too high. To some, Oklahoma seemed to offer greater opportunities than California. One of the most ardent partisans of California, Frank Petrovec, a young man of the type characterized by Germans as a Latin farmer, because he had been educated in a Latin school, was accidentally killed by a railroad train as the investigation committee neared the border-line of the land of promise. This tragic incident discouraged the members of the *Česká Osada*, who were never to taste the joy of resting beneath the orange tree after their daily toil.

A. F. Dignowity of Del Rio, Texas, invited the Čechs to settle on a ranch of some thirty thousand acres which he claimed he owned jointly with his brothers in Kinney County, seven miles from Fort Clark and Brackett.[1] Dignowity contended his land was as fertile as any in California. He wished the countrymen of his father, the late Dr. Anthony M. Dignowity, to avail themselves of the opportunity and establish a settlement on his land. Dignowity's appeal remained apparently unheeded, for no Čechs are known to live in that part of Texas.

The Čechs are not the only Europeans who have aspired to build up separate communities. The

[1] The *Pokrok Západu*, January 18, 1888.

NEW BOHEMIA IN AMERICA

Germans have made systematic and repeated efforts in that direction. Witness the Teutonic concentration in Pennsylvania. The Giesner Auswanderungs Gesellschaft schemed to make Missouri a German State. Read what vision Paul Follenius and Friedrich Münch, two Germans of culture, conjured to themselves: "We must not go from here [Germany] without realizing a national idea or at least making the beginning toward its realization; the foundation of a new and free Germany in the great North American Republic shall be laid by us. . . . Thus, we may be able at least in one of the American territories to establish an essentially German State, in which refuge may be found for all those to whom conditions at home have become unbearable — a territory which shall be able to make a model State in the great Republic."[1] Follenius and Münch and some followers secured land in 1834 in Warren County, but in a larger sense the plan ended in a failure.

In 1835, a society was organized in New York by the name of Germania. The main object of Germania was to introduce and foster here German customs and language. The promoters petitioned Congress to set aside a suitable area for exclusive colonization by Germans. Congress disallowed the petition; but the petitioners, undismayed, deter-

[1] Albert B. Faust: *The German Element in the United States*, with special reference to its political, moral, social, and educational influence, v. I, p. 433. 1909.

mined to pursue another course to attain their object. Immigrants from the Fatherland were to be advised to settle in enclaves picked out for them in advance; these enclaves were to be proclaimed German-language territories the moment German settlers had obtained the upper hand in them. The promoters, however, disagreed as to the choice of the State wherein the experiment was to be tried. While certain members favored Texas or Oregon, others thought the Middle West, somewhere between the Mississippi and the Lakes, the more suitable place. Franz Löhner, who had evinced considerable solicitude about the future of his countrymen beyond the seas, believed no country offered greater opportunities than the area between the basins of the Ohio and Missouri Rivers. The Irish, reasoned Löhner, made their homes in the large cities of the East; the Americans were scattered over the length and breadth of the continent. This distribution of races left to the Germans the Middle West in which were the choicest prizes — Wisconsin and Iowa. Upon Milwaukee was conferred the proud title, Deutsche Athen, German Athens. German settlers gained ascendancy in these Wisconsin counties: Milwaukee, Ozaukee, Washington, Grant, Sheboygan, Manitowoc, Jefferson, Outgamie, Fond du Lac, Sauk, Waupaca, Dane, Marathon, Waushara, Green Lake, Langlade, and Clark. What reader of older Čech newspapers will not readily recognize in several of these names old acquaintances? St. Killian is the home of a large settlement of Germans from northwestern Bohemia.[1]

Count von Castell, an aide to the Duke of Nassau, became convinced that prospects were excellent for the introduction of German kultur in Texas. Castell enlisted not only the sympathy, but what was more important, the financial aid, of a number of aristocratic families in Germany and Austria. In 1842 two delegates, Count Boos Waldek and Victor von Leininger, traveled to Texas in order to study the situation on the spot. And so enthusiastic was the report which these two nobles sent home that the Mainzer Adelverein agreed to sponsor the plan publicly. A systematic pro-Texas campaign was undertaken in Central Europe. Two years later (1844) Prince Carl Solms-Braunfels started for the new land with one hundred and fifty families by way of Bremen. The place which these pioneers chose as their headquarters was named New Braunfels, in honor of the leader of the expedition.

The agitation carried on by Solms-Braunfels had a direct bearing upon the immigration from Moravia a few years later. The principal seat of activity of the Mainzer Adelverein was at Mainz. Now, the Mainz fortress was until the Austro-Prussian War in 1866 garrisoned jointly by Austrian

[1] *Annual Report of the State Historical Society of Wisconsin*, pp. 58–59. 1890.

and Prussian soldiers. Čech soldiers served there among others, and the inference is a reasonable one that the projects of the Mainzer Adelverein were fairly well known to them. Besides, aristocrats who were interested in it as members or patrons, owned estates in Germany and Austria, as well as in Bohemia and Moravia.

It was not mere coincidence that the Čechs uniformly massed in those cities and country areas in which the Germans had been settled. Persons familiar with Čech psychology know that the march of the Čech pathfinders in the footsteps of the Germans had not been fortuitous, but a matter of careful premeditation. As explained on another page the Čechs were drawn to the Germans by a similarity, if not identity, in customs and mode of life; besides, educated as many of them had been in German-language schools, the pioneers felt pretty much at home among the Germans — notwithstanding old-country racial antagonisms. Wisconsin, we know, was intended to be a German State; we find Čech farmers settling there. The Čechs began massing in St. Louis in the middle of the last century; and St. Louis was one of the German strongholds in the Middle West. Other prominently German cities were Milwaukee, Cincinnati, and Detroit; strong groups of Čechs located in all these.

Could the Čechs with their incomparably small numbers and slender means hope to succeed where the Germans, having the advantage in numerical strength, superior organization, and powerful support, had failed?

Judging by the lessons of the past it is certain that communities which aim to perpetuate a language other than English will not thrive in the United States. The Slovaks at one time started a noisy campaign in their newspapers to divert miners and mill workers to a Slovak enclave in Arkansas. And the result? One village in Hazen County called Slovaktown attests the failure of the undertaking. Polonia in Wisconsin could tell its story of the shattered hopes of the Poles. A few decades ago the Scandinavians set out to dominate Minnesota. Now Minnesota dominates the Scandinavians.

No parish school, no church congregation, no foreign-language community can long withstand the *force majeure* of Americanization. In a measurable time the Bohemias, Germanias, New Braunfels, Polonias, and Slovaktowns, will be but a name and a memory.

CHAPTER X

GAMIN America has bestowed on certain of its
immigrants race-names, jestful or tantalizing,
over which the learned etymologist may well de-
spair. The Teuton is called "Dutchman," clearly
from "Deutsch," "Deutscher." In the olden times,
before the Yankee learned to differentiate between
the new-comers from Central Europe, every immigrant resembling the German in dress or looks was
unceremoniously dubbed by him a Dutchman.
For the son of Italy the gamin etymologist has
coined the somewhat cryptic appellations of "Dago"
and "Wop." Even one ignorant of the mysteries
of roots and terminations will readily understand
why he refers to the Mexican as "Greaser." The
Irishman is "Mick" and the Hungarian in Pennsylvania, "Hunk" or "Hunky." In some localities
Bohemians are called "Bohoes," in other "Bo-
hunks"; less familiar are the terms "Cheskey" and
"Bootchkey." A non-Bohemian finding himself in
a city quarter peopled by Bohemians cannot but
notice the word Český (pronounced Cheskey) leer-
ing at him from every store sign: Český pekař (Čech
baker), Český hostinec (Čech tavern), Český gro-
cerista (Čech grocer). Promptly he must see a

connection between *Český* and Bohemian. The word "Bootchkey," however, offers no such clue to the etymologist as "Cheskey"; to get at its hidden meaning one must know something of the moods of the New York street. The explanation is made that in a street warfare the Čech boys of the Upper East Side signaled to each other with the call *počkej*, meaning, in Čech, wait, hold on. To the ears of the non-Čech playmates this sounded very much like *bootchkey*. Hence, a Bohemian is "Bootchkey."

Thus far but one Čech word has made itself at home in the English language: *pantata*. The *Standard Dictionary of the English Language*,[1] page 1273, gives this derivation of it: "*Pan-tata.* (Slang U.S.) One having authority; a boss. Czech — *pan*, master, mister — *tata*, father. *Pantata, pan*—mister, and *tata* — endearing term for father (the true equivalent in Bohemian for father being *otec*), is ordinarily used in addressing one's father-in-law, though in a broad sense any elderly countryman may be spoken to as *pantata*. As understood in New York, where the word was first used in 1894, at the time of the Lexow Committee trial, it signifies a corrupt police captain."[2]

Has any one taken the pains to count the English words which have been injected into the Čech

---

[1] Funk & Wagnalls Co. New York and London, 1903.

[2] *Report and Proceedings of the Senate Committee*, appointed to investigate the Police Department of New York City, v. II, p. 1722.

language? Glance through the advertisement columns of a newspaper and you will begin to understand what inroad English is making into the Čech. The following words are taken from a short real estate advertisement in the *New Yorské Listy*: acre, improvement, block, lot, mortgage, assessment, canalization. It is superfluous to say that the Čech language has an equivalent for every one of the foregoing expressions, yet English is given preference.

Note how English looks when a foreign language — in this instance Slovak — tries to assimilate it. A Slovak weekly, *Národné Noviny* of Pittsburgh, complained in a recent article entitled, "Preserve the Purity of our Tongue," of the wanton corruption of the Slovak. As transliterated into the Slovak tongue, English looks queer to an American: jesser — yes sir; noser — no sir; sej — say; jes — yes; šúr — sure; olrajt — all right; kvoder — quarter; dajm — dime; skuner — schooner; viska — whiskey; pejda — pay day; boket — bucket; dinerka — dinner; štrita — street; revra — river; apštérs — upstairs; danštérs — downstairs. "The use of these and other corruptions," expostulates the editor of the *Národné Noviny*, "has gained such a hold on our people, that most of them are no longer aware they are using them." As an instance of the subduing force of English, the same editor tells of a social at which the guests present agreed to pay a fine of five cents for each English word uttered. In an hour's time $7.55 had been collected in fines.

In the homeland the purists try to keep the tongue free from the dross of the so-called Germanisms. Who will keep watch over the purity of the language here and shield it from Anglicisms, from erosion and corruption?

No name has caused its bearers greater discomfiture than Václav. Václav, be it remembered, is one of the patron saints of Bohemia. An ancient hymn which is still sung in the Catholic churches invokes "Holy Václav, Duke of Bohemian Land," to save his countrymen from extermination. Somehow or other the American Václavs — St. Václav has a host of namesakes on both sides of the ocean — are not content with the name. A number of the milder malcontents have given it a German or a Latin form: Wenzel, Venceslas, Venceslaus; the majority, though, figuratively speaking, have thrown Václav overboard, assuming in lieu of it William, Wesley, Wendel, James, according to the fancy of the bearer. Václav is, of course, as untranslatable as Roland, Kenneth, or Leslie.

The Americanization of names is a practice by no means infrequent, although it is not as widespread as popularly believed. Caprice or expediency prompt one to change his name. Sometimes a name is coined as a result of a fair exchange of values, Čech for English, provided it is translatable. Thus Jablečník is made Appleton, Studnička is transformed into Wells, Krejčí becomes Taylor, Zástěra hides himself behind Apron. In the majority of cases the man moulds his patronymic along the lines of Čech pronunciation: Kořista — Corrister; Anderlik — Underleak; Kučera — Goodsheller; Kočí — Cutshaw; Mrkvička — Murray; Křenka — Krank; Mosnička — Mason; Maršálek — Marshall; Nožíř — Norris; Čihák — Jayshaw; Hudec — Hudson; Tesař — Teaser; Přeučil — Prucil; Šimáček — Smack. A Nebraska politician trimmed his name from Lapáček to La Pache; Vančura, a plain Vančura, by a genial tug at his surname emerged from out of the purging process as Van Cura. Who would sense in Van Cura a Čech and not a descendant of a Knickerbocker family?

CHAPTER XI

ACCORDING to Austrian official statistics, 960.48 of every 1000 persons in Bohemia profess the Catholic faith, 21.77 are Protestants, 16.19 Jews, 1.12 Old Catholics, 0.20 without confession, 0.24 mixed. These figures, however, do not obtain in America. If we were to take the Čech residents of New York as an illustration, we should get approximately this result: Catholics, 254; Protestants, 110; Jews, 16; persons without any church affiliation, 620. Conditions, of course, vary in different States and places, due to various local causes. In some the strength of the Catholics and of the non-Catholics is about evenly balanced. Chicago is such a place. In others the Catholics predominate; the latter is believed to be the case in Texas, Wisconsin, Minnesota. It is within the truth to say that 50 per cent of the Čechs in America have seceded from their old-country faith. One author is convinced that the strength of the secessionists is nearer 60 or 70 per cent than 50.[1] Of the non-church faction, two distinct shades are recognizable; first, the negativists, and secondly

[1] J. E. Salaba Vojan: "Why should we American Čechs be Liberal-Minded?" pp. 425–28, in *Čech Reader*, edited by Vojta Beneš. Prague, 1912.

the dyed-in-the-wool anti-clericals who have subscribed to Havlíček's harsh formula as applied
to the priests: give them nothing, credit them
nothing.

From what class do the dissenters come? The
immigrant from the rural districts of the domestic and agricultural labor class has, on the whole,
remained loyal to the faith in which he was born
and reared. Not so with the worker from urban or
industrial centers. In his ranks, cases of dissent
are common. Among the *inteligence*, the educated
class, religious secession has been the rule, not the
exception. Indeed, so general was the secession by
the intellectuals that, before the mid-nineties, the
churchmen had no lay *inteligence* worth mention.

As between the Čechs from Bohemia and those
from Moravia, the first-named have manifested a
readier inclination to break away than their more
conservative kinsmen from Moravia.

Certain people professed to think that the schism
was but a whim and a fad and that when the nov-
elty of it wore off the malcontents would return.
Well-informed commentators did not share this op-
timistic view. The whim, if it were a whim, has
lasted altogether too long. Newspapers have been
made and unmade by reason of the controversy
between the churchmen and the secessionists. Determined to outdo the opposition, one faction has
built houses of worship, while the other with equal
perseverance has erected club-houses where men

and women could meet "free from the intrusion of clericalism."

What is the cause of this decatholization?

One writer[1] asserted that the rupture would never have taken place had not Joseph Pastor, editor of the weekly *Pokrok*, thrown a firebrand of discord among his countrymen. Before Pastor's time, he argued, the Čechs were of one mind, one faith.

Another was inclined to blame the clergy. The veteran priests, he charged, were wont to be domineering, and to show their resentment many parishioners ceased going to church.

Still another condemned Klácel and his subversive propaganda. Zdrůbek and Šnajdr and their liberal publications also came in for a share of censure.

A fourth writer thought that it was the scarcity of houses of worship in the pioneer years which led to the parting of the ways. Yet he failed to explain why the Poles did not falter in their faith under precisely the same untoward conditions. A Pole migrates from Catholic Poland to non-Catholic United States and he remains steadfast, notwithstanding the change of residence. The Čech, also a Catholic at home, becomes decatholicized overseas. Why?

An extremist in all things, Dr. Habenicht[2] held

---

[1] John Borecký: *Chapters on the History of Čech-Moravians in America*, p. 13.

[2] John Habenicht: *The History of the Čechs in America*, p. x.

to the view that "vulgar materialism" was at the bottom of the defection. According to him the liberals kept aloof from the churches for the reason that they were averse to supporting them financially.

An American student,[1] whose books on immigrants have elicited wide newspaper comment, has no argument to offer; however, he is scandalized that there are so many non-churchmen among the Čechs. "They are thoroughly eaten through and through by infidelity." If this writer had said that the Čechs were "thoroughly eaten through and through," not by infidelity, but by Hussitism, so far as Hussitism implies a challenge to unquestioning faith, he would have hit the nail on the head.

The primary cause, the *causa causans*, of the alienation lies deep in the nation's past. To contend that Pastor, or Klácel, or any one individual is responsible therefor is as reasonable as that John Brown's raid on Harper's Ferry was the cause of the Civil War.

First, there is Bohemia's Hussite past. Though he may not be conscious of it, the truth of the matter is that the Čech's inclination to dissent, to question, to challenge, to dispute, is largely inherited from his Hussite forefathers. In the American Čech these tendencies burst forth with elemental strength the moment he landed in America, where he could speak, act, and think free from the

[1] Edward A. Steiner: *On the Trail of the Immigrant*, p. 230.

oppression to which he was subject in his native land.

Von Ranke, the historian, avers that Emperor Charles IV (1316–78), was the greatest man born on Bohemian soil. Admittedly Charles was a wise, progressive sovereign. Under his rule many innovations were introduced, the foundation of the Prague University in 1348 being doubtless his most enduring achievement. Contrary to what von Ranke asserts, the Čechs believe that not Emperor Charles but John Hus was the greatest man born in Bohemia.

Non-Bohemian historians are apt to view and study Hussitism from one angle only, the religious. To the natives Hussitism has a deeper meaning. More than any other force it has kindled in them, keeping it alive for centuries, the feeling of national consciousness. The Austrian conqueror in the seventeenth century almost destroyed the nation, yet he was powerless to blot out the living memory of its glorious past, and it was under the light of this great past that nationalism revived in the middle of the nineteenth century.

The Hussites started out to correct certain abuses in the Church; but before long their leaders, broadening the programme, raised the banner of nationalism and struck at the Teutons, whom eventually they pushed everywhere to the very edge of the frontier. The defense of faith and the defense of language were not the only issues involved. In the course of time the dispute resolved itself into its elemental factors: a struggle between democracy, which the Hussites championed, the right of men to determine for themselves their system of government, their form of religion, and their scheme of social relationship; and aristocracy and Teutonism, represented by the anti-Hussites, which sought to impose upon the individual a privileged religion, government, and caste system. In the Čech of to-day Hussitism evokes emotions akin to those which move a Frenchman at the contemplation of the Great Revolution. The things the French did toward the close of the eighteenth century, the Hussites set out to achieve in the fifteenth century. That the Hussites failed, while the French three and a half centuries later triumphed, was due to causes wholly beyond the power of the Čechs to control.

Secondly, there are the country's Protestant traditions. That, too, is a weighty factor the influence of which should not be minimized. Up to the Thirty Years' War the Čechs had been a Protestant nation. When the victor had begun to recatholicize Bohemia following the disastrous Battle of White Hill in 1620, thousands, tens of thousands, preferred banishment to the renunciation of their faith. Several of the chief rebels lost their heads on the scaffold for a cause they believed to be a righteous one. Far from condemning the Protestants for having rebelled against the Hapsburgs, even though the ill-planned rebellion had almost cost the nation its life, every liberal-minded Čech of to-day admires as heroes and venerates as martyrs the men who on the Bloody Day at Prague, June 21, 1621, gave their lives for the Fatherland.

Thirdly, the fact should not be lost sight of that between the American protagonists of rationalism and the revivalists in the mother country the connection was not only close, but in many instances personal. The men who had worked for the regeneration of Bohemia since 1848, clergymen included, were thorough-going liberals, even radicals. One of the greatest leaders of this period, the man whom the American rationalists quote oftener than any other, was Charles Havlíček (1821–53), journalist and politician.

Not Ladimir Klácel, as is popularly believed, but Vojta Náprstek, was the first to disseminate rationalism among American Čechs. Náprstek, who was an admirer and personal friend of Havlíček's, published in Milwaukee, in the early fifties, a liberal weekly, the *Flug Blätter*. Though a German-language paper the *Flug Blätter* was read largely by Náprstek's fellow countrymen. Many of the patrons of the *Flug Blätter* became, in later years, stockholders, readers, publishers, editors, and supporters of the Čech press. As interpreted in the columns of the *Flug Blätter*, Náprstek's liberalism was strikingly like that espoused by Havlíček in the Prague *Národní Noviny;* that is to say, it was

THE ČECHS IN AMERICA

anti-clerical and anti-Austrian. "In 1854 the *Flug Blätter* was the subject of some heated debates in both houses of the Wisconsin legislature, where Assemblyman Worthington of Waukesha and Senator McGarry of Milwaukee offered resolutions prohibiting the legislative postmasters from distributing this publication to the members. These resolutions, however, were not adopted."[1]

Vojta Náprstek was born in Prague in 1828 and died in that city in 1894, mourned by the entire nation. He came to New York in 1849 as a political refugee. It is a mistake to think that Náprstek fled to America for political reasons only. In his mind's eye he pictured to himself an ideal Čech community in America. He weighed the matter carefully and noted in 1847 in his diary: "As soon as I am entirely ready, I shall start my agitation. In a year and half there shall be a Čech settlement in America."[2]

After wandering here and there he finally settled in Milwaukee, starting his publication in 1852. Although his stay in America was of a comparatively short duration, eight years in all, it sufficed to make an enthusiastic American of him. Upon returning to his native land in 1857, he missed no opportunity to familiarize his country with American ideas,

[1] Parkman: *Club Papers*, p. 236. 1896.
[2] Julius Zeyer: *Vojta Náprstek*. A lecture delivered on his seventieth birthday, p. 11. Prague, 1896. Vojta Náprstek: *Memorial Leaf*. Prague, 1894. Reprint of illustrated articles from the *Světozor*, Prague, XXVIII: 1420–21–22. J. R. Jičínský: *Osvěta Americká*, February–March, 1907.

VOJTA NÁPRSTEK AND "MRS. JOSEPHINE," HIS WIFE

American institutions, American methods. Americanism, it may truthfully be said, was Náprstek's life passion. When he came into possession of the family patrimony, which was considerable, he began to lay plans for what in time developed into the Náprstek American Museum, otherwise known as Náprstek Industrial Museum, in Prague. Woman suffrage had in him a warm advocate; the Club of American Women was organized and met in his salons. Náprstek's hospitable home was a rendezvous of emigrants and none were more heartily welcome than American Čechs. "That which the heart unites the sea shall not divide," was a motto prominently displayed in Náprstek's reading-rooms. He never sought the favor of the governing class, his democracy being too real and his religious views too radical. A New Yorker having once asked him what Americans he admired the most, the former editor of the *Flug Blätter* replied, unhesitatingly, Paine and Jefferson.

Now as to the part the press played in the secession movement.

The *Slowan Amerikánský*, *Národní Noviny*, *Slavie*, and the St. Louis *Pozor*, followed the old-fashioned programme of Čech nationalism. The *Pokrok*, which appeared in Chicago in 1867 under the direction of Joseph Pastor, struck out boldly and openly against clericalism. The *Pokrok's* challenge was taken up the same year by the *Katolické Noviny*, of which Father Joseph Molitor of Chicago was editor. Beginning with 1867 every newcomer in the journalistic field who had set out to serve the "interests of Čecho-Slavs in America" was obliged to choose between the one or the other camp. Neutrality was a word abhorred equally by both contentious factions. Matters progressed from bad to worse when Pastor resigned and Zdrůbek assumed his place as editor-in-chief of the *Pokrok*. During Zdrůbek's editorship, and due to his ignorance of the law, occurred the sensational libel suit which Father William Řepiš of the St. Václav parish in Cleveland brought against the editor. Trivial in itself, the libel caused a tremendous uproar everywhere; the "infidels" and the churchmen alike regarded it as a sort of test of their respective strength. One of the fruits of Řepiš's libel suit was the organization by the liberal party of the Liberal Union. The *Katolické Noviny* having passed out of existence for lack of support, Father Hessoun of St. Louis provided the Catholics in 1872 with another defender of their faith, the *Hlas*. The *Hlas* had retained almost unopposed the leadership among co-religionists until 1893–94. That year the order of the Benedictines established in Chicago two journals, since become influential, the *Katolík* and the *Národ*.

The Catholic adherents rallied around Hessoun's *Hlas*, while the *Pokrok* continued to fight the battles of the liberals. Even in Klácel's time the *Pokrok* was considered their organ, because the journalistic ventures of the aged thinker never enjoyed a wide circulation. After a stormy existence of eleven-odd years the *Pokrok* finally suspended publication in Cleveland.

The defunct *Pokrok* was replaced in the mid-seventies by two new pugnacious journals. One was the Chicago daily *Svornost*, which Zdrůbek founded in 1875 in partnership with August Geringer; the other was the weekly *Dennice Novověku* started by Václav Šnajdr in Cleveland. These two papers pledged themselves to uphold the cause of free religious discussion. Šnajdr sat in the editorial chair of the *Dennice Novověku* for thirty-three years. Zdrůbek held the reins of the *Svornost* for thirty-five years. Friend and foe alike will agree that Šnajdr and Zdrůbek kept the pact faithfully. Excellently edited, the *Dennice Novověku* boasted by far the most intelligent, though not the largest, community of readers.

Prior to 1891, the *Dennice Novověku* was the official organ of the Č.S.P.S. brotherhood. One can imagine what it meant to the cause of liberalism to get a fearless journal of the stamp of the *Dennice* into thousands of Č.S.P.S. households. In plain language it signified the winning over to the side of the liberals of as many partisans as there were members in the organization. The J.Č.D. sisterhood also adopted the *Dennice Novověku* as its organ; here again new territory had been conquered, new friends won.

The progressives scored a triumph when Klácel arrived in the United States, in 1869. Here was an author of distinction, a much-talked-of philospher and intimate friend of some of the greatest men and women of Bohemia. A report which preceded him from abroad that he was coming to America to found a commune of followers, added, if anything, to the magic of his name.

Even men who had studied theology or were duly ordained as priests, turned against their Church. Few of these endured more for a principle than Father Thomas Juránek. Coming to America in 1848 or 1849, a backwash of revolutionary Bohemia, Juránek tried hard to get a start at something that was more to his liking than the pulpit. He drudged for a time at cigarmaking in New York. Seeing no prospects in this occupation, he made his way to Milwaukee; there he became a fruit peddler. Saving a few dollars he bought a handorgan and with this instrument strapped to his back, he tramped along the Mississippi River to New Orleans and back to Wisconsin. He settled in Cooperstown, in Manitowoc County; there he established himself as a schoolmaster, cigarmaker, justice of the peace, and newspaper correspondent.[1] He died March 5, 1890.

Juránek was not the only priest to lay aside the

[1] Thomas Juránek: *The Contemplations and Reflections of an Old Čech Organ-Grinder toward the Close of the Nineteenth Century*. To all liberal-minded Čechs for careful perusal and investigation, dedicated by an apostate priest. Greenstreet, Wis., 1889.

cassock. Old settlers will readily recall the case of William Řepiš (or Revis, as he later anglicized his name), who in the seventies ministered to a thriving parish in Cleveland. Due, it is claimed, to bitter attacks by the radical press, Řepiš left the priesthood, married, and settled on a farm in Iowa.

Celebrated is the case of Ladimír Klácel. Educated for the priesthood, Klácel had taken the monastic vows of the Augustinian Friars and for a time taught philosophy at a school of that order at Brno, Moravia. But applying the philosophical deductions of Hegel, whose teachings he had embraced, to politics and religion, to Church and State, the brilliant pedagogue found himself, in consequence, in sharp opposition to his superiors. Expulsion from the school followed.[1] In order to "emancipate his mind from the shackles of slavery," as the ex-friar described his mental state, he decided to emigrate overseas at the risk of losing friends and imperiling a splendid literary reputation. At that time Klácel was in his sixty-first year, which would seem to indicate that his resolve to leave the Church was the outcome of seasoned judgment. The circumstance that he had quarreled with the

[1] Augustine Smetana (1814–51), a Cruciferian monk, was publicly excommunicated under circumstances recalling the dramatic and sensational expulsion from the Israelite Community, of which he was a member, of Baruch Spinoza, the Dutch philosopher. In this connection one is reminded of the case of another Cruciferian monk, Karl Anton Postl, known to American literature as Charles Sealsfield, born in Moravia. Postl was a fellow inmate with Smetana in the monastery of that order in Prague.

hierarchy and that the hierarchy had disciplined him added, if anything, to the luster of his name in the opinion of the American rationalists.

Toward the close of his life, due, no doubt, to worries and cruel disappointments of all kinds, Klácel turned mystic and visionary. As a social reformer he shared Fourier's communistic ideas. Fourier, as we know, proposed what he termed phalansteries, consisting of a fixed number of persons who should live together, combining the result of their labor. Klácel's pet scheme was the organization in the Middle West (he had his eye on the Black Hills country in South Dakota) of Svojanov communities composed of his followers who should work the land on the coöperative basis — precisely Fourier's project. Fortunately for Klácel none of his communities of which he dreamed were realized; had they become actualities it is certain they would have collapsed as did most of the undertakings of this kind, as for example the most noted one, Brook Farm in Massachusetts. When Klácel finds a competent biographer who will edit an informing synopsis of his philosophy, the historian will be better prepared to assign a place to this remarkable man in the evolution of thought in America.

F. B. Zdrůbek (1842–1911), "the arch-propagandist of atheism," was the son of poor, struggling parents who sent him to a Catholic seminary to be educated for the priesthood. Having, as he tells us,

LADIMÍR KLÁCEL

experienced a change in religious faith, Zdrůbek left the Catholic for a Protestant seminary, from which latter he duly graduated. Settling in Chicago and taking up journalism as a profession, he began as lecturer, writer, and journalist, "to combat the menace of bigotry and superstition among his countrymen."

Few journalists waged a more relentless warfare against the clergy than Joseph Pastor, editor of the *Pokrok*, who served a novitiate with the friars of Želiv Abbey.

John V. Čapek, author of the humorous life of St. Anthony of Padua, in verse, spent a school semester or two with the Franciscans in Prague. Čapek asserted that it was in the monastic cell that his theological ideals underwent a change.

Bartoš Bittner and Alois Janda both took a course in Catholic theological seminaries, both rebelling in the end.

Dr. Frank Iška started his career as a priest. Unable to believe what he preached, he went over to the Old Catholic Church. In 1902 he arrived in the United States with the idea, it is said, of organizing in Chicago a congregation of Old Catholics. Failing in this, he returned to his native country, but the following year came back, establishing a permanent residence in Chicago. Casting aside Old Catholicism, he avowed his adhesion to the principles for which Klácel and Zdrůbek fought all their lives — freedom of religious expression.

THE ČECHS IN AMERICA

J. B. Erben of St. Louis, the oldest living Čech journalist in the country, is said to have run away, as a student, from a Benedictine monastery in Bohemia where he was being educated. Embracing the evangelical faith, Erben, who knew German as well as his mother tongue, gave himself to religious work among the Germans in the United States.

Tragic was the end of John C. Hojda, spiritual head of the St. Václav parish in Baltimore. Resigning his charge and at the same time renouncing his faith, Hojda eked out a scanty existence on the Baltimore *Telegraf*, a struggling Čech weekly. Subsequently he took up horticulture for a living. In a fit of insanity, due, it is said, to brooding over family matters, he killed two of his children. He was placed in an asylum, where he died in 1898.

Rationalistic tenets, so far as known, claimed two converts from among the Protestants. One was a minister by the name of Joseph Kalda, a restless, discontented spirit. For a Chicago publishing house Kalda edited a book of *Funeral Speeches* for the use of those who wished non-church burial. Kalda died in want in Chicago under particularly distressing circumstances. A recent convert to rationalism is V. Mineberger, editor of the Baltimore *Čecho-Slovan*. Mineberger announced that it was his resolve to leave the Church in whose teachings he no longer believed. Like Zdrůbek, Mineberger, too, was originally a Catholic.

A strange case came to the notice of the public

about eight years ago. The secretary of a New York liberal association, Anton Vlček, died following a short illness. Vlček's occupation was that of a bookkeeper in a downtown business house. After his death the members of the society were astounded to learn that their radical-minded official had been none other than Father Anton Vlček, formerly pastor of the St. Prokop Catholic parish in Cleveland. The surprising part of it was that Vlček contrived to guard the secret of his former life even from intimates.

Rev. Václav Vaněk, a well-known Protestant divine, formerly attached to a parish in Baltimore, but now located in Chicago, originally studied theology in a Catholic seminary; finding himself in dissent from Catholic teachings he joined the Chicago coterie of journalists, of whom the late B. Bittner, liberal thinker, was one.

Čech rationalism [1] in the United States is the

[1] T. G. Masaryk: "Čech Liberals in America," *Naše Doba* (Prague), October, 1902, pp. 1–7; Rev. F. Tichý: *Thoughts on New Religion.* An answer to L. J. Palda. Probed into and submitted to an impartial examination. 88 pp.; *Čech American Liberalism*, 1907–11, or, *Discussions, Deliberations and Resolutions passed at the Convention of Liberals*, 135 pp. New York, 1911; *Discussions, Deliberations and Resolutions passed at the Convention of Liberals*, held June 13, 14, and 15, 1907. Chicago. 182 pp.; *Lectures by T. G. Masaryk*: Published by the Executive Committee of the Liberal Union. 61 pp. Chicago, 1907. Contents of the lectures: "Havlíček and the Liberal Movement; "Liberalism and Religion"; "Religion and Human Society"; "The Principles adopted at the Convention of Čech Liberals in America"; "The Evolution of Liberalism"; "The Political Situation of the Čech Nation and Austria"; "The Woman and her Position in the Family and Public Life."

after-growth of political repression and narrow-minded paternalism. Náprstek's *Flug Blätter* fought not creeds, but the Church as a political institution, as a partner of the Hapsburg State. Euphemistically Havlíček defined this one-time fellowship of the Hapsburg State and the Church as a "union of the saber and the aspergill." Now, when the fetters of bondage are shattered and in his homeland the Čech is as free as he is here, whence will the militant rationalist derive his inspiration and his slogans?

CHAPTER XII

SOCIALISM AND RADICALISM

L. J. PALDA is entitled to be called the father of Čech socialism in the United States. In his autobiography Palda states that his admiration for Lassalle and Marx dates from the time he worked as a factory hand, a weaver, in Switzerland and Saxony. This statement is open to doubt, for at the time of his arrival in New York, in 1867, Palda was a youth barely twenty years old. The more reasonable supposition is that the socialist cult obtained a firm hold on him not in Switzerland or Saxony, but in the United States, during his development into maturer manhood, when the laboring class, yielding to his forceful personality, acclaimed him as one of its chiefs. Just how deeply Palda was read in the party's literature, we glean from the following sentence: "At the house of friend Borovička (New York) I came across Havlíček's *Duch Národních Novin* and a treatise on socialism and communism by Klácel."[1] Together with Frank Škarda he founded in Cleveland in 1875, *Dělnické Listy* (the Workingmen's News).

[1] L. J. Palda: *From Times Past*. These reminiscences, in Čech, were published serially in the *Osvěta Americká* in 1903. Borovička, here referred to, was an intelligent New York workman, reader of good books, and, at the time of Palda's first stay in New York, a caretaker of the library belonging to the Slovanská Lípa Society.

The motto of the paper was "Equal duties, equal rights." The title-page bore the significant legend that the Workingmen's News was being published as the "Organ of the Socialist Workingmen's Party in the United States." Precisely what socialist party the paper claimed to be the official spokesman of, and who the members of the party were, has not been made clear. Joseph Buňata,[1] a contemporary and a party man, admits there were Čech socialists in the country at that time (1875), yet he recalls nothing of an organized socialist party. For instance, Leo Meilbek, a member of the Illinois legislature, classified himself as a social democrat. Palda's business partner, Frank Škarda, was nominated, though not elected, on the socialist ticket for Lieutenant-Governor of Ohio.

Two years later (1877) the *Dělnické Listy* was removed to New York City, the publishers correctly surmising that the metropolis offered to a socialist paper a wider field than an inland city of the size and location of Cleveland.

In Palda's reminiscences we are told that soon after the removal of the paper to New York, its editor started organizing socialist clubs. The warcry, "Proletarians of the world, unite," demanded not words, but action, he informs us. "The group I helped to organize bore the name, Čech-Slavic International Workingmen's Association of New

---

[1] Joseph Buňata, a journalist living at Ennis, Texas, has long ago renounced his adherence to socialism.

L. J. PALDA

York." The principal members (besides Palda) were V. Jandus,[1] George Šrétr, Joseph Buňata, and Bílý. The last-named was an arrival from Paris.

In justice to Palda, it should be said that in his advocacy of socialism he was conciliatory. He was well aware of the fact that the doctrine was foreign to the mass of his countrymen, most of whom had emigrated from rural districts, and he was a patient teacher. Like all socialists, he believed, of course, that our social and economic order was unjust; yet he held consistently to the viewpoint that society had it in its power to purge itself, not by revolution, but by evolution. Moreover, he was not convinced that in obedience to the party's behests he must renounce his Čech nationalism. In this last regard he was what we might call a Nationalist Socialist. As his mind ripened, his views ran more along the lines of scientific socialism; that is, he predicted the coming of socialism as the result of gradual economic evolution. Younger comrades, who were eager for action, tried more than once to discredit Palda in the esteem of the party. Pettifogger, capitalist in disguise, were some of the epithets hurled at him in their press. Palda's missionary work in America would have, in all likelihood, come to naught, had not events occurred at home which gave socialism here a firmer footing. In 1879 social democrats

[1] V. (William) Jandus, since 1876 a resident of Cleveland, published in the English language a forceful study, *Social Wrongs and State Responsibilities*. Cleveland. Horace Carr. 1913.

held in Prague a secret meeting which has become known in the annals of the party as the St. Margaret's Congress. (St. Margaret was the name of a hall in Prague.) Convoked without a permit, the Congress was dispersed by the police and a number of the leaders arrested and thrown into prison.

Once on the police black-list, the more prominent of the socialists found existence in Bohemia unendurable. So they removed to other parts of the empire, not a few leaving it altogether. Some went to Budapest; others escaped to Switzerland; still others chose as their future homes great industrial centers in Europe and America: Paris, London, New York, Chicago. On January 30, 1884, martial law was proclaimed in Vienna. A direct result of this measure was the suspension of the constitutional rights of trial by jury (non-political cases excepted), freedom of association of citizens, and freedom of the press. With a stern hand the police dissolved political clubs, suppressed newspapers, arrested or expelled the leading agitators. So rigorous was the clean-up that by 1885 social democracy in Austria was laid prostrate.[1] Comrade Josef Hybeš[2] reckoned that in the period between 1878–87

---

[1] Dr. Edward Beneš: *The Labor Movement in Austria and Bohemia.* 47 pp. Brandýs n. L. 1911.

[2] Josef Hybeš: *The Initial Days of the Propaganda among Čech Comrades.* 64 pp. Brno, 1900. Hybeš gives account in his pamphlet of their connection with the propaganda in Prague and Vienna of comrades Mikolanda, Milý, Zoula, Choura, all of whom had emigrated to America.

the police, employing all those devices favored by the secret police of autocracy, had ruined the existence of some 2000 socialists. According to Josef Steiner [1] the political police had to its credit 4086 arrests and convictions between 1880–89. A look at Steiner's revelatory statistics will enable one to understand why Emperor Franz Josef nursed a personal grudge against social democrats.

STEINER'S TABLE

Sentenced for	1880	1881	1882	1883	1884	1885	1886	1887	1888	1889
Unlawful association	41	41	91	92	93	93	145	11	2	14
Treason		1	1	3	27	11	9	2	1	5
Lèse majesté (person of Emperor)	364	367	332	335	306	302	250	283	246	240
Lèse majesté (members of reigning house)	8	23	17	39	30	16	22	19	25	73
Disturbing peace	10	2	10	17	17	3	4	5	3	2
Unlawful collection of funds		4		5	11	1	5	5	1	1
Total....4086	423	438	451	491	484	426	435	325	278	335

All accounts agree that one of the first fugitive socialists to arrive in America was Leo Kochmann (1844–1919), who escaped on the eve of going to jail to serve a sentence for active participation in the St. Margaret's Congress. Frank Škarda, who at that time (1882) was looking about for an editor, promptly gave Kochmann employment on the *Dělnické Listy*. From this time on until he retired

[1] Josef Steiner: *The Martyrdom of Čech-Slavic Social Democracy and the Progress of the Party in Austria.* 178 pp. Prague, 1902.

from journalism (1913), Kochmann resided in New York uninterruptedly, and the colony of social democrats in that city came to regard him as one of its strong men. Far below Palda in intelligence, possessing but an elementary-school education, diffident as a speaker, upright, but in his earlier years inclined to be fanatical, Kochmann was tolerably well posted on the aims and literature of social democracy. However, his party was his world, and beyond the sky-line of that world he had neither the ambition nor the courage to look. The revolutionary verses appearing under his pen name, Vive la Liberté, were sincere and on occasions spirited. In collaboration with Frank J. Hlaváček and Bernard Herc, Kochmann rendered into Čech (1890) Blos's *French Revolution*. For a quarter of a century he was editor-in-chief of the New York daily, *Hlas Lidu*.

In 1882 Johann Most came to the United States. He had just finished a jail term of sixteen months in England for having glorified, in his journal, the assassination of Alexander II, Czar of Russia. Before that time Most had served terms in Austrian, Saxon, and Prussian prisons. Soon after his arrival, he undertook a speaking tour through the country. Social democrats were surprised at the large number of followers who flocked everywhere to Most's standard. In several cities in the United States, where Most delivered his harangues, anarchist clubs were established. A convention of radicals was held in Pittsburgh in 1883; and the New York police having in the meantime taken measures to check the local Most agitation, the headquarters of the party were transferred from New York to Chicago. Then followed, in 1886, the Haymarket tragedy which aroused and angered American public opinion as no other similar event has ever done. A number of the organizers of the riot suffered the death penalty. At the same time the authorities launched a crusade against the anarchists from which they have never recovered.[1]

The fact cannot be denied that Johann Most found ardent sympathizers among those Čech social democrats who were dissatisfied with the orthodox, scholarly socialism of Marx and Lassalle, and who clamored for deeds. Literature and party newspapers prove this irrefutably.

The protagonists of revolutionary socialism were, with a few exceptions, workmen, but workme of the more intelligent and well-paid class — furriers, tailors, machinists, typesetters, — who had learned their trade or worked at it in large cities. The earning power of these craftsmen was comparatively

---

[1] Hillquit thus differentiates between the socialist and the anarchist: "The anarchist sees the highest state of development in the absolute sovereignty of the individual, and considers all social restraints upon the personal and untrammeled personal liberty as injurious and reactionary elements in human civilization [p. 231]. The socialist regards society as an organic body, of which the individuals are but separate organs performing different functions for the organism as a whole and in turn deriving their strength from the well-being of the entire organism" (p. 230). Morris Hillquit: *History of Socialism in the United States*. 234 pp. New York, 1903.

high; in intelligence they towered far above the un-skilled agricultural and domestic labor from the non-industrial districts of Kutná Hora, Tábor, Písek. Association with men and women of other races lent these men that air of cosmopolitanism which is the envy of the provincial. Not a few were glib talkers, if not effective, persuasive impromptu debaters; when oratory failed to convince the doubter through presentation of reasons, they were ready to try to sway the wavering ones by appeal to passion and prejudice. Most idealists, as we know, possess the gift of eloquence to an unusual degree. In addition to the vernacular, almost all, if not all, were versed in German. This enabled them to read German-language newspapers, and associate freely with German comrades. Those who had been em-ployed in Paris brought with them to America a smattering of French. The members of the small London colony learned English. Comrades with a literary turn of mind, on coming to the United States translated almost exclusively from German sources; seldom from English or French, never from Russian. This made apparent the dominating influ-ence of the several Volkszeitungs, Arbeiterzeitungs, and Volksrechts on the American Čech socialist editors. But few of the journalists knew English enough freely to translate from it. This meant that they judged America in the light of a foreign dogma and sought to reform it through the medium of a foreign language.

SOCIALISM AND RADICALISM

Proselytism by means of the press reached its high-water mark between 1885 and 1890. New York City was the center of the movement; less active was the field of the radicals in Cleveland and Chicago. By far the busiest publishers were:

The Čech groups of the International Workingmen's Union of Chicago (České skupiny Mezinárodní Dělnické Jednoty v Chicagu). Series, *Epistles of Revolution.*

The American Workingman (Dělník Americký). Series, *Workingmen's Library.*

The Group Anarchy (Bezvládí) of New York. Series, *The International Library.*

The Group Self-Rule (Samospráva) of NewYork. Series, *The Epistles of Freedom.*

The Literary and Debating Club Progress (Pokrok) of New York.

The Čech Workingmen's Educational Society No. 2 of New York (Českodělnický vzdělávací Spolek čís. 2 v New Yorku).

The Čech Social Democratic Section in New York (Česká sociální demokratická sekce v New Yorku).

The Group Bezvládí attained a considerable position as a publisher. While not strong numerically, its membership was made up of self-conscious young men who knew that to carry on a propaganda with results costs money, but they were willing to pay for it. Members taxed themselves from $1 to $5 monthly according to the wages they

145

earned. Now and then London and Paris sent in small gifts of money; even comrades in Bohemia contributed their mite. The main burden of financing the propaganda was borne and ungrudgingly paid by the New York units.

Save a few revolutionary songs by Norbert Zoula, Joseph B. Pecka, Leo Kochmann, and F. J. Hlaváček, the Čech book literature of social reformers, which, by the way, is surprisingly copious, consists of translations. Not one creative thinker, not one self-directing reasoner appears among them. The catalogue shows translations — unskilled translations at that — from Michael Bakunine, Adolf Douai, Peter Kropotkin, Paul Lafargue, Enrico Malatesta, Karl Marx, Johann Most, J. A. Popengiesel, Élisée Reclus, A. Retté, A. Schäffle, Pierre Ramus, Ferdinand Lassalle.

In due time the consequences of the propaganda began to be manifest. The New York community split into two antagonistic factions: the nationalists and the radical socialists. The first-named party stood for Americanism; as a subordinate issue, it defended Čech nationalism as interpreted by Jonáš and by the other editors. Agreeably to the tenets of their creed, the socialists inclined toward internationalism, which, as the name implies, spurned national separatism. From radical socialism to anarchism was only a small leap and there were many reformers who embraced the creed of anarchy openly.

SOCIALISM AND RADICALISM

Thoughtful and observant men, Palda among them, warned the radicals, clustered around the *Proletář* and the *Dĕlnické Listy* [1] in New York and around the *Budoucnost*, in Chicago, to be moderate. The agitation, they pointed out, was doomed to end in a fiasco if not supported by the American press. Who was it that sympathized with the radicals, they argued? Not the American workman, nor yet the farmer; these two classes remained deaf to their seductive catchwords. The farmer and the mechanic read none save the English-language papers, which discussed the timely topics of trade-unionism, tariff, pension, currency. Radical socialism found favor and support in large industrial places only, and then in the foreign quarters thereof. "Anarchy is hopelessly discounted," argued Palda, "so long as the carriers of the doctrine are confined to Volkszeitungs and to other foreign-language newspapers."

But a writer in the *Proletář* reproved the father of socialism for interfering in a quarrel the merits of which he, a capitalist (!) and a westerner, had ceased to understand.

The advent in New York of Norbert Zoula, [2] a silversmith from Prague, is chronicled in 1883. Zoula spent a year and a half in an Austrian prison

---

[1] This *Dĕlnické Listy* must not be confounded with Škarda's paper of that name. The *Dĕlnické Listy* here mentioned was the property of the International Workingmen's Union of New York, edited by F. J. Hlaváček.

[2] According to one account Zoula was by birth a Slovene, not a Čech.

awaiting trial; after finishing a sentence of ten months, he repaired to Switzerland, from which country he emigrated here. After a comparatively short stay in New York, he proceeded to Chicago to edit in that city the *Budoucnost* (Future), "organ of anarchists of the Čech-Slavic language." His associates in the management of the paper were Joseph Pondělíček, Jacob Mikolanda, Joseph B. Pecka. The vigorous police censorship which followed the Chicago Haymarket outbreak forced this journal, like many other anarchist papers, to suspend. The year the *Budoucnost* sang its swan song, Zoula died in California of tuberculosis, "the common malady of the proletariat," a newspaper commented at the time: and he died in utter want, deserted by his comrades.

Joseph Boleslav Pecka, moulder by trade, made his appearance in Chicago in 1884. As the recording secretary of St. Margaret's Congress, he brought upon himself in the motherland the anger of the police. For this with thirty other comrades he was put into prison. His "portion" was eighteen months and he served his term in full. Having been active in Vienna as collaborator of the *Dělnické Listy*, he needed no urging to do his share in the press propaganda of the party in America. He died in Chicago in 1897, in his forty-eighth year. Two years after his death, comrades published his *Sebrané Básně* (Collected Songs). Pecka's style as a journalist was vigorous and clear. The *Collected Songs* (92 pages) are the revolutionary rhapsodies of the downtrodden proletarian.

Jacob Mikolanda, a baker, migrated in 1882 or 1883. He became connected with the Chicago *Budoucnost*, and when this radical paper was forced to the wall, he wrote for the *Právo Lidu* (People's Rights), a weekly of more moderate tone than the *Budoucnost*. For alleged complicity in the Haymarket affair Mikolanda was sent to the workhouse for six months. His death occurred in Cleveland.

Frank J. Hlaváček, now on the editorial staff of the Chicago daily *Spravedlnost* (Justice), began life as a miner. Having had a certain degree of newspaper training at home, Hlaváček from the outset (he came to New York about 1887) gave himself wholly to journalism. With several friends he set up in New York in 1893 the *Dělnické Listy*, the publisher of which was nominally the International Workingmen's Union. By common consent the *Dělnické Listy* was regarded as the organ of revolutionary socialists. For want of support the paper was forced to give up its existence in New York. It was removed to Cleveland, where, under the editorship of V. Kudlata, it finally went under. Disillusioned, Hlaváček quit New York and went to Chicago. There he returned to his old allegiance — social democracy. With the downfall of the *Dělnické Listy* the radical wing of social democrats, the party of action in New York, lost its greatest support.

Thereafter the decline of this faction in New York was rapid and its ultimate break-up inevitable. Among other small things, Hlaváček published a collection of workingmen's songs in Čech, *The Torch* (214 pages) and a rhymed narrative of the *Creation*, "accurately according to the version of the Bible." Though Hlaváček is not above the average rhymester in skill, one cannot but concede, reading his humorous tale of the *Creation*, that he possessed a certain store of robust humor. Zdrůbek tried to tell much the same story in verse, but his *Bible to Laugh* is incomparably inferior to Hlaváček's.

Edward Milý, a typesetter, was expelled from Bohemia and later from Vienna as a political undesirable. He went to Budapest, removing in 1884 to London. Later he came to New York. Milý did effective work on the *Volné Listy* (Free News),[1] and translated, besides, several pamphlets.

The youngest refugee was William Kroužilka, a student from Prague. A ready debater and a clever newspaper reporter, Kroužilka, despite his youth, rose quickly to prominence in the party. In Chicago, whither he went from New York, he published creditable pamphlets, one of which was a *Life of Darwin*. He died in Chicago a few years ago.

Václav Kudlata, said to have been a student of theology in Bohemia, delivered in 1897 a lecture "on the occasion of the tenth anniversary of the

---

[1] The *Volné Listy* originated in 1890 in Brooklyn. Suspended in the first months of the war.

death of the Chicago Martyrs," which was that year printed in pamphlet form under the heading *After Ten Years*. Another brochure by Kudlata is entitled, *Half-hearted and Whole Liberalism* (1897). Kudlata died in 1917, at Elizabeth, New Jersey.

None of the reformers had a more enthusiastic following in the debating clubs than Gustav Haberman. During his second stay in the United States, in the early nineties, Haberman helped to father the radical *Volné Listy* in New York. "Later I dissented from the extreme policy of this paper," we read in his memoirs.[1] Returning to Bohemia, Haberman rose to a commanding position in the working-men's councils and he was elected on the socialistic ticket to the old Austrian Parliament.

Of Frank Choura (a miner living in a small town in Pennsylvania) Dr. Soukup has this to say: "He was a witness and a participant in the Pačes drama. After the arrest of Pačes, Rampas and Christopher Černý, he (Choura) fled to America. On this man rested the terrible suspicion of having informed on his comrades. The events of the last few years have, however, fully exonerated Choura."

Because he had a guilty knowledge of the existence of Pačes's unlicensed printing shop and had omitted to inform the police, Frank Janota, a tailor, became, in the eyes of the law, Pačes's accomplice after the fact. Janota saved himself from arrest by

[1] Gustav Haberman: *Z mého Života* (From my Life). 253 pp. Prague, 1914.

a hurried flight to Switzerland. From the Swiss Republic he went to London, and there published sheets which he called *Pomsta* (Revenge) and *Revoluce* (Revolution). Reaching New York some time in 1894, he became associated with the *Volné Listy*, remaining at the head of this paper for about five years. Janota signed his articles with the pseudonym "Rebel."

In the little cemetery at Neligh, Nebraska, lies buried a martyr-workman whose tragic life-story, because true, is more gripping than that of Jean Valjean, in *Les Misérables*. Whereas in Hugo's masterpiece the villain was the sergeant Thénardier, in the case of Joseph Pačes, the Čech Jean Valjean, it was the State, as typified by secret police, which played the villain's rôle.

Joseph Pačes was a simple workman, whom social and national wrongs had made a rebel — rebel against society and state. Jean Valjean stole a loaf of bread and for this was sent to the galleys; Pačes did not steal, cheat, or rob. He was a political criminal, though a desperate one, according to the viewpoint of the Austrian police. What crimes did Pačes commit? First, he set up a secret printing press in northern Bohemia to further the propaganda of social democracy. Because he did this without a license from the authorities (who, of course, would not have granted it), he violated certain strict police regulations. Then he was guilty of *lèse majesté*. The Government prosecutor charged him with treason,

JOSEPH PAČES

besides. When in prison, Pačes in a moment of desperation attacked a brutal jail-keeper with a knife; this constituted a new crime: assault with intent to kill.

On the occasion of his discharge from prison (altogether Pačes had given eighteen years of his life to the cause of social democracy), his comrades in Prague arranged a reception in his honor. "Here we saw him for the first time," writes Dr. Francis Soukup.[1] "A bent, pale-faced man, looking as if he had just arisen from the grave. With face seamed, a haunted look, proud flesh around one eye. Hands trembling as if palsied, knees wabbly. Eighteen years spent in an Austrian prison at hard labor had left its marks on this living skeleton. . . ." Dr. Soukup visited Pačes's grave at Neligh. "Here Pačes came to find his resting-place. . . . On these vast plains, in the heart of America, far from the people who had taken away from him all he had, wife, children, youth, health, life. . . . Such had been his life, such is his grave; great as a man, greater still as the martyr of the Čech proletariat. . . ."

Anarchism among the American Čechs is dead. The Haymarket event dealt it a knock-out blow from which it never recovered. The older generation of immigrants, who had the opportunity to note at close range its corrosive tendencies and the vicious methods employed by its votaries, recall it as a

[1] Dr. Francis Soukup: *America; a Series of Pictures from American Life*. Prague, 1912.

hideous vision. Both the leaders and the followers are anxious to forget the past.

The socialists have four newspapers to further their cause, namely, the *Spravedlnost* (Justice) and the *Zájmy Lidu* (Interests of the People) in Chicago, the *Americké Dělnické Listy* (American Workingmen's News) in Cleveland, and the *Obrana* (Defense) in New York.

CHAPTER XIII
THE ČECH AS A SOLDIER

IN the Civil War the Čechs provided the United States Army with more musicians than generals. At any rate, the historian is certain of the existence of the former, whereas a most thorough search of the register of officers from 1789, the year of the organization of the Army, to 1903,[1] failed to unearth a single general. The Poles presented to the struggling Republic two fighters of note, Kosciuszko and Pulaski. A number of Polish officers are known to have served in the Civil War. The name of V. Krzyzanowski, who held an independent command, comes to mind. No Austro-Hungarian nation, however, has paid such generous tribute to Mars, the god of war, as the Magyars.[2] This is of course explained by the circumstance that many Magyar officers were living here in involuntary exile, following the suppression of the Hungarian Rebellion in 1849. Among the list of officers serving in the Union Army and claimed to be Magyar one notices such suspiciously un-Magyar names as John T. Fiala and Anton Pokorný. The last-named

[1] Francis B. Heitmann: *Historical Register and Dictionary of the U.S. Army, from its Organization, September 29, 1789, to March 2, 1903.* Published under Act of Congress, March 2, 1903. Washington. Government Printing Office.

[2] Eugene Pivány: *Hungarians in the American Civil War.* Cleveland, 1913.

was major of the Eighth and lieutenant-colonel of the Seventh New York Infantry.

Pridefully the Chicago Čechoslovaks point to the fact that their first club (1860) was a military organization styling itself the Slavonian Lincoln Rifle Company. Several of the Čech members having dropped out before the volunteers had been called into service, the club corrected its name to Lincoln Rifle Company. Géza Mihalóczy, according to one version a Slovak, but according to another (Piványi), a Magyar, is remembered as its organizer. Whether Magyar or Slovak, Mihalóczy died a brave soldier's death on the battle-field. He lies buried at Chattanooga. Before the war he was quite a conspicuous figure in the Chicago circles.

But two officers, in the *Register* and *Dictionary* have given Bohemia as their birthland: John Pilsen (seemingly an assumed name from the town of Pilsen), captain of a New York regiment of volunteers, and John Rziha. Elsewhere, Rziha is referred to as John Laub de Laubenfels. The *Slavie* prints a communication dated March 19, 1862, from private J. Zajíček, stationed at Hunter's Chapel, Virginia, in which occurs this passage: "In our regiment of volunteers, that is the 8th of New York, we have only a handful of Čechs, eight all told. The first in command of Company B. is F. Werther,[1] by

---

[1] Frederick Werther owned a liquor saloon in New York, much patronized by Čechs. He took active interest in the social activities of his blood brothers.

birth a Slovak, who is attached heart and soul to his ancient race." In another letter, also published in the *Slavie*, bearing the date December 5, 1862, the same soldier (Zajíček) writes: "When the 28th Wisconsin Regiment passed through (Hunter's Chapel) we lined up by the roadside. We were surprised to hear that so many Čechs were enrolled in that regiment. Presently a comrade rushed to tell us the joyful news that he had recognized several friends in the 28th Regiment, with whom he had spent enjoyable days in Chicago and Milwaukee; Lieutenant Landa was there and with him no less than sixty Čechs." The *Slavie* that year was sending out about twenty copies to soldiers in the field. From this it would seem that there were not many soldiers in the camps; or that Čech fighters had been braver soldiers than newspaper subscribers. Just how many had shouldered the musket in defense of the Union, one cannot say, for the muster rolls did not tabulate the nationality of the private. The subjective and often more confusing than illuminating reminiscences of Čech soldiers, which we find reprinted in Joseph Čermák's book,[1] offer no basis even for an estimate, much less for accurate computation. A monument has been erected in the Bohemian National Cemetery in Chicago to commemorate their participation in the great struggle.

We have said that the Čechs had contributed

---

[1] Joseph Čermák: *The History of America*. From various sources. Chicago, 1889.

more musicians to the Army than generals. In corroboration of this we find in the local history of the Poles [1] this bit of interesting information: "A deputation of Poles headed by Officer Ludwig Zychlinski wished to pay the compliments of their people to President Lincoln, who was staying in camp not far from St. Louis. General Hooker undertook to introduce the delegation to Lincoln. The President asked how many Poles were serving in the army; and recalling some of the Polish officers by name, Krzyzanowski first of all, he praised their valor." On this occasion, relates Zychlinski, "a toast was drunk to the health and good luck of the Poles, and the musicians, among whom were Čechs and two Poles from Warsaw, played the anthem, 'Jeszcze Polska nie Zginela' (Poland has not yet perished) which moved all to tears."

"So far as I could make out from the scanty material at my disposal no Čech in the Union Army wore a higher brevet than Adolph B. Chládek (born 1838 in Vamberk, Bohemia, died 1887 in Chicago). He served with the Ninth Wisconsin Infantry, early receiving the commission of second lieutenant. At first he was attached to the staff of General Schofield; later he served on that of General Weir. [2]

Čermák believes that American Čechs sent a con-

---

[1] *History of the Polish National Union*, p. 23. Chicago, 1905.
[2] Joseph Čermák: *The History of America*. Part III, *The History of the Civil War*. Chicago, 1889.

siderable number of their sons to the ranks. Precisely how many, he fails to state; his narrative accounts for these numbers serving in the Union Army: Iowa, 29 men [1] (p. 198); Wisconsin, 26 (p. 181); Maryland, 19 (p. 182); Illinois, 13 (p. 78); Michigan, 10; and so forth. Čermák leaves it to be inferred that, except a handful of conscripts in the Confederate Army from Texas and Louisiana (the only Southern States having Čech population), they were all fighting for the Union.

John Wagner, a not over-veracious writer,[2] assumes that Captain Lesdegar Kinsky (conceivably a member of the aristocratic family of that name) was a Bohemian. Kinsky served in the war until 1864 when wounds and sickness incapacitated him. He died in Boston in 1891. Another soldier of fortune from Bohemia with a Civil War record was Count Edward C. Wratislaw, Lieutenant-colonel of the Forty-fifth New York Infantry.[3]

Čeněk Paclt, a rolling stone and a globe-trotter, whose inextinguishable desire for adventure had led him to explore the ends of the earth, is the only soldier of Čech nationality serving in the Mexican War of whom we have any record. Having enlisted

[1] B. Shimek: (e) *The Bohemians in Johnson County*, on pp. 6–7, gives the names of 57 Čechs serving in the 6th, 12th, 14th, 15th, 22d, 46th, 47th Iowa Infantry and 1st, 2d, 6th, 8th, and 9th Iowa Cavalry, in addition to 6 regulars.

[2] John Wagner: *Transatlantic Gossip*. 41 pp. Prague, 1898.

[3] F. B. Heitmann: *Field Officers of Volunteers and Militia in the Service of the United States during the War of the Rebellion; 1861–65;* p. 827.

in the United States Army in 1846, Paclt claimed to have taken part in several of the battles that ended in the seizure, by General Winfield Scott, of Mexico City in 1847. Discharged from the Army in 1853, this restless wanderer resumed his globe-trotting. He died in 1887 in Zululand.[1]

Hundreds of Čech volunteers and enlisted men shouldered the musket in the Spanish-American War, doing their duty honorably in Cuba, Porto Rico, and the Philippines. A comrade in arms, a United States regular, told their collective story.[2]

In the war just ended Čechoslovak volunteers (at home they call them legionaries), fought the Central Powers under Russian, French, Italian, Serbian, Canadian, English and United States colors.

How many legionaries served in the armies of the Allies? Soon after his arrival from Russia President Masaryk in a speech delivered in Carnegie Hall, in the summer of 1918, asserted that 50,000 Čechoslovaks in Siberia were under arms and that another 60,000 were awaiting to be armed.

The Čechoslovak unit in France numbered 15,000 men. This was made up of volunteers from the United States and deserters and released prisoners of war from the Russian and Serbian fronts.

The contingent in Italy, composed wholly of de-

[1] *Čeněk Paclt's World Travels.* By Dr. Jaroslav Svoboda. Mladá Boleslav, 1888.

[2] Matthew Mašek: *The Spanish-American War of 1898.* Illustrated. 48 pp. August Geringer. Chicago, 1899.

serters from the Austro-Hungarian Armies, was mentioned in the dispatches as having over 20,000 men.

Some 1000 took part in the operations on the Balkan fronts.

A writer who has made a close study of published reports computes the strength of volunteers and enlisted men in the United States at 100,000. In the opinion of the same writer the loss in man power on the Allied side was 34,000. By far the heaviest losses were sustained in the Russian campaigns and in the terrible march with the Serbian Army across Albania.

Putting the estimate of the losses in the Austro-Hungarian Armies at 220,000, we obtain a total of 254,000 men killed.[1]

A popular legend in Bohemia says that the knights slumbering in the cave of the Blaník Mountain would awaken and with St. Václav leading them would fall upon the enemy at the hour of the Fatherland's direst peril and would confound and destroy him.

The knights of the legend did awaken and they did come out of the Blaník Mountain at the time the Fatherland was in supreme peril. That was in July, 1914. The knights were the legionaries who gave their lives to the end that democracy might triumph and that their native land might be freed from the yoke of the Hapsburg oppressor.

[1] Otakar Charvát: *The Pokrok*, July 16, 1919.

161

THE ČECH AS A SOLDIER

On July 18, 1919, President Woodrow Wilson reviewed in Washington a detachment of invalided veterans returning home from Siberia. On this occasion the President addressed the following eulogy to "Major Vladimir Jirsa, officers, and men of the detachment of the Čechoslovak Army," which will always be read and treasured by Čechoslovak legionaries.

"It gives me great pleasure to have this opportunity to review this detachment of your valiant army and to extend to you, its officers, and the brave men associated with you, a most cordial welcome. Though we have been far away, we have watched your actions, and have been moved by admiration of the services you have rendered under the most adverse circumstances. Having been subjected to an alien control, you were fired by a love of your former independence and for the institutions of your native land, and gallantly aligned yourselves with those who fought in opposition to all despotism and military autocracy. At the moment when adversity came to the armies with which you were fighting, and when darkness and discouragement cast a shadow upon your cause, you declined to be daunted by circumstance and retained your gallant hope. Your steadfastness in purpose, your unshaking belief in high ideals, your valor of mind, of body and of heart evoked the admiration of the world. In the midst of a disorganized people and subject to influence which worked

162

for ruin, you constantly maintained order within your ranks, and by your example helped those with whom you came in contact to reëstablish their lives. I cannot say too much in praise of the demeanor of your brave army in these trying circumstances. Future generations will happily record the influence for good which you were privileged to exercise upon a large part of the population of the world, and will accord you the place which you have so courageously won. There is perhaps nowhere recorded a more brilliant record than the withdrawal of your forces in opposition to the armies of Germany and Austria, through a population at first hostile, or the march of your armies for thousands of miles across the great stretches of Siberia, all the while keeping in mind the necessity for order and organization.

"You are returning now to your native land, which is to-day, we all rejoice to say, again a free and independent country. May you contribute to her life that stamina which you so conspicuously manifested through all your trying experiences in Russia and Siberia, and may you keep in mind after your return, as you had kept in mind heretofore, that the laws of God, the laws of man, and the laws of nature require systematic order and cool counsel for their proper application and development, and for the welfare and happiness of the human race."

CHAPTER XIV

JOURNALISM AND LITERATURE

A N American writer who examined the bibliography of Čech books, pamphlets, year-books, memorials, and newspapers published here since 1860, expressed genuine astonishment at its bulk. Not knowing the language, however, he was unable to differentiate between original productions and publications which are mere reprints, translations, or adaptations. The truth is that original works catalogued are but few. The book output of the socialists, for instance, is made up of translations. Several of the most productive authors — to mention one, Zdrůbek — were translators, not original writers.

Is it possible to create in America a distinctive German, or Swedish, or Čech literature? More intensively than any other race the Germans cultivated letters in their national tongue in America; yet what really great writers have they produced since Peter Zenker's time? "The hopes of a German-American literature, entertained by some of the enthusiasts of 1832 and 1848, have never been realized," so answers this query Gustavus Ohlinger. "It would be difficult to find a German book," he continues, "which the Germans themselves would claim was entitled to even an humble place in liter-

164

THE FIRST NUMBER OF THE SLOWAN AMERIKÁNSKÝ

The first Čech Newspaper in the United States

ature. Very few native-born German-Americans have become German writers of even average ability."

Perhaps Swedish, Italian, or Čech authors may yet create a work of striking and enduring value, but in view of the absorbing force of Americanism one is certain that other than English-language literature will not thrive here.

Journalism preceded book literature.[1] The first newspaper, *Slowan Amerikánský*, came out January 1, 1860; the first publication in book form, of which we have authentic record, was issued in 1865.[2] From the first the newspapers had the upper hand. To improve them the publishers spared neither time nor expense; book literature, unfortunately, remained an afterthought. Like Cinderella it was forced to mope in the corner, while the publisher spent all his spare cash to dress up the pampered daughter, the newspaper, in most attractive finery. Of course, one must reckon with the high-pressure life of the average American, who finds just time enough to read the daily paper. That book-publishing continued to be neglected was due,

[1] ......th (F. K. Ringsmuth): "Čech Literature in America," *Květy Americké*, September 29, 1886.

[2] *Pravda*, etc., The Truth, or an open discussion of events and of progress in the nineteenth century, as viewed in the light of history and from other sources, by Charles Procházka. Racine, 1865. A year before, that is in 1864, Charles Jonáš brought out a *Spelling Book and First Reader for Čech Slavic Youth in America*, and Anton Elsner, in St. Louis, a *Reminder of the Fatherland*. The two last-named publications, however, were reprints.

largely, to a lack of a purchasing public. August Geringer in Chicago, John Rosický in Omaha, Anton Novák in Milwaukee, and Charles Jonáš in Racine published quite a number of books and might have published more if the public had shown more appreciation — in buying them.

A New York bookseller, on being asked what class of people purchased Čech books, replied: "My best customers are clergymen and socialists. Old settlers seldom buy a book; their children never."

Useful handbooks antedated belles-lettres. Dictionaries and interpreters were as indispensable to the immigrant as a plough is needful to the farmer or tools to the mechanic. Five years after the American type foundries had cast type with Čech diacritic marks, Charles Jonáš compiled for the use of his countrymen a *Bohemian-English Interpreter*. By 1870 F. B. Zdrůbek had gotten out an *English Grammar*. Both publications were woefully deficient textually and crude typographically. For that matter, everything that came off the press in those days, whether a pamphlet or a newspaper, bore tell-tale marks of apprenticeship.

In the winter of 1852–53 arrived in Boston, on the ship Amor, a small company of home-seekers, several of whom were destined to play a noted part in the history of Čech immigration. One of them was Frank Kořízek (1820–99),[1] stonemason and

[1] *Květy Americké*, August 18, 1886. Biography and portrait.

J. B. ERBEN

FRANK KOŘÍZEK

JOSEPH PASTOR

FRANK MRÁČEK

odd-job man from Letovice, a provincial town in Moravia. At one time Kořízek had been a turnkey in the château of Count Kálnoky. It hardly need be added that he was, in addition to all his varied accomplishments, a self-taught musician, who was glad to earn a florin or two at country dances and weddings.

Kořízek settled in Racine — Watertown was his objective — and earned the distinction of being the Nestor of Čech journalism. His daughter, Christina, married Charles Jonáš; the other daughter, Cecilia, was given in marriage to Václav Šnajdr, a name inseparably linked with the evolution of the rationalist movement.

Another of the Amor's passengers was John Bárta (also called Letovský, from Letovice, his birthplace), Kořízek's fellow townsman and schoolmate. Bárta (1821–98, Iowa City), who had rendered invaluable help to Kořízek, in his initial struggles with the *Slowan Amerikánský*, established in 1869 at Iowa City a weekly bearing almost the same name as Kořízek's journal. The paper founded by Bárta still continues to be issued in Cedar Rapids, whither it was removed from Iowa City. Its name is *Slovan Americký* (*American Slav*).

Charles Jonáš, in the biography [1] of Kořízek, asserts that his father-in-law made up his mind to become a publisher after reading the life-story of Benjamin Franklin. The famous American philoso-

[1] Jubilee issue of *Slavie*, November 4, 1885.

pher started his career as a printer's apprentice; why could not Kořízek begin the same way, even though he was a married man and father of a growing family? In this resolve, Jonáš tells us, Kořízek was strengthened by the study of Charles Havlíček's [1] editorials loaned to him by a friend.

While it is conceivable that Kořízek found an inspiration in the life-stories of Franklin and Havlíček, and was eager to emulate, in his own humble way, the example of these great men, yet there is one essential fact which Jonáš omitted in telling of Kořízek's achievement, namely, that years before another fellow countryman in the United States had striven hard to establish here a newspaper in the Čech language. That man was Vojta Náprstek. In 1857 Náprstek addressed a meeting of interested parties in St. Louis on the subject. He urged New Yorkers to help, and he is known to have corresponded with Chicagoans toward the same end. Náprstek even outlined the future policy of such a paper. It should be liberal and fearless, somewhat like Havlíček's *Národní Noviny*. Náprstek's return to Europe in 1857 alone prevented him from realizing this pet project. Notwithstanding this clear and convincing evidence, we are asked by Jonáš to be-

[1] Charles Havlíček, or Charles Havlíček Borovský (from Borovany, his birthplace), was a noted publicist, whose journal, *Národní Noviny* (National Gazette) the Austrian Government suppressed as revolutionary. A volume of selected editorials was published under the caption, *The Spirit* (the essence) of the *Národní Noviny*.

KRISTINA KOŘÍZEK, JONÁŠ'S BRIDE

CHARLES JONÁŠ AT 30

JONÁŠ'S BIRTHPLACE AT MALEŠOV, BOHEMIA

lieve that his father-in-law derived all his resolve and drew all his inspiration from Franklin and Havlíček and none from Vojta Náprstek, his near neighbor and contemporary (Náprstek lived in Milwaukee, Kořízek in Racine). Posterity will do justice to Vojta Náprstek as the originator, the mental sponsor, of the idea; Kořízek will be remembered as the mechanic who consummated it.

Kořízek learned to set type in the shop of the *National Demokrat*, a German weekly in his home town, Racine. Hearing that stored behind the sacristy of a Milwaukee church was a hand printing press, the property of a priest, Kořízek decided to buy it. The price of the press was $140. He had a few dollars laid aside, which he had earned as a musician, and, with loans and gifts from friends, he succeeded in raising $40. For the balance of the purchase price, that is $100, Kořízek gave the priest a mortgage on his cottage.

The first number of Kořízek's weekly was dated January 1, 1860. It bore the name *Slowan Amerikánský*. The type was German, or "kurent" (current), as the old folks used to call German script. Twenty-four numbers of the paper Kořízek edited and set up alone, with only such small outside help as Joseph Satran (tailor) and Václav Šimonek (school-teacher) were able to render. In the daytime he worked in the printing shop; evenings he was kept busy reading and writing by candlelight, except when he was engaged to play, for music still assured the sole dependable means of a livelihood and he felt he must not neglect it.[1]

Kořízek's *Slowan Amerikánský* was three or four weeks old, when the St. Louis Čechs launched forth another weekly, the *Národní Noviny* (National Gazette). This paper was meant to be the first journal published in America, but owing to the dilatoriness of its promoters, it really was the second. The St. Louis paper was a joint-stock enterprise which had been in the making for upward of three or four years. In a way the *Národní Noviny* was Náprstek's paper, inasmuch as its stockholders were following the plan previously laid out by him. By acting quickly, Kořízek forestalled the St. Louisians by less than a month, reaping as publisher whatever advantage accrued from priority.

Before long the *Slowan Amerikánský* and the *Národní Noviny* felt keenly the adverse economic conditions incident to the Civil War, and friends having advised merger as the only means of saving both properties from bankruptcy, a meeting of representative men was arranged in Caledonia, Wisconsin, with the result that the rival concerns joined forces. The *Slowan Amerikánský* and the *Národní Noviny*, title names and all, were thrown into the melting-pot out of which emerged on October 30, 1861, a weekly, that was christened the

[1] *Slavie*, November 4, 1885. *Květy Americké*, September 18, 1886. Biography written by Charles Jonáš.

Slavie. Racine prevailed over St. Louis as the home office of the new journal.

Between January, 1860, and the spring of 1911, 326 Čech journals had come into being, representing every shade of public opinion.[1] Socialists, anarchists, Protestants, Catholics, agnostics, Republicans, Democrats have had their say in them. Of these 326 journals some 85 survive and to-day clamor to be heard. The *Hlasatel* (Herald) of Chicago claims a circulation of 25,000, if one is to take the advertising agent at his word. The *Hospodář* (Husbandman), an agricultural bi-monthly, with a home in Omaha, is said to be a regular guest in 30,000 households. The year 1875 witnessed the issuance in Chicago of the first daily, the *Svornost;* now four dailies serve the needs of readers in that busy Western metropolis alone. One champions the cause of the socialists, another proclaims itself the organ of the Catholics, the tendency of the third is anti-clerical, the fourth seeks to be independent. Cleveland and New York support two dailies each, Omaha one.

"Published in the interest of the Čecho-Slavs in America" is a legend that is printed under the headlines of pretty nearly every journal, irrespective of religious or political affiliation. Usually, if not always, the paper is being issued in the interest of one Čecho-Slav — namely, the publisher.

[1] Thomas Čapek: *Padesát Let českého tisku v Americe* (Fifty Years of Čech Letters in America), p. 185. New York, 1911.

THE ČECHS IN AMERICA

To the dictates of the American political parties the Čechs responded readily and loyally. Democrats and Republicans were, of course, always represented in the press. The old Prohibitionist party never made any conquest among them. The *Slavie* under Jonáš's management was a stanch Democratic partisan. The *Pokrok Západu*, while John Rosický owned and edited it, was a steadfast Republican adherent. A dyed-in-the-wool Republican among the veteran editors was John A. Oliverius, who was never happier than at election time when he could measure swords with Jonáš in a newspaper encounter.

He was a fortunate publisher, indeed, who owned a printing press. Generally the beginner had only sufficient funds to buy a modest stock of type, cases, galleys, and stones. The paper was set up in the shop, but sent out to an American or German pressroom to be printed. It was only after a time that the publisher, if his venture proved successful, was able to buy a printing press, usually on the installment plan. Bruce's type foundry in New York was among the first in the country to yield to the demand for Čech type. To the great misery of typesetters, Bruce and later Spindler cast no other than lower and upper case type. Accented job type was supplied by the foundries at a much later date. Typesetters who knew the trade from the old country were few. Most, if not all, the printers were initiated into the mysteries of this craft in America.

NEWSPAPER HOMES
The Svornost, Chicago; The Hospodář, Omaha; The Hlasatel, Chicago

JOURNALISM AND LITERATURE

Every pioneer newspaperman, publisher, and editor knew in detail the tricks of the business and could, in case of an emergency, such as a strike, not only edit, but set up and print his own paper. Long is the roster of editors who rose from the case to a seat in the editorial *sanctum sanctorum*. Proud was the publisher, jubilant the typesetters, appreciative the readers, when the paper appeared dressed in brand-new type from Bruce's or Spindler's foundry. Every one on such an occasion had a word of praise for the publisher's spirit and enterprise. However, such events were exceedingly rare. Many papers, alas! never lived to wear a second suit of clothes. A Cleveland weekly, now happily defunct, will be remembered with a shudder for its battered type and general ragged looks.

Editor! Journalist! A time was when the editor not only wrote for the people; he literally thought for them. His advice on matters relating to the affairs of the community never failed to command attention. Grumblers there were, of course, who dissented from the editor's views, but sooner or later the opposition was sure to fall victim to the mighty man's wrath.

The editor was invariably picked out to umpire quarrels, many of which, by the way, were of his own making. He was chosen as orator to address meetings and conventions; played leading rôles at amateur theatricals; taught the local Čech language school; helped to organize new lodges; was called upon to write funeral orations, political speeches, and banquet toasts.

When Jonáš was in the heyday of his power, his word in the *Slavie* was law and his decision admitted of no appeal. Now lawyers, doctors, teachers, merchants, and professional politicians help the editor to mould public opinion.

In towns where there were two or more rival journals there were bound to be two or more contentious factions. The editor, in each case, was the fixed star around which the lesser lights circled.

Stories of Indian life were as popular with the veteran reader as are the conventional detective thrillers of the present day. Without an exception every paper fed its patrons on them. The scribe who translated them into fustian Čech seemed to revel in them no less than the reader himself. The curious feature of it was that the border settler, who should have been the last person in the world to entertain romantic notions about the redskin, was most fond of stories of Indian adventure. Singularly enough, not one of the devotees of this trashy reading seemed to know enough to translate the wholesome tales of James Fenimore Cooper. Instead, they wasted their time on such worthless rubbish as the *Dragon of Silver Lake*, or the *Old Backwoodsman*, *Hukah Jim, the Cruel Modoc, Wild Katie*, or the *Prairie Outlaw*. If reproved, the editor excused his course by arguing that first you must teach people to be readers before you begin to educate their taste.

JOURNALISM AND LITERATURE

The Russo-Turkish War (1877) and the occupation by Austria-Hungary of Bosnia and Herzegovina happily diverted the readers' attention from the redskin and the cowboy to the South Slavs. Promptly the Indian fell into disfavor, and the editor, answering the call of Slavic blood, turned to the life of the Balkan Slavs and their age-long struggle against the Turkish master. Then it was that Prokop Chocholoušek,[1] a writer whose romantic tales from South-Slavic countries had enjoyed great popularity in Bohemia, came to his own. There was hardly a paper which did not, during the period of the Russo-Turkish War, lend generous space to Chocholoušek's South-Slavic heroics.

With the rise of modern Čech literature, novels by Alois Jirásek, Karel Rais, Václav Hladík, and other writers of recognized ability, began to dominate more and more the columns reserved for fiction. It is no secret that Čech-American publishers are dependent for this sort of reading matter on the literary output of the mother country. Copyright laws have no terrors for the publisher or the editor, accustomed to literary pillage. When the book market abroad was poor, as it was thirty or forty years ago, the reader here was made to starve in a literary sense. One can imagine what dearth of reading matter there was half a century ago when the St.

[1] Prokop Chocholoušek (1819–64) was a writer who imitated Walter Scott. His stories, though lacking the finish and preparation of his favorite master, exercised a powerful spell over the reader, particularly of the younger set.

THE ČECHS IN AMERICA

Louis *Pozor*, a weekly circulating among the working classes, was driven by dire need to reprint Klácel's unpalatable *Dobrověda*. Of the old-time romances none were in greater demand by the publishers than Herloszsohn's *The Last Taborite, or Bohemia in the Fifteenth Century*.[1] We dare say that this historic novel will be found reprinted in every paper dating back to the seventies.

Anti-clerical journals, the *Pokrok, Dennice Novověku, Svornost*, and *Šotek*, maintained a special column in which the editor registered, or reviewed, each week, the transgressions of the clergy. Bittner's "Clerical Peep Hole" in the *Šotek* made uncomfortable reading for the priest who happened to get into the focus of the "Peep Hole."

Of sensational disclosures by nuns who had made their escape from convents, there were published several variants. Sister Lucy tells in the *Svornost* of her harrowing experiences in an English convent. Sister Agatha confesses her troubles to the *Dennice Novověku*. Sister Thérèse bares the alleged secrets of her life, also in the *Svornost*. Zdrůbek translated, for the *Svornost*, Chiniquy's *Priest, Woman and Confessional*. Exposures, confessions, revelations are

---

[1] George Charles Reginald Herloszsohn, in Čech Herloš, was born in Prague in 1804; died in Germany in 1849. Although his stories were written by him in German, he betrayed his nativity in every historic novel. A passionate admirer of Bohemia's past, he liked to sketch the stern heroes of the Hussite Wars, when Bohemia hurled defiance at papal Europe. Though uncritical, his historic novels are still popular.

many; there is the *Confession by Pope Alexander VI*, by Altaroche; *Priest's Victims*, by J. E. Ball; the *Secrets of the Spanish Inquisition*, by M. V. Fereal; *Hierarchy and Aristocracy*, by F. Hassaurek.

Discussing some of the commercial aspects of journalism Václav Šnajdr, has this to say: [1] ". . . Two or three Čech houses established a reputation as steadfast and dependable advertisers. The firms of Severa (Cedar Rapids) and of Triner (Chicago) settled their bills promptly on the day and on the hour. The checks from firms like these made it possible for many a newspaper to meet its expenses.

"Forty-five years ago typesetters were paid twenty-five cents per thousand ems. Of course, much depended on the typesetter himself and on the locality where the paper was published. Girls who had been trained for the work by the publisher received less.

"The wages of typesetters on the *Dennice Novověku* were $15, later $18, payment being made promptly on wage day. I would rather have left the shop empty-handed myself on Saturday, than not to have paid the employees. I know, however, that certain publishers treated their men scandalously in this respect. When daily papers began to gain a firm footing and Čech typographical unions had organized their men, the wages of typesetters rose so markedly that many a reporter gave up his job

[1] Specially communicated in 1915 to the author by Václav Šnajdr, at present living in retirement in Cleveland.

at the desk and took to typesetting. At the case the reporter felt he was more independent; the publisher did not require him to attend, in the interest of his paper, dances, amateur theatricals, concerts, meetings. Furthermore, as a typesetter, he was secure from the impertinence of petty demagogues, who made miserable the life of the editor.

"The *Slavie's* high-water mark in the matter of subscribers was 4000. The highest figure reached by the *Dennice Novověku* was 3000. Considering the paper's radical policy, this was considered as enviably large. But in time a recession came. Publishers started to manufacture 'patent inside' weeklies and bi-weeklies filled with material taken bodily from the dailies. Against these factory-made weeklies, as they might be called, the genuine weeklies could compete in everything save in the quantity of reading matter.

"Except for occasional help, the *Slavie* never employed a salaried associate editor. It was always a partnership, or a profit-sharing arrangement of one kind or other. Kořízek and Bárta had agreed to divide the profits; but as matters were there was nothing to divide. On the contrary, the paper would have been run at a loss but for extras earned by Kořízek as a musician. After the merger of the *Národní Noviny* and the *Slowan Amerikánský*, Mráček and Bárta were to have drawn a certain salary. This salary was not paid as agreed, for the simple reason that there were no available funds.

VÁCLAV ŠNAJDR

JOURNALISM AND LITERATURE

Mráček and Bárta, as you know, went to Russia on a special mission. In Jonáš's and Kořízek's time, the old system of profit-sharing was again put into practice and continued until 1868, when I bought out Kořízek's share. After that Charles Jonáš and I drew $50 a month each. The profits, if any, we divided at the end of the year. My salary as associate editor never exceeded $50 per month. About the same stipend was paid to J. V. Sládek who worked for the *Slavie* a few weeks. Joseph Jiří Král received a compensation of $60 or $65 a month. I am not certain how much other publishers were paying, but my impression is that John A. Oliverius did not receive more on the *Pozor* than $45 or $50. Zdrůbek began with $50. Joseph Pastor had a promise of more on the *Nová Doba* of Chicago; however, the receipts were never such as to warrant the extra compensation. In those days $50 a month was generally thought a fair honorarium. As to your inquiry concerning circulation. Until 1865 readers were counted by the hundreds only. The *Slavie* probably had at that time 2000 subscribers. When I bought out Kořízek in 1868 the circulation was 2500; readers began to increase after the seventies. Advertisements were at first inserted not so much for revenue as to fill the space. In 1870 advertisements netted the *Slavie* $200. Later there was a steady accession of advertising matter. The best-paid advertisement was that of the North German Lloyd — $25 yearly.

THE ČECHS IN AMERICA

"What the Bártas doled out to Klácel as editor of the *Slovan Amerikánský*, I do not know, but it could not have amounted to much, for the old professor never wearied complaining to his friends that he was in want and that his pay was beggarly.

"After his return from Europe, where he had gone to report on the Franco-Prussian War, Jonáš began publishing a small weekly, a sort of a supplement to the *Slavie*, which he named the *Amerikán*. He was enough of a business man to see that the *Slavie* could not keep two editors busy, and he was anxious to earn an extra dollar from this new enterprise. The typesetting on the supplement was done almost entirely by his wife Christine, who, like her younger sister, Celia, later my wife, had become a skilled typesetter.

"Meantime Edward Rosewater,[1] who had served for a time in the Civil War as a field telegraph operator, issued in Omaha, besides his daily paper the *Bee*, a Čech weekly, the *Pokrok Západu*. One of the contributors to the *Pokrok Západu* was carpenter Vodička. The sheet led a precarious existence, being more of an advertising medium of land speculators than a purveyor of news. Obviously this state of things did not tend to raise the paper's reputation among its readers. Seeing that the Čechs were beginning to settle in Nebraska in increasing numbers, Rosewater decided to raise the standard of the

[1] *Květy Americké*, September 28, 1887. Biography and portrait. Rosewater was born in 1841 and arrived in 1854.

JOURNALISM AND LITERATURE

Pokrok Západu, and he offered me, upon whose advice I do not remember, the editorship, at a weekly salary of $25, in addition to giving me lodging in the printing shop. This salary Rosewater paid me regularly; and to show my gratitude, I toiled night and day, taking charge not only of the editorial columns, but of business correspondence as well. Advertisements were few, because Čech business men, other than saloon-keepers, grocers, bakers, and butchers, were but a handful. That publishers accepted advertisements at ridiculously low rates is true. Some papers were content to receive almost any price; again others were satisfied to be paid by the advertiser in kind — clothing and footwear for the printers, dress material for the women folks. The *Dennice Novověku* in the initial years owed its existence to profitable advertisements which I solicited personally in my off hours, after my editorial duties were done. Subscriptions from readers came in tardily and were inadequate to keep the paper going."

As they have lived so they have died — in honorable poverty. Bittner, the greatest talent of them all, left his family in utter destitution. Janda, another gifted journalist, died pitifully poor. A charitable relative drove the proverbial wolf away from Oliverius's door more than once. Klácel was all but a public almoner living on the scant pittance of his admirers. The income from the newspaper drudgery barely sufficed to keep soul and body together.

Palda repeatedly jeopardized his business interests by his unconquerable passion for journalistic work. In his memoirs Palda laments: "If times were hard in Cleveland they were intolerable in New York. The employees, to be sure, had to be paid promptly. We three publishers divided the income as follows: John V. Čapek, being single and having supposedly smaller needs, drew five dollars weekly; I received eight wherewith to support myself, wife and three children; Škarda and his wife kept the balance." Believing he was taking a final leave of the profession Čapek in the last number of the Cleveland *Národní Noviny* (1873) says with ill-concealed bitterness: "I throw away my pen with which I have wasted here three of the best years of my life." To Pastor, ambitious and clear-headed, the outlook appeared so dismal that he made haste to withdraw while still young and turn his energy to a more gainful employment. Zdrůbek was one of the few favored ones who accumulated a competence. But Zdrůbek's main revenue was derived, not from journalism, but from paid functions incident to his position as Speaker of the Liberal Union in Chicago.

No ordinary journalist was Frank Mráček [1] (born in Moravia in 1828, died, 1896, in Odessa, Russia), whom the publishers of the St. Louis *Ná-*

---

[1] John Borecký: *Chapters on the History of Čech-Moravians in America*, p. 9. Cedar Rapids, 1896. The *Pokrok Západu*, March 10, 1896.

ANTON MALINOWSKI

JAN BÁRTA LETOVSKÝ

rodní Noviny called in 1860, to edit that paper. His biographer said of him that he had been sentenced to serve a twenty-year term in the military prison at Kufstein, in the Tyrol, for having taken an active part in political agitation in Prague. After the amnesty in 1857 Mráček emigrated to the United States. In the first years of the Civil War, a farming element, discontented with conditions here, conceived the somewhat fantastic plan of migrating to Asiatic Russia. Mráček and Bárta Letovský were chosen as envoys to go to the Czar's land, there to pick out a suitable region for the future New Bohemia. Happily, the contemplated emigration to Russia never took place; so far as is known only one emigrant settled in Russia pursuant to the plan. That emigrant was Mráček himself. To his countrymen in the United States Mráček's leave-taking was a real loss, for he was a cultured gentleman, a born leader and organizer. Mráček's widow, who is still living (or rather was living before the war) in Russia, draws a pension from the United States Government; he served in the Army during the Civil War.

Charles Jonáš (1840–96), the "first Čech in America," as Carl Schurz was the "first German," came to the United States in 1863, as an undergraduate of the Polytechnic at Prague. To save himself from arrest for actively participating in the Čech national movement, Jonáš had fled to London; from that city friends invited him to come to

183

Racine to take charge of the *Slavie*. When he assumed editorship of that paper he was but twenty-three years old, an alarmingly immature age for an editor. Yet Jonáš's youth was not without its compensations, for it enabled him to master more quickly the English language and to grow up, so to say, with the surroundings. Even before he came to America he had evinced a marked liking for public affairs, to which in the United States he could give free rein.

In his student days he wrote a political pamphlet in German wherein he sought to prove that a confederacy of free nations was the only solution of the Austrian problem. His quick wit told him he must master the English language before he could aspire to leadership among his people here. At a time when others were still hesitating whether they should stay in America or emigrate to Amur, Jonáš busied himself with English. Though a mere youth, he was sagacious enough to recognize the unwisdom of opening the columns of the *Slavie* to religious disputes. That the temptation to do so was strong is easily believable, for Jonáš was a liberal through and through, and there was no mistake as to where his sympathies lay. Among his journalistic colleagues he attained an exceptional position: friend and foe alike learned to look up to him as an authority, from whose decision but few had the courage to appeal. Such was the weight of his word that his views and his opinions on matters relat-

CHARLES JONÁŠ

ing to the national life of the Čechs in America were regarded as final; not perhaps that he was always right, but because it was Jonáš who said it. About 1872 the *Slavie* ranged itself openly on the side of the Democratic Party, with the result that probably the majority of Čechs followed Jonáš willingly and embraced the creed thereof. His literary work was entirely of the useful kind. Though he had been trained, as stated, for the career of a technicist, he plunged courageously into philology and lexicography. His initial volume was the *Bohemian-English Interpreter*, published in 1865.[1] In 1876 appeared the Bohemian-English and English-Bohemian dictionaries. The fact that these dictionaries have gone through sixteen editions, in each case amplified and improved, is the best testimony of their merit and usefulness. In 1884 followed the *New American Interpreter;* in 1890 *Bohemian Made Easy. The American Law* and *Golden Book for Farmers* are compilations. Other Čechs have achieved higher political honors than he; Jonáš was state senator (1883), consul to Prague (1885), lieutenant-governor of Wisconsin (1890), consul to Petrograd (1894), consul to Crefeld (1894). Yet in

[1] Adolph William Straka, political exile living in London, preceded Jonáš by three years with his *English Grammar*, published in Prague in 1862. This is the first book of its kind in the Čech language. Inasmuch as Jonáš came to Racine from London and had associated in the English capital with Straka, the inference is that it was Straka's example which inspired Jonáš to devote himself in America to the same line of literary work.

the estimation of the old-timers, Jonáš was without a peer. He died at Crefeld, Germany,[1] and was buried in Prague. His tombstone bears this inscription: "Charles Jonáš, first United States Consul of Čech nationality, born October 30, 1840, died January 15, 1896. I have one wish. Bury me in the loved Čech land, for which I have fervently longed and for which I have sacrificed all." [2]

Journalism will not forget the name of Joseph Pastor, the fighting editor of the ultra-radical weekly *Pokrok*. Pastor was born in 1841, and after graduation from a Latin school (gymnasium), being too poor to continue his studies in the university, he joined a religious order. He appeared in New York in 1866. There he earned a niggardly living at cigarmaking. Later he entered the service of the New York *Staatszeitung* as a stenographer.

---

[1] In order to set at rest the stories current as to the cause of Jonáš's death, the author addressed a letter of inquiry to the State Department. Here is the answer:

Department of State, August 10, 1918

Mr. Thomas Čapek.

DEAR SIR: In response to your inquiry of July 29th I regret to inform you that the Department's records show that Mr. Charles Jonáš, American Consul at Crefeld, Germany, died of heart failure, January 15, 1896.

HERBERT C. HENGSTLER,
Acting Chief, Consular Bureau

[2] The *Květy Americké*, July 15, 1885, autobiography and portrait; the *Slavie*, January 22, 1896, obituary by J. J. Král and portrait; the *Světozor*, Prague, XXXII: 120–21, portrait of tombstone; the *Slavie*, May 31, 1912, eulogy by J. E. S. Vojan, on the occasion of the unveiling of a monument to Jonáš in Racine.

Pastor was a thorough German scholar. His letters from New York to the *Slavie* attracted the attention of Jonáš and of Kořízek, who offered him the editorship of the *Pokrok*. While no one questioned Pastor's ability and sincerity, the more cultured element deplored his rough-and-tumble style of handling his adversaries. Father Joseph Molitor, of the Chicago *Katolické Noviny*, was a particular sufferer at Pastor's hands. Wearied of the miseries of journalism, he removed to Hamburg, where he established himself as a steamship ticket agent. During his residence in Hamburg he issued in 1884 a periodical, the *České Osady v Americe* (Čech Settlements in America), containing much useful statistical information. Pastor was a warm admirer of America and of its free institutions.

The *Květy Americké* (American Blossoms) [1] had this to say of Václav Šnajdr, from 1877 to 1911 the publisher and editor of the *Dennice Novověku:* "He holds a notable rank in our national life, enjoying the esteem and confidence of the liberal element among Čechs in America. After the retirement of Jonáš from active journalism, Šnajdr occupied without doubt a foremost place as a newspaper writer; as a poet he has not been equaled (among his countrymen here). Pity, though, that the exhausting work of journalism has stifled in him the poet."

[1] The *Květy Americké*, August 17, 1887. Biography and portrait; Thomas Čapek: *Fifiy Years of Čech Letters in America*, pp. 120–21, autobiographical note.

Šnajdr, who was born in 1847, came to the United States the same year as did Klácel. Preparatory to his taking charge of the *Dennice Novověku*, which he founded in 1877, he received journalistic training on the *Slavie*, *Pokrok Západu*, and *Pokrok*. Several of his compilations — his favorite author appears to have been Ingersoll — were published in pamphlet form. The estimate of Šnajdr by the *Květy Americké* is correct in the main, except for the assertion that he ranked next to Jonáš as a journalist. The truth is that disciplined readers appraised Šnajdr as the abler newspaperman of the two. This estimate of Šnajdr's abilities was sustained as Jonáš, in later years, began to neglect journalism for the more exciting, though not profitable, game of politics. Šnajdr was always frank, at times disagreeably so. Jonáš as an aspiring politician was necessarily wary, diplomatic. Except for a few pamphlets, all Šnajdr's literary production is stored in the *Dennice Novověku*, and the thought is a mournful one — a tragic feature of the journalism of a small nation — that a man's life effort should be bound up in the archives of a newspaper of which there exists but one copy, the copy which is called the editorial file.

An original personality among the old standard-bearers was John Borecký (1828–1908).[1] Though he received no more than a village school education

---

[1] The *Květy Americké*, November 10, 1886; *St. Louiské Listy*, January, 1909.

VÁCLAV SNAJDR AND
JOSEPH V. SLÁDEK (left)

VÁCLAV ŠNAJDR AND
HIS BROTHER-IN-LAW
CHARLES JONÁŠ (standing)

and notwithstanding the fact that he was a stranger to the mysteries of Čech orthography, to quote a journalistic opponent, Borecký was capable of writing thoughtful, and if the subject-matter related to the doings of pioneers, exceedingly informative, articles. Aggressive to rashness, Borecký was unafraid even of Klácel, if he believed himself in the right. In newspaper disputes he had no hesitancy in attacking Šnajdr, Zdrůbek and Palda. His great gift was his remarkable memory which, even in his extreme old age — he died at Little Rock, Arkansas, in his eightieth year — served him unerringly. If a controversy arose over the details of some long-forgotten event, all that was needed was to knock at the door of old man Borecký and he promptly supplied the missing facts. His scrap-book was deadly and men with shady pasts felt uneasy when Borecký became reminiscent. It was he who silenced Hynek Sládek,[1] a poor newspaper scribe; it was he who made J. B. Erben, the first editor of the St. Louis *Národní Noviny* and the intimate of his youth, disgusted with journalism.[2] In addition to articles

[1] For details from Sládek's life, see article, "One of the Pioneer Čech editors," the *Květy Americké*, Omaha, July 10, 1902; another account, the *Květy Americké*, November 10, 1886. Hynek Sládek should not be confounded with J. V. Sládek, the poet.

[2] J. B. Erben was born in 1837, and according to latest advices, lives with his daughter in retirement in St. Louis. His past has been the subject of heated controversies, in which Borecký, his chief detractor, invariably led the opposition. *Osvěta Americká*, January 16, 1907, and Borecký's letter, dated March 15, 1907, published in the *St. Louiské Listy*.

scattered in various newspapers, he wrote a brief treatise, *Kapitoly* (Chapters on the History of Čech-Moravians in America). Only that part of the tract which contains the personal reminiscences of the author is of value; the rest, in which Borecký debates with the protagonists of liberalism, is rambling. Following a newspaper quarrel, Borecký left the liberal party and joined, in theory at least, the socialists. He came to the United States as a journeyman tailor and resided alternately in Milwaukee, St. Louis, Chicago, and Little Rock.

John A. Oliverius (1843–1904) was not nicknamed "newspaper grave-digger" without reason. His name is associated with sixteen papers on which he had been active as editor or in which he was interested as publisher. Not one newspaperman could boast of such a record. Oliverius's head was ever afire with lofty ideals and far-reaching plans, the latter invariably aiming to save from racial extinction his countrymen in America. Among other things he advocated the founding of a New Bohemia, preferably in Oregon, where it would be protected on one side by the sea. Charles Jonáš, his political adversary — Oliverius championed the Republican Party while Jonáš was a Democratic partisan — was wont to call him a visionary and a fool; yet Oliverius was far from a fool. On the contrary, he was, on occasions, a shrewd judge of men, far-sighted, almost prophetic in some of his conclusions. In a newspaper *mêlée*, it is true, he often lost all sense of proportion. Despite his long residence in America (Chicago), he never learned the art of making money, a circumstance all the more remarkable, since he had been trained in his youth for a merchant's career. But for the charitableness of a relative abroad he would have suffered what Klácel bitterly termed, vulgar want. His nickname, "newspaper grave-digger," was not wholly undeserved, yet it was Oliverius's cash and his alone, which went to pay for all the newspaper graves that he dug. In 1890 he published in pamphlet form a lecture on the *Cultural Meaning of the Queen's Court and Green Hill MSS.* (144 pp.). In view of the fact that both of these manuscripts were proved to be spurious, the treatise has but an antiquarian interest. Not even his opponents questioned his probity or his rugged patriotism. "Oliverius was impracticable," "Oliverius was an idealistic visionary," was the worst they could say of him. He died in poverty and is buried in Prague.

Ladimír Klácel [1] created nothing in America of enduring value. Driven by dire need to seek a living in unprofitable and unappreciated newspaper work, again and again changing his residence,— he

[1] The *Květy Americké*, September 15, 1885, biography and portrait; Václav Šnajdr: *Ladimír (Francis) Klácel: His Life and Teaching.* 49 pp. Cleveland, 1908; same, the *Dennice Novověku*, April 9, 1908. The monument above his grave in Belle Plaine bears inscriptions in Čech, English, and Latin. The English text is: "Professor Ladimír Klácel, the Čech Patriot, Philosopher and Freethinker, born at Česká, Třebová, April 7th, 1803. Died at Belle Plaine, March 17th, 1882. Erected by his grateful countrymen."

191

lived successively in Iowa City, Chicago, Cooperstown, Kossuthtown, Keewaunee, Krok, Milwaukee, Belle Plaine,— Klácel lacked that repose of mind and sense of security which, if not indispensable, are yet conducive to scholarly pursuits.

Šnajdr, who visited Klácel in his flat in Chicago, thus describes the plight of the hapless philosopher: "He occupied one room partitioned off by a screen; the front part was used as a kitchen and sleeping-place by the housekeeper, Mrs. Moll. In the other lived Klácel surrounded by his books. Dejection and poverty were reflected in his sorrowing eyes. 'We subsist on bread and milk and at times we lack even that; besides, my clothes are falling apart,' he complained, pointing to a black alpaca coat, such as the clergy wear. Neither I nor my companion could repress our emotions. I shall not forget this visit."

A fellow countryman found Klácel weeping on the steps of a country church in Wisconsin, in which, in his utter destitution, he was compelled, as a means of earning a scant pittance, to conduct services to a motley congregation. What poignant suffering it must have caused him to again put on priest's vestments and repeat before the altar the ceremony which he had often ridiculed.

To a friend he wrote that he wished to publish in America a newspaper "serving the needs of a cultured people, who strive after truth, righteousness, love. Yet, what do I find? Every lofty ideal meets

EARLY NEWSPAPERS

with derision. Nevertheless I persist and try to please the minority, at least, hoping that in the end victory may be our reward. But it is disheartening to have to struggle with vulgar want." And this in a communication to an admirer: "How deeply grieved I am that they [the Bártas] should treat me as if I were a day laborer, from whom they accept what suits them, paying me what they please for services rendered. All too readily do they forget that the 1500 subscribers [of the *Slovan Amerikánský*] are due to my endeavor."

"Klácel's American writings," comments Anton Novák of Milwaukee, "were printed in editions at no time exceeding 500; of this number about one half was sold, the remaining half was knocked about on the shelves for years until I gave the stuff away or threw it out on the rubbish heap, in order to gain shelf-space for other books. It was very poor business; there were issues that did not bring in enough to pay the cost of the print paper. The *Věčný Kalendář* (Perpetual Calendar) had about 150 subscribers; the *Historie Spojených Státu Amerických* (History of the United States) barely 100. That under such circumstances I could not go on with other of Klácel's publications is self-evident."

One cannot speak of Klácel as a journalist. Judging his work in the retrospect, we get the picture of a sorrowing old man, captivated by dogmas; one who had no adequate conception of the realities of American life. Is it to be wondered that readers grumbled that "Klácel wrote too learnedly"? In the *Hlas Jednoty* spoke not an American journalist, whose function is to record the events of the day, but an old-fashioned schoolmaster.

Among self-made men, who, to use a homely but an expressive phrase, pulled themselves up by their boot-straps, the best known was L. J. Palda (1847–1912). An eloquent speaker, an independent thinker, a gifted journalist, an indefatigable organizer, Palda might have risen high, had he been able to tear himself away from the diminutive world to which his birth had chained him, but which he adored above all else. He had many of the faults and virtues of the great men, of the Mirabeaus, Gambettas, Cavours, and Riegers of history. His life gave every evidence of his strong personality. He organizes workingmen, advocates socialism — he is rightfully called the father of Čech socialism — by appealing speeches tries to sustain, when and wherever called, the waning courage of strikers, drudges as editor and as pamphleteer. It is hard to decide which of his achievements deserve higher praise. Is it his work as a publicist? Or his efforts as an organizer of labor? Even his enemies — and Palda had plenty of them (he was vainglorious, they said) — will not gainsay his splendid gift of eloquence. Socialists will not detract from his merits, though the more radical element repudiated him, at one time, as a reactionary. An idealist and humanist despite unending disappointments, Palda wrote, in 1902, a remarkable booklet, which he entitled *Myšlenky o novém náboženství* (Thoughts on New Religion). In it the thinking man sets out to analyze his creed; not satisfied with evasion he demands solution of the perplexing problem of religion. He arrives at the conclusion that mere non-belief, negativity, is not enough. "I yearned by this exposition of my faith partly to ease my troubled mind, partly, if possible, to assist in the approaching regeneration of our liberal party. I see this possible only in a new religion, which shall embrace all our desires, all our ideals, our teachings, our views. . . . I realized more and more that mere negativity, renunciation of the beliefs, will not suffice to fill a spiritual void." Palda's *New Religion*, however, pleased neither the orthodox among the rationalists nor the old-fashioned believers. The latter challenged the author through the person of Father Tichý of Minnesota,[1] who was of the opinion that there was no need to go in search of new creeds. All that was necessary was an abiding constancy in the old, the true faith. As for the rationalists, they passed a scathing resolution in which they, metaphorically speaking, ejected Palda from their ranks as an apostate and undesirable. Palda's last years were spent in Cedar Rapids, where he operated a cigar factory on a small scale. By trade he was not a cigarmaker; he came to the United States in 1867 as a journeyman weaver. Journalism always attracted him and he yielded to

[1] *Odpověď Paldovi* (A Reply to Palda). 1906. A pamphlet of 88 pp.

its allurements, though his business often suffered in consequence. He received but little more than a common school education; yet those who had the good fortune of knowing him intimately agreed that he was not only an amiable companion, but a cultured man. A well-stocked library was his only college. As a journalist he towered far above Zdrů-bek and as a student he outranked Jonáš, who had more of a practical than contemplative mind. His tragic death occurred in Cedar Rapids in 1912.[1]

Frank Boleslav Zdrůbek was born in 1842 of a poor family. He was sent to a Catholic theological seminary to be educated for the priesthood. Having, as he says, experienced a change in religious faith, Zdrůbek left the Catholic for a Protestant seminary, from which latter he graduated. Emigrating before the seventies to the United States, he took charge, at Caledonia, Wisconsin, and at Wesley, Texas, of evangelical congregations of Čech-Moravian Brethren. But his career as a minister of the gospel was of brief duration. The parishioners complained that their pastor was too radical in his views; the pastor again was dissatisfied because his flock was not progressive enough. When Joseph Pastor resigned from the anti-clerical weekly *Pokrok*, Zdrůbek gave up the pulpit, removed to Chicago, and "notwithstanding his

[1] The *Květy Americké*, August 15, 1885, autobiography and portrait; Dr. F. Soukup: article in Prague *Právo Lidu*, reprinted in *Hlas Lidu*, July 10, 1913; article in Prague *Čas*, reprinted in *Hlas Lidu*, July 8, 1913.

FRANCIS B. ZDRŮBEK

retiring disposition and his aversion to public life,"
accepted the post of editor of that paper. "He did
this all the more readily, as he felt that as a minister
of the gospel he could not make an honorable living
unless he chose to make of his vocation a vulgar
traffic and practice from the pulpit pious extor-
tion." [1]

Zdrůbek was an iconoclast who believed in no
miracles save those which science performed.
Though a pulpiteer of considerable experience, it
could not be said of him that he was an orator.
As a journalist he was distinctly commonplace.
Most prolific of all the Čech *literati*, he was, in fact,
not a creative writer, but a translator. Yet in the
end Zdrůbek managed to raise himself to the foremost place among his countrymen and the liberals
bowed to him as their chief. What was the secret of
his success? Zdrůbek was a man who triumphed not
by reason of genius, for he was not above medioc-
rity, but rather because all his life he had been a
hard, conscientious worker, a man of unblemished
reputation. The liberal ideas which he imbibed
from Voltaire, Paine, Ingersoll, Klácel, and other
thinkers, he espoused with a zeal, which no one
would have suspected in this meek and humble ex-
pastor. His life-work proceeded along two dissimi-
lar lines: like Jonáš he compiled dictionaries and
grammars. At the same time he combated, orally
and in writing, clericalism in all its forms. The

[1] The *Květy Americké*, June 23, 1886, autobiography.

English Grammar came out in 1870. Then followed successively, *How to Pronounce in English, Čech English Interpreter, Pocket Dictionary of the English and Čech Languages,* and a grammar or two for Čech elementary schools. His translations from English and German include: *Das Leben Jesu,* by David Friedrich Strauss (1883); *The Age of Reason,* by Thomas Paine (1884); *Die Konventionellen Lügen der Kulturmenschheit,* by Max Nordau (1885); *Kraft und Stoff,* by Ludwig Buechner (1889). Then there are the *Sermons,* delivered on various occasions, but chiefly as a Speaker of the Liberal Union in Chicago between 1879 and 1894. His rhymed *Comic Bible* (1885) is maladroit. In 1877 he took part in a public disputation with Father V. Čoka, a Chicago priest. Zdrůbek's contribution to this debate was printed under the title, *Two Religious Disputations,* etc. Jointly with August Geringer he founded, in 1875, the Chicago *Svornost,* remaining uninterruptedly at its head up to his death in Chicago in 1911. An adversary thus epitomized Zdrůbek's life-work: "With tireless energy worthy of a better cause, he propagated the teaching of infidelity, and he admired greatly the doctrines of that American agnostic, Robert Ingersoll."

The roster of pioneers would be incomplete without the name of John Rosický of Omaha.[1] A self-

[1] *A Souvenir,* published in memory of John Rosický, American Čech journalist and patriot. 90 pp. Omaha, 1910.

JOHN ROSICKÝ

made man, Rosický came to be recognized as one of the forceful members of the journalistic profession. In 1871 he took over from Edward Rosewater the weekly *Pokrok Západu* (Progress of the West), then a small sheet, without influence and without readers. In time Rosický raised the *Pokrok Západu* to the front of Čech weeklies. That his tastes were higher than mere commercial journalism, he proved in 1884, when he set up the *Květy Americké*, the first genuine attempt at a Čech literary periodical. Bravely the *Květy Americké* strove to live up to the programme outlined in the prospectus of the publisher. But the most ambitious plans of a publisher are doomed to miscarry if the reading community fails adequately to support him. Tiring of the recurrent deficits, Rosický was forced to modify his original plan with the *Květy Americké*. Out of the compromise emerged, in 1903, a publication called the *Osvěta Americká* (American Culture), half commercial, half literary. By far the most profitable of Rosický's ventures proved to be an agricultural paper, the *Hospodář* (Husbandman). This publication now claims a larger circulation than any other agricultural paper printed in the Čech language. Rosický was a newspaper man and not an author. Only one brief booklet — businesslike and to the point — bears his name, *Jak je v Americe?* (America as it is), compiled "for the guidance of newly arrived compatriots in America." A man of compelling individuality, he rendered helpful service to settlers west of the Missouri River. He was born in 1845, came with his parents to America in 1861, and died in Omaha in 1910.

John V. Čapek was a humorist whom no Čech writer in America has yet equaled. His homely humor was of that rustic grain — Čapek was peasant born — which, like a happy after-dinner speech, provokes both good feeling and mirth. His ready pen turned out droll rhymes with the same astonishing ease and neatness with which a magician pulls things out of his hat. The comic *Life of St. Anthony of Padua* (New York, 1883) in verse is fairly indicative of Čapek's skill in this respect. The life of the Italian saint, by the way, is not a translation of Wilhelm Busch's *Der Heilige St. Antonius von Padua*. Only the illustrations are borrowed from that German writer-artist. The text is original. Čapek's humorous weekly, the *Diblík* (Puck), will long be remembered by discriminating lovers of clean, sparkling humor. As a journalist and writer of fiction, he was thought of highly by contemporaries, and would have added considerably to Čech letters here, since he was a man of fine culture and broad views, had not experiments in electricity lured him away from literature. He was born in Bohemia, in 1842, studied in the University of Prague, and came to America in 1871 in answer to a call from the publishers of the Cleveland *Pokrok*. He died in New York in 1909.

F. K. Ringsmuth possessed more than a versi-

JOHN V. ČAPEK

fier's adroitness at turning out rhymes. He, too, had in him the material of which genuine poets are made. Marital troubles were accountable for Ringsmuth's complete desertion of literature. Pecksniffian colleagues called him a turncoat; in a sense, Ringsmuth was a turncoat. From a social democrat and a rationalist, which he was in his younger years, he turned for consolation to the Scriptures, becoming first a missionary, later a Protestant minister. The *Kytice Básní* (Bouquet of Poems, New York, 1882) discloses a man of decided poetic talent.

Josephine Humpal-Zeman (1870–1906), a newspaper writer, and advocate of woman's suffrage, was the very opposite of Frances Gregor. An unfortunate marriage forced her to earn her own living. Incidentally, marital experiences lent a sharper angle to her estimate of the new woman. Mrs. Zeman first obtained entrance into American circles through the good offices of certain women interested in a Chicago settlement house. One of these, Mary Ingersoll, Mrs. Zeman called, in a book dedication, "My second mother." Presumably due to the generosity of this woman, Mrs. Zeman was sent to a seminary. From the seminary she brought home two very valuable assets: first, a fair command of the English language, and secondly, a broader general knowledge. Later in life, when she put herself at the head of the woman suffrage movement, she was enabled to make excellent use of these acquirements. With other women she founded in Chicago, in 1894, a weekly paper, the *Ženské Listy* (Woman's Gazette). Aside from journalism she was active as a lecturer, speaking to audiences in English or in her mother tongue, as circumstances required. She was the pioneer in this work. Ungallantly, Bartoš Bittner was wont to chaff her in the *Šotek* with the sobriquet, "Mrs. General." Mrs. Zeman was a type that shone to greatest advantage on the lecture platform championing the rights of her sex, or in woman's clubs, where her readiness as a debater was a great asset. We have only one book from her, *Amerika v pravém Světle* (America in its True Light), published in Prague in 1903. "The book contains three of the lectures I delivered while on a visit to my native land, in some thirty towns in Bohemia, Moravia, and Silesia." The "three lectures" is a pamphlet full of bright *bon mots*. The observations in *America in its True Light* are cleverly phrased but superficial. She died in Prague in 1906.

Using the popular history by Benson John Lossing as a model and "from various other sources," Joseph Čermák of Chicago has compiled a *History of the United States*. In the preface Čermák asks the forbearance of the critic, his compilation being, as he explains, "an extra work, done at odd evening hours, in addition to the hurry-up work of a newspaper editor." Even the most indulgent reviewer will readily agree with the compiler that his *His-*

Catherine M. Čapek

Josephine Humpal-Zeman

Frances Gregor

Dr. Anna F. Novák

PROFESSIONAL WOMEN

tory of the United States was done as extra work. A standard history of the United States, preferably a translation by a competent translator of some approved textbook used in our schools, is one of the existing needs of American Čech literature. And this need, unfortunately, Čermák's history does not fill. Čermák is an authority on the technique of physical training and his book (412 pp.), *Physical Training; Being a Practical Aid to Čech American Instructors of Youth,* has earned the praise of Sokols here and in Bohemia.

No visitor has written so many glaring inaccuracies and screaming untruths about America as John Wagner (1856–1905, in Prague). The man simply could not treat America seriously or soberly; he only knew America as the land of "unlimited impossibilities," America farcical and grotesque. Wagner was a Čech Munchausen, and judging from some of his performances one is inclined to believe that if Bill Nye's *Comic History of the United States* had fallen into his hands, he would have pronounced it a genuine history of America. Wagner should have known better, for he was not a Sunday tourist who studies a country by looking at it from the window of a railroad train and then describes it. He lived in the United States for a considerable time, doing newspaper work in New York, Omaha, and Chicago. His pamphlet, *Transatlantic Gossip,* was published in Prague in 1898.

Frances Gregor was born in Bohemia in 1850, but

was brought to this country when an infant. In Wisconsin, where her parents settled on a farm, she became a school-teacher. Ambitious to better herself, she entered Cornell University, from which she graduated with honors. The supreme wish of her life was realized when friends enabled her to go to Prague, there to devote herself to literary work and, incidentally, to improve her knowledge of the Čech tongue. The fruits of her stay abroad were, first, a translation of Božena Němcová's charming story from rustic life, *Babička* (Grandmother), and later, the *History of Bohemia*. In translating Němcová's *Babička* into idiomatic English — the first storybook by a Čech author, so honored — Frances Gregor rendered a real service to literature. Many an American Čech youth has had his or her first glimpse of Čech rural life from the English version of *Babička*. Gregor's *History of Bohemia* has since been superseded by abler historical narratives. An incurable malady not only interfered with her literary work, but made life, especially towards the end, unendurable. She died in 1901, in Colorado.

Literary critics will assign to Bartoš Bittner (1861–1912) [1] a leading place as an essayist. Bittner was intended for the law; but tiring of the Austro-Čech Blackstone, he gave up his law studies and entered a Catholic theological seminary. From this

[1] Quill and Vojan: *Orgán Bratrstva, Č.S.P.S.*, May, 1913; "Reminiscences of Bartoš Bittner," *Č.A.T.K.*; "Leave-Taking of Bartoš Bittner," *Hlas Lidu*, May 10, 1912.

BARTOŠ BITTNER

JOURNALISM AND LITERATURE

he ran away and came, in 1884, to this country.
Soon after arriving, he secured a position as a
teacher in a language school in Cedar Rapids.
Journalism, however, attracted him, and presently
we find him at it in New York and later in Chicago.
In the Western metropolis he set up a humorous
and satirical weekly, the *Šotek* (Imp), which soon
achieved marked success. He reached the height of
popularity about 1894, when the Chicago Benedictines, angered by his philippics — Bittner's
raillery was particularly aimed at Abbot Jäger —
brought a suit for criminal libel against him.
Though as poor as the proverbial church mouse,
Bittner was able promptly to raise among his admirers $20,000 bail. The winning of the suit still
more enhanced his reputation. Having lost the
Šotek, owing to poor business management, Bittner
became a literary free lance, working for whom he
pleased and when he pleased; that, for one of his
capricious temperament, meant that he worked
irregularly, often not at all. But whatever issued
from his facile pen bore unmistakable evidence of
a talent of high order. He employed political satires
with great effectiveness. As a matter of fact there
were two Bittners; one, who at times was given to
conviviality. This Bittner was introspective, brooding, wretched, a grave study for the psychologist.
The other Bittner was a poet and a thinker, a master of Čech diction, who defied the greatest lumi-
naries among his countrymen. His essays, poems,

and humorous discourses, if edited, would fill volumes. His end was as tragic as had been bohemian the life he elected to lead. Separated from his family he died alone, unrecognized, in a squalid Chicago lodging-house.

Dr. Aleš Hrdlička, who is in charge of the Division of Physical Anthropology in the United States National Museum in Washington, was born in Bohemia, 1869. He immigrated with his parents as a lad. In New York he studied and for a short time practiced medicine. From the general practice of his profession he soon turned his attention to the anthropology of the insane and other defective classes. His writings, notably those on the antiquity of man in North and South America, are numerous and acknowledged by scientists as authoritative. Hrdlička did research work in Europe, Argentine, Peru, Panama, Mexico, Siberia, China, Egypt. He is a member of many scientific bodies in this country and in Europe, of the Čech Academy of Sciences among them. Since 1918 he has edited the *American Journal of Physical Anthropology*, of which publication he is also the founder. Readers of the *Dennice Novověku* have not forgotten the instructive articles in Čech which Dr. Hrdlička contributed years ago.

Čech America has had but a few talented writers of fiction. Three names have found an echo in the old country, Paul Albieri (1861–1901), John Havlasa, and J. R. Pšenka. Albieri came to America

DR. ALEŠ HRDLIČKA

with the reputation of a successful narrator of stories of military life. In time he might have achieved distinction as a journalist, his fitness for newspaper work being undeniable, if only his restlessness, ever driving him into new ventures, had not set at naught every serious effort that he made in that direction. That he was a poor judge of men and a worse critic of things he proved time and again by his notes on America, published in Prague papers. Bohemian in a double sense (that is, by birth and by habits) he was withal a delightful companion and a gifted conversationalist. He met death in a railroad accident in Texas.

A Chicago girl (Vlasta Charlotte Kozel, 1873–1901), writing under the name of Pavla Čechová, contributed to newspapers colorful articles of striking originality. Though born and bred in Chicago and notwithstanding the fact that she had never seen the inside of a Čech schoolroom, Miss Čechová acquired a remarkable command of Čech, preferring to compose in that language exclusively. Though it is uncommon for American-born children to use the Čech for literary expression, Miss Čechová was by no means an isolated case. Miss Rose Rosický, who was born in Omaha and educated in the schools of that city, and who has only a book acquaintance with the native country of her parents, never having been in Bohemia, edits with ability the woman's page in the Omaha *Květy Americké*. Mrs. Ludmila Kuchař-Foxlee, a New

Yorker by birth and schooling, writes excellent Čech. Miss Šárka B. Hrbkova, a native of Iowa, was formerly professor of Čech in the Nebraska State University. For a while she was editor-in-chief of a college students' monthly, the *Komenský*.

Alois Janda, a theologian, actor, journalist, teacher, was more than an everyday versifier; he was a gifted poet. Janda's first offering in book form, *Českým Duším* (To Čech Souls; St. Louis, 1894), proves it beyond all doubt. When maturer years had tempered his judgment, Janda wrote articles for the Chicago *Svornost* remarkable for depth of thought and dignity of expression. He died in penury in Chicago, in 1911.

J. J. Král, for years editor of the socialist daily *Spravedlnost* (Justice) in Chicago, now an employee of the Government in Washington, belongs to the younger set of writers. His most ambitious literary effort is a volume called *Víra a Věda* (Faith and Science), 213 pp. Neither Klácel, nor Zdrůbek, nor Šnajdr can claim authorship to anything equaling Král's *Víra a Věda*. The book is replete with telling arguments and seemingly unanswerable facts. Král's other brochures are, the *Life of Abraham Lincoln*, *Life of Ladimír Klácel*, *American Law* (the author was admitted to the bar), Darwin's *Descent of Man and the Law of Natural Selection*.

John Vránek, a Catholic clergyman in Omaha, published in Chicago a volume of poems, *Na Americké Půdě* (On American Soil), 263 pp. Among

THOMAS ĆAPEK

the Catholic clergy with literary tastes, Vránek ranks high. The life which country priests are constrained to lead, notably those in charge of congregations of foreigners, is sufficiently dreary and monotonous to silence the talent of the most ambitious ones. Father Vránek's lyric muse is too true to be silenced.

John Stephen Brož (1865–1919), a studious and learned Nebraska priest (died at South Omaha) did research work in anthropology. No scholar was better informed on the subject of skeletal remains of the aborigines in Nebraska than Father Brož. On the anthropology of Indians he read papers before scientific societies to which he belonged. He was, besides, an authority on the history of Čech immigration to Nebraska.

V. A. Jung resided in the United States a number of years. He received his journalistic training on Rosický's *Pokrok Západu*, some time in 1882. For a Prague house he translated from Byron and from Russian and Polish poets. He is the author of unabridged English-Čech and Čech-English dictionaries. None of his books were published in America.

E. St. Vráz, a traveler, author and lecturer, who makes his home in Chicago and collaborates on the *Svornost* and the almanac *Amerikán*, has written extensively on travel. He is well posted on conditions in South America, having lived in the tropics for years. All his travel books have been published in Bohemia.

THE ČECHS IN AMERICA

Who did not know or has not heard of Dr. John Habenicht (1840–1917), the author of the *Dějiny Čechův Amerických* (History of the Čechs in America)? Countless are the anecdotes which the professional humorist relates about the amiable doctor: of his innocent stage affectations and mannerisms and of his other notable failing, that is, an aggravated case of *wanderlust*. In his prime an amateur actor of no mean ability, Dr. Habenicht was never happier than when he got a chance to talk over the histrionic triumphs in the past of himself and of his stage cronies. The amateur stage was an obsession with him; a close acquaintance said of him that he knew the heroes and the villains of Shakespeare dramas better than the master minds of medicine and surgery. The *wanderlust* led him to try, in a professional way, Chicago, Detroit, Cleveland, Baltimore, and towns in Texas, Nebraska, Minnesota. Chicago, however, was his favorite stamping-ground and to Chicago he unfailingly returned. It was on his itineraries through the Southwest, he asserts, that he picked up the data on Čech immigration for the *Dějiny*. Faulty and biased, the history is not without merit, particularly as regards the names and biographies of old settlers. The "unbelievers" and the "materialists" the author excoriates with gusto.

Although only thirty-eight years of age, John Havlasa has a whole row of volumes to his credit. Havlasa's predilection for the uncanny and the occult has been pointed out by the critics. During the war he spent a few months in an Austrian detention camp for presuming to criticize the Government. He completed a tour around the world in company with his wife and had planned to lecture in his native country on what he had seen and experienced in America (for several years he resided in California), Tahiti, Japan, and elsewhere, when the war broke out. Apropos, his wife is a granddaughter of John Heřman, a Wisconsin and Nebraska pioneer. Havlasa came to the United States at the time of the St. Louis Exposition (1904) and liked this country so well that he stayed until 1914.

Ladislav Tupý (1872–1918) was an ardent collector of old-time newspapers. From time to time the need of an American Čech museum has been considered; if the project is ever put through Tupý's invaluable collection of journals should be acquired for it. Another of his fancies was to keep a record of the doings (and of misdoings as well) of men and women prominent in the public eye. This record Tupý kept with punctilious attention to details in much the same way as a merchant makes entries of sales and purchases in his ledgers. Tupý had been associated with Bittner on the *Šotek*, and at the time of his death (he died in a train accident near Chicago) was publisher of the *Slavie*.

The war has been the making of the reputations of some men; on the other hand, it has been the undoing of others. Dr. Frank Iška, editor of the defunct *Vesmír* (Universe), is one of the idols whom the war has brushed down ruthlessly from the high pedestal of public favor.

At the outset Iška, like every Čech journalist in the country, was whole-heartedly against Austria and Germany. By degrees, as the war progressed, his paper, the *Vesmír*, was noticed to swerve to the side of the Austrophiles. Readers of the paper were puzzled. Associated with Iška on the *Vesmír* was an obscure journalist, A. C. Melichar, a pre-war arrival, who was strongly suspected of maintaining friendly relations with Austrian officials in Washington and in New York.

Dr. Iška gravely compromised his reputation, not so much by reason of charges made against him on January 26, 1916, by the *Providence Journal*, as that in the *Vesmír* he pursued a policy that was distinctly pro-Austrian. By this Dr. Iška has put himself in a class all by himself. Fifty-odd years of Čech journalism in the United States does not record a single instance of a paper having taken its cue from official Austria. That the obloquy which Dr. Iška brought on his name will react unfavorably on the rationalist movement, of which he was, until the war, one of the strong men, is obvious.

The ghost of Clement Wenzel Nepomuk Lothar, Prince of Metternich, the crafty diplomat and statesman of the Austria of bygone days, must have been rudely shocked when Charles Pergler was

CHARLES PERGLER

appointed Commissioner in the United States of the Čechoslovak Republic. Think of it, the representative in Washington of sixty-six per cent of what was Austria before the war a commoner, an out-and-out Čech, a diplomat schooled, not in the Vienna Terezianum, but in the law office of a town in the Middle West — Cresco, Iowa!

Before the war a Čech stood small chance of getting a consular post and none whatever of a diplomatic appointment in the service of the old Austro-Hungarian Government. The diplomatic and consular service was reserved for German barons, Magyar counts, with now and then a Polish szlachtic. Austro-Hungarian embassies and consulates everywhere were regarded by Čechs as enemy territory. The Austro-Hungarian Consul-General in New York was once asked what he thought of the American Čechs. "Of all the races of the Hapsburg monarchy we like the Čechs best. Why? Because they never come here and they never bother us for favors."

When the Bohemian National Alliance, which was then in its swaddling clothes, began to issue manifestoes to the public at large signed by men representing various factions, certain New Yorkers asked inquiringly, "Who is Pergler?" All that New Yorkers knew about him was that he had written a handbook on American civics, a brief biography of Wendell Phillips, and that he had been on the staff of the Chicago *Spravedlnost*. One day Pergler came to New York to address a meeting of nationals. He spoke on his usual topic, Čech emancipation. After this meeting censorious New Yorkers no longer asked, "Who is Pergler?" He has been heard many times since, and every appearance has strengthened the conviction that as a speaker Pergler has no peer among American Čechs. Palda had the reputation of being a speaker of rare gifts, but Palda was handicapped in that he spoke in his mother tongue only, while Pergler is equally at home in both English and Čech.

Like Palda and other American Čechs who acquired prominence he is a self-made man. He was eight years old when his parents emigrated to the United States. In Chicago he graduated from the public schools. A year or two later his widowed mother returned from Chicago to Bohemia with the family. In Prague Pergler clerked in a store for a while. Even as a youth not yet out of his teens he took a keen interest in public affairs, writing items for party organs, and on occasions delivering fervid speeches at meetings of the younger set of the Social Democratic Party. At twenty-three we find Pergler back in Chicago once more, doing responsible work on the daily *Spravedlnost*. From journalism to law was the next step in his career. He was a country lawyer in Iowa when he was drafted for the work of the Bohemian National Alliance.

The lectures and talks he has delivered before chambers of commerce, economic leagues, bar associations, college clubs, legislative bodies, and before men of affairs generally, contributed in no small degree to a clearer understanding by the thinking American people of the past history and future aspirations of the reborn Čechoslovak State.

In addition to all his absorbing duties he found time to write virile articles for magazines and booklets on Čechoslovak subjects. The *Heart of Europe* and the *Czechoslovak State* are his best publications.

Vojta Beneš, since 1916 general secretary of the Bohemian National Alliance, is by profession a school-teacher. Before the war the Matice Association invited him to the United States, first, to reform the Čech language schools, and secondly, to provide these schools with up-to-date textbooks. As a result of his sojourn here a Prague publishing house printed in 1912, "for the Patrons of the Liberal School in New York," *Česká Čítanka* (Čech Reader, 430 pp.) "for the use of Čech-Slavic Youth in America." Later two more readers were brought out by Beneš. Returning to the United States in the late summer of 1915, Beneš at once joined in the work of political emancipation of his nationals. In 1916 the Bohemian National Alliance appointed him its organizer and general secretary in place of Joseph Tvrzický, who was transferred by the Alliance to the Publicity Bureau. The *Readers* are not Beneš's only books; he has set down his war impressions in several brochures.

As a young man Dr. Jaroslav F. Smetanka, editor

of the *Czechoslovak Review*, thought he wanted to be a minister of the gospel, and so, upon graduation from a gymnasium in Bohemia, he matriculated in the Union Theological Seminary in New York. The seminary course finished, Smetanka began to take more than a layman's interest in Blackstone's Commentaries. The upshot of it was that, instead of putting on the cloth, he entered a college out West and took up the study of the law in earnest, securing in the end a doctor's degree. When the world war started, Smetanka had a well-established law office in Chicago. In the winter of 1917 the Bohemian National Alliance decided to publish a monthly in English. The executive of the Alliance offered the post of editor to Smetanka, who accepted, and closing his law office, he became henceforth a journalist. A man of broad views, Smetanka edits the *Czechoslovak Review* ably and conservatively. Recently the Czechoslovak Government named him Consul in Chicago. Francis Kopecký, Consul General in New York, was the first consular appointee to this country.

Informed opinion is that J. E. S. Vojan, Joseph Tvrzický, Karel Horký, and F. J. Kuták, stand at the head of the journalistic profession.

Jaroslav E. Salaba Vojan, former editor of the Prague *Nová Česká Revue*, is a writer of subtle intellect and of pronounced artistic tastes. In a newspaper polemic he is distinguished by that urbanity and dignity which men like Pastor misinterpreted

DR. J. F. SMETANKA

DR. J. E. S. VOJAN   JOSEPH TVRZICKÝ

as weakness or as fear of an adversary. Vojan's *Česko-Americké Epištoly* (Čech-American Epistles; Chicago, 1911) is an illuminative review of the so-called national life in America, of its bright and dark sides. Though all the deductions in the *Epistles* are not to be unquestioningly accepted, the author's courage and sincerity are worthy of praise. Vojan's articles written in Čech are noted for faultless phrasing and literary finish.

Joseph Tvrzický, of the Czechoslovak Information Bureau in Washington, rendered a peculiarly helpful service in the crystallization of public opinion in the first years of the war. Over his colleagues Tvrzický has the advantage that he knows personally many of the men prominent in literature and politics in Bohemia. In Prague he had been a potential force in the club life of academic youth.

From Karel Horký, who landed in the fall of 1916, the public expected much and not without reason, for the reputation of a capable writer preceded Horký from the other side. *Teď anebo Nikdy* (Now or Never), a brochure on Bohemia's aspirations, made Horký's name a by-word in every household. Soon after his arrival, Horký started a weekly in New York, the *Poděbradka*. This journal might have prospered, if the publisher (Horký) had been half as clever a business man as the editor (Horký) was. On the spur of the moment he rushed out a pamphlet, which on the face of it was a defense of his father-in-law, Dyrich, a disavowed leader of the Čechoslovak troops in Russia; in reality the pamphlet turned out to be a vitriolic attack on the men who were directing in foreign countries Bohemia's propaganda for independence. For good measure the pamphleteer slapped back at American Čechs. Horký's fall, as a result of the pamphlet, was as sudden as had been rapid his rise in public favor. Charles Dickens, it is said, never ceased regretting the authorship of the *American Notes*. The time will come — if it is not already at hand — when impressionist Horký will repent having published his pamphlet, *Dyrich's Nation and Beneš' Public* (52 pp., New York, 1917).

F. J. Kuták is a well-poised newspaperman who has a way of going straight into the essentials of a topic. His articles are relished by readers who appreciate the value of clarity, order, and arrangement. Kuták is editor of the *Orgán Bratrstva, Č.S.P.S.* He conducted the *Rozhledy* (Review), an illustrated weekly which he established in 1905 in Chicago.

If fiction writing assured to authors not wealth, but sufficiency, J. R. Pšenka, editor of the Chicago *Svornost*, and author of *Washington Závora* and other romances from the life of American Čechs, would have in all probability given up journalism for fiction writing. Pšenka served in Africa in the French Foreign Legion and in one of his stories he describes his adventures as a legionary.

Journalists who are looked up to are: Hynek

Dostal, of the St. Louis *Hlas*, conceded to be the ablest of the Catholic laymen; Václav J. Petrželka, of the *Svornost;* Joseph Martínek, of the *Americké Dělnické Listy* in Cleveland; F. Holeček, editor-in-chief, and his associate, A. J. Havránek, of the Chicago *Denní Hlasatel;* Otakar Charvát, of the Omaha *Pokrok Západu;* Stanislav Šerpán, editor of the *Bratrský Věstník* (Fraternal Bulletin); Joseph J. Nový of the *New Yorské Listy* and B. Grégr of the *Hlas Lidu.* The latter two are New Yorkers. There are two veteran journalists in Texas: Joseph Buňata, a free-lance contributor to the liberal press, and L. W. Dongres (Just A. Man). J. J. Kárník of New York, who is interested in Čech language schools, wields a trenchant pen.

A large and steadily increasing group of books comprises literature of the useful kind: Pocket Dictionaries, English Instructors, Interpreters, Readers, Spellers, Almanacs, Memorial Books (published chiefly by fraternal organizations to record their anniversaries), Cook Books, Books of Toasts, Guides in Household Economy, Farmer's Guides, Manuals of Felicitations, Patriotic and Folk Songs, Handbooks of Declamations for Sociables, Handbooks of Speeches and Ceremonials for the use of Clubs and Fraternal Societies, Handbooks of Funeral Addresses for use at non-church burials (by F. B. Zdrůbek, J. Kalda, B. Pavlíková), and so forth.

There are no less than six manuals on American

civics discussing American judicature, immigration, and naturalization laws. They are by Charles Jonáš, J. J. Král, Charles Pergler, Vladimír A. Geringer, J. F. Smetanka, Louis Pacák. The manual by Pacák is the newest and most comprehensive of all.

The output in prose and verse as a rule does not get beyond the newspapers, but there are, of course, a few exceptions. The published collection, in addition to the books enumerated in the foregoing, include: F. J. Škaloud, *Bordinkáři* (Boarders, a bit of romance from the life of Chicago Čechs); J. A. Trojan, *V boji za ideál* (Battling for an Ideal); Otakar Charvát, *Kresby a Povídky* (Portraits and Tales); F. Staňková-Bujárková, *Po stopách české krve* (On the Trail of Čech Descendants, a Civil War narrative); Jiří Mařín, *Pod Mrakem* (Beneath Dark Clouds); Joseph Mach, *Na obou polokoulích* (In Both Hemispheres).

This chapter would be incomplete without mentioning writers of Čech birth or extraction who seek to express themselves in both languages or who write in English only.

Anna V. Čapek: Bibliography.

Thomas Čapek: Bibliography, history, politics.

Thomas Čapek, Jr.: Journalism.

Jaroslav Císař: Politics, translations of poetry.

Anthony M. Dignowity: Memoirs.

F. Francl: Grammar.

Frances Gregor: History, translations of fiction.

Jeffrey D. Hrbek: Poetry.

Šárka B. Hrbkova: Literature.

Aleš Hrdlička: Ethnography, anthropology.

J. R. Jičínský: Sokol body culture.

Charles Jonáš: Dictionaries, grammars.

CLARA VOSTROVSKÝ WINLOW
Author of "Our Little Czechoslovak Cousin"
"The Story of the Slav Races," etc.

JOURNALISM AND LITERATURE

R. J. Kerner: Bibliography.

Otto Kotouč: Translations of poetry.

J. J. Král: Folk-music, biography, translations of fiction, economics, grammars.

Antonie Krejsa: Translations of fiction.

L. Zelenka Lerando: Music.

Beatrice M. Měkota: Translations of fiction.

J. V. Nigrin: Grammars.

Charles Pergler: Politics, history, economics.

Godfrey R. Pisek: Medicine.

Vincent Pisek: Translations of folk-songs.

E. F. Prantner: Politics, economics.

Charles Recht: Translations of poetry, drama.

Rose Rosický: Translations of fiction.

B. Šimek: Politics.

Joseph Šinkmajer: Ecclesiastical history.

Jaroslav F. Smetanka: Politics, journalism.

Anthony M. Soukup: Dictionaries, language manuals.

Edward O. Tabor: Political economy.

Ladislav Urban: Music.

J. E. S. Vojan: Art, music.

Clara V. Winlow: Child study, juvenile fiction, history.

F. B. Zdrůbek: Grammars, dictionaries.

Jaroslav J. Zmrhal: Grammars, civics.

That American Čechs of the younger generation have not, heretofore, taken a more general interest in English Bohemica is both surprising and regrettable. They have shown their mettle in commercial and professional pursuits — why the aloofness from literature? [1]

[1] For a complete list of English Bohemica, see Thomas Čapek and Anna V. Čapek: *Bohemian (Čech) Bibliography.* 256 pp. Illustrated. Fleming H. Revell Company. New York, 1918.

CHAPTER XV

A BRASS band or a symphony orchestra without a Čech is unthinkable. At Fortress Monroe, at Presidio, at West Point, Annapolis, the Brooklyn Navy Yard, in the Philippines, Hawaii, Porto Rico, at Western army posts, where there is a brass band a Čech musician is certain to be around. Joseph Buchar, veteran of the Civil, Indian, and Spanish-American Wars, was bandmaster at the Academy at West Point. William Emanuel Boleška (Bolech) was bandmaster at the Brooklyn Navy Yard. He had served with the Navy since 1874. During the Civil War he was bandmaster of the Sixth Regiment of United States Infantry. Bandmaster Vondráček (Von Drack), from New York, wielded the baton for a quater of a century at various army posts. Hanzi Lochner, also a New Yorker, was bandmaster aboard a man-of-war stationed off Guam. Jaroslav Jícha conducts on the battleship South Carolina; F. Karásek, at the Arsenal in Columbus, Ohio; Jacob Schmidt was, during the war, bandmaster at Camp Cody, New Mexico. V. F. Šafránek, formerly at Fort Snelling, is conductor at Fort Kamehameha, Hawaii. Before that he was attached to a post in the Philippines. M. Torovský leads a band at Annapolis. Major

MUSIC

Vincent F. Faltis, now an American citizen and resident of New York, was a bandmaster in Cairo. He wears a number of British, Egyptian, Bulgarian, and German ribbons. "Kryl and his Band" is an organization of recognized merit in the Middle West. The Mudra and Zámečník bands of Cleveland were in their day unrivalled in Ohio.

If it were possible to enumerate all the musicians who are dependent wholly or partly on income derived from music at dances, funerals, and amateur theatricals, one would get a formidable total. At one time (1903) there were eleven Čechs in the Theodore Thomas Orchestra.

When in 1883 a certain fledgling of the Prague Conservatory of Music was leaving the Čech capital for a concert tour to the United States, John Neruda memorialized the event by one of his inimitable *feuilletons* in the Prague *Národní Listy*, so unusual was the occurrence, so venturesome appeared the project! Who could count all the pupils and graduates of that conservatory now connected with the various musical organizations, or earning their living as teachers?

Instances of musical families are not uncommon. Take the Ondříčeks. The founder of the family renown was Francis Ondříček, violinist, who visited the United States in 1895. He went back, but four of his kinsfolk came here to live. Emanuel has a music school in Boston; Charles, who had been a member of the Kneisel Quartet, is established in

Toronto. One sister, a violinist, is married to Karel Leitner, piano teacher in New York; the other sister, a piano teacher, is the wife of Bedřich Váška, a cellist with the Eastman Quintet in Rochester. Váška is said to have organized the Ševčík Quartet, an organization well known in Europe. The Ondříčeks have inherited their gift from their father, whom old Prague remembers as an inveterate fiddler.

The Ersts, of Chicago, grandfather, father, and son, three generations of musicians, were all graduates of the Prague Conservatory of Music: the grandfather, Stephen Erst, in 1846 as clarionetist; the father, Stephen Erst second, as vocalist in 1883; the son, Stephen Erst third, in 1910 as pianist. Stephen Erst second is choirmaster in a prominent church in his home city.

How many musical families in the United States can equal the record of the Hrubys of Cleveland? Local No. 4, American Federation of Musicians, has enrolled twelve Hrubys as members. Lagging somewhat behind the Hrubys in numbers, yet a force to be reckoned with, is the Zámečník clan of the same city: John Zámečník (honorary), John S. Zámečník, Joseph Zámečník (honorary), Joseph E. Zámečník, Joseph J. Zámečník. The directory of membership of Local No. 4 contains 179 Čech names.[1]

Bohumir Kryl of Chicago, a popular cornetist, has two daughters who are accomplished musicians.

[1] *American Federation of Musicians*, Local No. 4, Cleveland, p. 78.

MUSICIANS

Josy Kryl, a pupil of Ysaye, is a violin virtuoso; Marie Kryl has won recognition as a pianist. Joseph Kryl, Bohumir's brother, plays the French horn with the Chicago Philharmonic Society.

Francis Ondříček and Jan Kubelík lead as violinists. Kubelík's first visit occurred in 1901. One year after that Jaroslav Kocián came. "Before my time," writes J. H. Chapek, violin teacher in Chicago, "no Čech violinist had given concerts in this country except Wenzel Kopta. In 1866 Kopta was soloist with the Theodore Thomas Orchestra and the New York Philharmonic Society. The following year he traveled with Max Strakosch. He married Flora Pauline Wilson of Philadelphia, returning thereupon to his native country. In Prague Kopta and I belonged to the same musical organization and Antonín Dvořák often came to hear us play. If my memory serves me right, Joseph Kašpar of Washington, D.C., toured the country in 1879–80."

Many years ago Kopta removed with his family from Bohemia to southern California and he died in the coast State in 1916. His wife has translated a volume of Čech poems into English.

The largest colony of artists is of course found in New York.

Wenzel A. Raboch, in former years organist in the Trinity Church, is frequently heard at organ recitals, and critics have declared that on the organ, his favorite instrument, Raboch has not many equals.

THE ČECHS IN AMERICA

Joseph J. Kovářík, of the New York Philharmonic Society, was pronounced by Safonov, the Russian conductor, one of the best viola players in the country. An intimate friend of Dvořák, — it was at Spillville, Iowa, Kovářík's birthplace, that the great composer put the finishing touches to the "New World Symphony," — Kovářík is thoroughly familiar with Čech music. In the Prague Conservatory, he made the personal acquaintance of many prominent Čech composers.

There is in the metropolis, Joseph Stransky, conductor of the Philharmonic Society of New York.

Rudolf Friml, pianist and composer, began his career as Kubelík's accompanist. Friml now devotes himself entirely to composition and in his light creations he has met both with professional and financial success. The musical comedies "Firefly," "High Jinks," "I Love You," and others, have attained wide popularity, notably in New York.

Victor Kolář, violinist, who on occasions conducted the Damrosch Symphony Orchestra, aims higher as a composer of music than mere commercial profit. He writes serious music, and those who know this striving young musician predict he will make a mark for himself. His better known compositions are: "Lyric Suite," "Hiawatha," "Indian Scherzo," "Fairy Tale," "Americana," and "Symphony D-dur." Kolář introduced himself to musical America some dozen years ago, when he came over with the "Čech Trio" (Kolář, violin, Reiser,

VÁCLAV KOPTA, violinist

J. J. KOVÁŘÍK, viola

J. H. ČAPEK, violinist

V. A. RABOCH, organist

violoncello, Volavý, piano). The story is that Jan Kubelík "discovered" Kolář in Budapest.

Alois Reiser (Kolář's colleague from Prague), won in 1918 the Elizabeth Coolidge (Berkshire String Quartet) second prize in composition.

John Mokrejs, a piano teacher, has composed a number of piano suites. He is the author of *Lessons in Harmony* and *Lessons in Rhythm*.

Ladislav Urban, composer, wrote the booklet, *Music in Bohemia*.

Ludvik Schwab, teacher and composer, came to New York as Kubelík's accompanist.

Margaret Volavý, pianist, teacher in the Volpe School of Music was schooled in Vienna, while Marie Mikova received her training in Paris.

Emil J. Polak, composer and accompanist, has a clientele largely among the Metropolitan Opera singers.

Ludmila Vojáčková-Wetché, pianist, is a graduate of the Prague Conservatory; so is Joseph Franzl, instructor on the French horn in the Institute of Musical Art, and Anna Fuka-Pangrác, organist.

Last but not least, Otakar Bartík is master of ballet in the Metropolitan Opera.

A composer of unquestioned ability was the late Otakar Nováček, who played first violin with the Boston Symphony Orchestra, later with the New York Symphony Orchestra. He died in New York in 1900.

Music teachers, as may be inferred, are most

numerous in cities populated by their nationals. *The Directory of Bohemian Merchants and Traders* of Chicago contains the cards of twenty-two conservatories and nineteen bandmasters. However, enterprising talents are found everywhere.

Pupils of the Prague Conservatory who have helped to make Čech music better known are: Charles Rychlík, John S. Zámečník, and Edward Krejsa, of Cleveland. All three have studied under Dvořák and all three compose.

Joseph Čadek is master of a conservatory of music in Chattanooga. He gave a violin recital in the White House during McKinley's administration. On this occasion for the first time Čech music was heard in the official residence of the Presidents. Marie Herites-Kohn teaches the violin in the Agricultural and Mechanical College at Stillwater, Oklahoma; August Mölzer is head of a school of music at Lincoln, Nebraska; J. Gerald Mráz, author of *Systematized Intervals*, a work on violin technic, is the founder of the Mráz Violin School in Oklahoma City; Vratislav Mudroch is with the Mudroch School of Music in Nashville. The Málek Music School in Grand Rapids, Michigan, takes its name from Otakar Málek, pianist, formerly assistant conductor of the Berlin Philharmonic Society. Though born in Egypt, Emil Straka has not lost through the accident of his birth the inherited bent of his race for music. Straka's music school is in St. Paul. Before he settled permanently in America,

MUSICIANS

L. Zelenka Lerando was concert harpist to the Duke of Devonshire and later at the court of Detmold, Lippe. He toured America in 1911–15.

A Čech by birth (on his father's side) was Joseph Mischka, for more than half a century a teacher of music in Buffalo. Born in 1826, Mischka settled in that city with his parents in 1853. John Borecký, who knew Mischka personally, counts him as a fellow countryman, spelling his name Myška. He died in Buffalo in 1913.

Born in the same year as Mischka and like him a teacher among the Germans was Hans Balatka. In Milwaukee Balatka achieved wide renown as author, conductor, and musical critic (writing for the *Illinois Staatszeitung*). In former years he was happy to get into touch with his nationals. He did not deny his Čech birth; environment, he declared, had made him a German.[1]

A genius in his own way was John Reindl, who came to New York in 1869, with Slavjansky's Russian Concert Company. In Prague Reindl sang in the Russian Cathedral with the wife of Antonín Dvořák. For a time he was soloist in the Russian Cathedral in San Francisco and while in that city he took up the study of Chinese, and friends claim he was the only Čech who could carry on a conversation in that language. Reindl died in New York in 1906 in poverty.

Singers almost forgotten by the present genera-

[1] The *Pokrok Západu*, April 25, 1899. Balatka's obituary.

tion are Anna Dráždil (Drasdil) and Clementine Kalaš.

Anna Dráždil, contralto, was the pioneer songbird to appear in the United States. Her greatest success is recorded from Philadelphia, where she sang in the Academy of Music, September 20–27, 1876, with Theodore Thomas. To Peter Čapek, a Milwaukee musician, she confided that she was born in Budějovice and that she first visited the United States in 1872, arriving from London. In the early eighties she married a New York merchant after which she retired from the concert stage.[1]

Clementine Kalaš, a contralto and composer "of rare literary attainments and esthetic culture," belonged to Colonel Mapleson's operatic *ensemble*. She died in Brazil while on a concert tour, in June, 1889, sincerely mourned by the literary and artistic set in Prague. Vrchlický wrote a poem in her memory, "E Morta." The Clementine Kalaš foundation, in the Čech Academy of Sciences and Arts, awards prizes for the best compositions.

On "Bohemian Day," August 12, 1893, at the Chicago Columbian Exposition, two masters of music conducted their own compositions; one was Antonín Dvořák, the other Vojtěch I. Hlaváč of Petrograd. Hlaváč returned to Russia, the country of his adoption, where he died a few years ago. To the American musical public Antonín Dvořák,

[1] *The Pokrok Západu*, October 27, 1875.

ANNA DRÁŽDIL

FRANCES R. JANAUSCHEK

composer of the "New World Symphony," requires no introduction. He came to New York in 1892, to take charge of the National Conservatory of Music, founded by Jeannette Thurber, remaining until 1895.

Ernestine Schumann-Heink is not a Čech, though born in Libeň, near Prague; the same is true of the late Gustav Mahler, whose affiliations had been with the Germans of Bohemia, not with the Čechs.

Frances Janauschek (1830–1906) was a Čech, notwithstanding the fact that she had never acted on the Bohemian stage, having played first in German and later, when she mastered English, in that language. The author had many interesting talks with Madame Janauschek in 1899 and corresponded with her. She frankly admitted to him that her people had been of pure Čech stock. But her dramatic training was German, as indeed Prague at the time of her girlhood had the veneer of a German city. Upon one visit, when Madame Janauschek was already gravely ill, she surprised the author by saying the Lord's Prayer (Pater Noster) in fluent Čech, though, as she remarked, she had lived the greater part of half a century outside her native country. In the national tongue the name is spelled Janoušek.

Joseph Šmaha, *régisseur* of the National Theater in Prague, gave a number of readings and dramatic performances (with the support of amateurs) in the larger Čech communities, notably in Chicago, the

year of the Columbian Exposition. The sojourn
of this noted actor was productive of much good;
the amateur enthusiasts (no community, however
diminutive, is without these) had an opportunity
to study at close range Šmaha's histrionic art and,
incidentally, to better their own.

An event of unusual importance was the arrival
in 1893 of Ludvík's Theatrical Company from
Bohemia. Heretofore the burden of producing plays
in the Čech language rested entirely on the shoulders of the much-worked amateur clubs. Ludvík
came over with an *ensemble* of twenty-two men and
women and after he had toured pretty thoroughly
all Čech America, amid the acclaim of people, most
of whom had not seen a play acted in their mother
tongue by professional actors in years, if ever, Ludvík settled in Chicago, where his company has
remained ever since. It is the only Čech dramatic
organization of professionals in the United States.
In 1898 Ludvík took his actors on a trip to Bohemia and if the press agent's accounts can be
trusted, they captured theater-goers with their
répertoire of American plays translated. [1]

In the winter of 1898 there arrived in New York
the Čech Humoristic Troupe consisting of Henry
Kovář, Joseph Wanderer, Rudolph Průša, Engel-
berta Heisler, Rose Breicha. They toured the larger

---

[1] *1893–1903. Memorial of Ludvík's Theatrical Company*, published
on the occasion of the tenth anniversary of a Čech playhouse in
Chicago. Illustrated. 52 pp.

settlements with success. The Čech Singing Quartet (Mikoláš, Černý, Novák, Svojsík) paid a professional visit to their American nationals in 1902.

Two American actresses of Čech descent have been flatteringly noticed by dramatic critics: Blanche Yurka of New York and Adelaide Novak of Chicago. Blanche Yurka's high talent was recognized in "Daybreak," in which play she achieved conspicuous success. There is still another Novak, namely Jane, a well-known photoplay star.

Four or five of the visiting musical artists bear European reputations: Jan Kubelík, violin virtuoso, Emmy Destinn, prima donna of the Metropolitan Opera in New York, Carl Burian, tenor, who will be remembered by the older patrons of the Metropolitan Opera. Newspapers have put down Leo Slezák as a Bohemian tenor, though he professed to be "Internazional."

One season (1915) the roster of the Metropolitan Opera in New York contained the name of Erna Žárská, soprano.

Bogea Oumiroff, baritone, at present living in Paris, visited the United States three times. During the winter season of 1903, Oumiroff, accompanied on the piano by Rudolph Průša of New York, sang Čech and Slovak folk songs in the White House before President Roosevelt. "This appearance in the White House I consider one of the artistic triumphs of my life," declared Oumiroff. Čech folk songs, by the way, were again heard in the White House; this time they were sung by Louise Llewellyn, an American soprano, whose interpretation of them, critics agreed, was exceptionally felicitous.

Rose Matura, a dramatic and operatic artist of the National Theater in Prague, gave a number of recitals here in 1903. Later two Prague singers, W. Florjanský (accompanied on the piano by Francis Veselský) and Bohumil Pták toured the country. Such as they were, their artistic successes were confined to audiences of nationals.

The high position of Čech graphic art is ably sustained in the United States by three names, Preissig, Růžička, Vondrouš.

Rudolph Růžička of New York is credited as being without peer among wood engravers plying the art in America. He is president of the Czechoslovak Arts Club in New York.

J. C. Vondrouš, etcher, also a New Yorker, belongs to the Anglo-American school, a classification of which he may well be proud.

No collection of American war posters can be complete or representative without the colored posters which Vojta Preissig designed for the Bohemian National Alliance. Preissig's posters are animated, masterful. The artist, full of patriotic wrath, is seen inflicting unsparing chastisement on Austria-Hungary, "the embodiment of centuries-old crime against the liberty of mankind." Preissig is professor in the Wentworth Institute in Boston.

Albin Polášek and Joseph Mario Korbel are the

two foremost sculptors of Čech birth in America. Polášek is professor in the Chicago Art Institute. Korbel is a New Yorker with a growing patronage among the wealthy.

Illustrators of Čech birth or extraction are many. A pioneer illustrator is Emanuel V. Nádherný, for more than twenty-five years member of the art staff on the New York *Herald*. Vincent A. Svoboda of New York specializes in poster drawing; some of his genres, however, have been genuinely admired. Harrison Fisher inherited his talent from his Čech father. The elder Fisher, who died in California, was a painter though not as successful as his son.

Joseph Mrázek of New York is the leading representative in the United States of Čech peasant art. Jan Matulka, also a resident of New York, won the Joseph Pulitzer prize in the Academy of Design.

Next to New York Chicago has the largest community of artists. A veteran among these is Marie Koupal-Lusk, painter. She immigrated with her parents in 1867 and studied in New York and Paris. A. Štěrba, painter, and Albin Polášek, sculptor, teach in the Chicago Art Institute. Some of the other painters, designers, illustrators, and sculptors are, Rudolf F. Ingerle, Thomas F. Ouška, Oldřich Farský, August Petrtýl, Rudolf Bohuněk, A. Lukáš, Jarka Košař.

Of the visiting artists Alfons M. Mucha is by far the most widely known. While in America Mucha received a commission from Charles R. Crane, of

Chicago and New York, to paint a cycle of allegories symbolical of the evolution of the Slav. When completed, the canvases are to be presented by Crane to the municipality of Prague.

Bohuslav Kroupa, illustrator, traveler, author, lecturer, knew the Northwest and the American cowboy and Indian as intimately as any native. He illustrated the publication, *From Ocean to Ocean; Sanford Fleming's Expedition through Canada in 1872.* His experiences of travel and of life among the Indians he stored in an English publication, *An Artist's Tour in North and Central America and the Sandwich Islands.* (London, 1890.) The Prague illustrated papers printed many of his sketches.

That America is an object of ever-increasing concern to the people on the other side is apparent from the long list of transatlantic visitors — publicists, artists, business men.

The earliest known guests were the Reverend Heřman z Tardy and the Reverend L. B. Kašpar who came in 1869 in the interest of the Čech Reformed (evangelical) Church. The Reverend Kašpar described the journey in a *Report of Pilgrimage undertaken to America 1869.*

Joseph V. Sládek, one of Bohemia's major poets, a Shakespearean scholar, a translator of Bret Harte, Henry W. Longfellow, Frank Richard Stockton, Thomas Bailey Aldrich, Lord Byron, Robert Burns, S. T. Coleridge, spent a few months in the

CHARLES J. VOPIČKA, OF CHICAGO
United States Minister to Rumania

United States (1869–70), to the enduring profit of his country's literature.

Another stranger was Dr. Joseph Štolba, whose volume, *Beyond the Ocean*, published upon his return in 1873, long retained primacy among books on American travel. Like all Štolba's travelogues, *Beyond the Ocean* is written in a light, rather humorous vein, making no attempt at deeper research.

The Chicago World's Fair (1893) brought hither a number of travelers, two authors of prominence among them: Francis Herites and Joseph Kořenský. The latter-named set out from Chicago, with his friend and traveling companion (Řezníček), on a tour around the world, which he described in two large volumes, *Travels around the World in 1893–94*. Herites's study of American conditions was favorably commended at the time for its fairness and accuracy.

Dr. Emil Holub delivered a series of lectures on his African travel and discoveries before ethnographic and geographic societies in 1894.

An exceptional interest attached to the visit in 1902 of Thomas G. Masaryk, then the leader of the realist party in Bohemia. Five years later Masaryk returned. He spoke on political, national, economic, and philosophic topics. Incidentally Masaryk lectured at the University of Chicago on the "History of a Small Nation."

The Louisiana Purchase Exposition and the Inter-Parliamentary Congress, held in St. Louis

(1904) were attended by engineers, manufacturers, and men of affairs generally. George Stibral, Superintendent of the Art and Industrial School in Prague, jointly with Architect John Kotěra, had charge of the arrangement of the technical part of the Austrian section of the exposition.

President Masaryk is not the only one who knows America from close-at-hand study; three ministers of his first cabinet — Václav J. Klofáč, Minister of National Defense, the late General Milan R. Štefanik, Minister of War, Dr. Francis Soukup, Minister of Justice, have traveled here more or less extensively — while a fourth (Gustav Haberman, Minister of Education) lived in the United States long enough to have been entitled to citizenship. None appeared to be more profoundly impressed with the industrial potentialities of the New World than Dr. Soukup. His volume, *America; a Series of Pictures from American Life*, which he published in 1912, stamps the author as a wide-awake, astute observer, though by no means a flatterer. To Dr. Soukup, who is a social democrat and who sat as deputy in the old Austrian Parliament, was accorded the privilege of speaking before the House of Representatives in Washington.

Gustav Haberman toiled in New York and in Chicago on socialistic newspapers. He made three journeys to America, in 1889, 1892, 1913, as one learns from his volume, *From my Life*, published in 1914.

VISITORS FROM ABROAD

Štefanik traveled across the continent for the first time in 1910 bound for Tahiti for the purpose of making astronomical observations on that island. During the war Štefanik twice revisited America.

The Čech Sokol Union paid to the American Sokols a long-deferred visit in 1909. The "Sokol Excursion to America," as the Sokol annalists call it, was led by Dr. Joseph Scheiner, the president of the organization. At least three of the excursionists set down in print their observations. Dr. Scheiner's book is entitled, *Sokol Excursion to America in 1909.*

At the instance of the Čech Press Bureau in Chicago, Count Lützow in the winter of 1912 delivered lectures in American universities and colleges on the "Bohemian Question." His subjective ideas Count Lützow embodied in a pamphlet, written in German, *Amerikanische Eindrücke.*

Other visitors who wrote their impressions of America were: Čeněk Křička, architect, lately elected to the National Assembly (published his notes in the *Pražská Lidová Revue*, 1905–06), and J. F. Votruba, writer on economical subjects. Dr. George Guth, John Havlasa and F. Sokol Tůma were commissioned by Prague papers to "write up" the Louisiana Purchase Exposition. Havlasa found California, to which he repaired, so congenial that he prolonged his stay for years. The American rationalists asked Dr. Theodore Bartošek (1907) and Charles Pelant (1908), both active in the rationalist movement in Bohemia, to lecture to them.

THE ČECHS IN AMERICA

A delegation of the Prague Chamber of Commerce came in 1912 to repay a visit that had been previously made by the Boston Chamber of Commerce. Not only merchants, but scientists joined the delegation.

Dr. Charles Veleminský made a fruitful study of the American school system in 1912. Dr. Veleminský, who holds a responsible position in the Ministry of Education, purposes introducing in the Czechoslovak Republic many of the school features thought to be distinctively American.

CHAPTER XVI

THE LANGUAGE SCHOOLS: TEACHING OF ČECH

THE Slovanská Lípa Society in Milwaukee opened a Čech language school June 22, 1862.[1] Joseph W. Sýkora, in a letter from Cleveland to the *Slavie*, announces that July 24, 1864, after the saying of the mass, instruction to children would be given in spelling, reading, and arithmetic, in the schoolrooms of the St. Joseph Church.[2]

The first language school in Chicago was organized in the fall of 1864. "Instruction in the mother tongue will be conducted every Saturday from 10 A.M. to 2 P.M.; Sundays from 1 P.M., for adults in the Hall of the Slovanská Lípa."

New York's first school dates from September 24, 1865, and we are told that thirty-nine children were in attendance at the opening.[3]

In 1881 the *Slovan Americký* began agitating the question of founding a Čech College somewhere in the Middle West, in or near some larger settlement. A society for that purpose was incorporated in Johnson County, Iowa, and the *Slovan Americký*, the originator of the idea, undertook to raise a foundation fund. But the *Slavie* — because the idea had not emanated from the editor of that paper, the

---

[1] The *Slavie*, June 18, 1862.
[2] *Ibid.*, July 14, 1864.　　[3] *Ibid.*, May 22, 1867.

241

THE ČECHS IN AMERICA

Slovan Americký charged — while not openly hostile to the scheme, expressed grave doubts concerning its feasibility. "Our opinion is that we can venture into it with a fair hope of success," commented the *Slavie*, "if we raise $20,000 to start with. If American Čechs want the college, they will no doubt subscribe this sum." The $20,000 endowment fund was not subscribed, and the college was not founded.

At the instance of the American (Congregational) Home Missionary Society, Oberlin College organized in 1885 a Theological Seminary in connection with its Slavic Department. Through the Anne Walworth bequest of 1905, Oberlin College came into possession of a fund, the income of which is sufficient to provide for the instruction and maintenance of about ten students.[1] Professor Louis Francis Miškovský is chairman of the faculty committee of the Slavic Department.[2] The Reverend J. Průcha of Cleveland is certain that of all American higher institutions of learning Oberlin College was the first to introduce in its curriculum the study of Čech. "Our mother tongue has been taught in this school for more than five years," he wrote in 1894.[3]

At Lisle (Du Page County, Illinois), the Benedictines have established what the college syllabus describes as the only higher Čech-Slavic educa-

[1] *The Bulletin of Oberlin College*, March 10, 1916, p. 6.

[2] The establishment of the Slavic Department was due to the untiring efforts of the Reverend H. A. Schauffler.

[3] Communication by the Reverend J. Průcha, the *Pokrok Západu*, February 7, 1894.

ST. PROKOP COLLEGE, LISLE, ILLINOIS

tional institution in America. This college was opened in 1887, in Chicago, but was removed in 1901 to Lisle, where a more suitable building had been erected for its needs.[1] The founders dedicated the school to St. Prokop (Procopius), whose name it bears.

Between the language schools, which the liberal element support out of voluntary gifts, and the Catholic parochial schools, there is the essential difference that while the Catholics give full instruction to children, the liberals practically confine their school courses to teaching the Čech language only, sessions being held after public school hours. The liberals, needless to say, are opposed to sectarian instruction, contending that children should not be deprived of the advantages which the public school offers.

All told the number of children receiving instruction in the liberal schools is from 7500 to 8000. Chicago, with its suburbs, maintains nineteen schools, attended by 1340 pupils.[2] The school in New York City is attended by 800 pupils. Cleveland sends 700 children to the language schools.

"In five years we have succeded in getting into our organization 69 schools with 5292 children," says J. J. Kárník.[3]

[1] *Annual Report of St. Procopius College, at Lisle.* 1908–09.
[2] *Directory and Almanac of the Bohemian Population of Chicago,* p. 66. 1915.
[3] *Česká Škola,* v. XVIII, p. 16. Published by the Česká Americká Matice Školská in 1915, in commemoration of the death of a great

THE ČECHS IN AMERICA

The University of California has had a lecturer on Čech (George R. Noyes) since 1901. During the year 1919–20 courses in elementary Čech with exercises in conversation, reading, and composition will be given in Columbia University (A. B. Koukol). For a time B. Prokosch taught it in the University of Wisconsin and L. Z. Lerando in the Ohio State University. Prokosch also lectured on Čech and Russian in the University of Chicago. Coe College in Iowa (Anna Heyberger) and the State University of Texas (Charles Knížek) give courses. The best organized departments teaching not only the fundamentals of the grammar, but the reading of more difficult texts, prose and poetry, with exercises, are found in the Dubuque College and Seminary (Alois Barta), the St. Procopius College (Kosmas Veselý), and Oberlin College (Louis F. Miškovský).

A Čech department was established in the University of Nebraska in 1907. The late Jeffrey D. Hrbek was put in charge. After his death, his sister, Šárka B. Hrbkova, succeeded him, remaining at its head until 1919, when it was abolished.

Between 1913–15 instruction in the language was given in the State University of Iowa (Anna Heyberger).

Čech is taught in one or two high schools in Chi-

Čech, Master John Hus. Edited by J. J. Kárník; Discourses on school subjects and pedagogical manuals of the Čech American School Association (Matice). Last pamphlet is numbered v. XXI; Vojta Beneš: *Contribution to the Reform of the Čech Schools in America*, vs. IV and v. 88 pp. Cleveland, 1914.

ŠÁRKA B. HRBKOVA

cago, in the high schools at Wilber, Prague, Crete, Clarkson, Brainard, Fremont, Verdigre, and Milligan, in Nebraska.

"In addition," writes Dr. R. J. Kerner, of the University of Missouri, "Harvard University (Dr. Leo Wiener), University of Michigan, University of Notre Dame, University of Pennsylvania, University of Wisconsin, gave courses in Slavic languages and literatures usually Russian, in the case of Notre Dame, Polish."[1]

[1] For much of this information the author expresses his gratitude to Dr. Kerner, Dr. Lerando, and Professor Hrbkova. Professor Meader of the University of Michigan wrote in 1913 for the *Russian Review* (published by the University of Liverpool) a short, but good, account of the origin of Slavic work in the United States.

CHAPTER XVII

THE CHURCHES

THE strength of Catholics and of Protestants may be approximated by the number of congregations and pastors which they respectively support.

According to their official organ,[1] the Catholics had, in 1917, 270 priests administering 320 parishes, missions, and branches. Several of these were

[1] The *Katolík*. Čech American Almanac for the year. *Register* of Čech priests in America, pp. 194–97. *Register* of Čech Catholic Settlements in America, pp. 197–207.

Reading: Rev. Anton Peter Houšť: *The Čech Catholic Settlements in America*. St. Louis, 1890. Rev. Joseph Šinkmajer: (e) "The Bohemians in the United States." *The Catholic Encyclopedia*, v. ii, pp. 620–22. Rev. Valentine Kohlbeck: (e) "The Bohemian Element. Short History of the Bohemian Catholic Congregations in Chicago," *The New World*, pp. 136–40. April, 1900. *The First Annual Report*, or a catalogue of the St. Prokop College in Lisle, Illinois, for the year 1901–02. Rev. J. G. Kissner: (e) "The Catholic Church and the Bohemian Immigrants," *The Charities*, Dec., 1904. New York. Rev. Valentine Kohlbeck: (e) "The Catholic Bohemians in the United States." *The Champlain Educator*, January–March, 1906. *The First Čech Catholic Convention*. Held in the St. John Nepomuk Church, in St. Louis, September 24–26, 1907. 54 pp. Rev. Prokop Neužil: *Memorial of the St. Prokop Congregation*. Twenty-five Year Jubilee of the Consecration of St. John Prokop Church, pp. 7–29. Chicago, 1908. Rev. Prokop Neužil: *Twenty-five Years of Endeavor*. Report on the work of Čech Benedictines of the St. Prokop Abbey in Chicago, from the year of their coming to Chicago in 1885 to 1910. 73 pp. Chicago. Dr. John Habenicht: *The History of the Čechs in America*. St. Louis. 1904. Rev. John Rynda: *A Guide through the Čech Catholic Settlements in the Archdiocese of St. Paul* (Minn). 233 pp. Chicago, 1910.

ST. PROKOP CHURCH
Allport and Eighteenth Streets, Chicago

mixed; that is, Čech-German, Čech-Irish, Čech-Polish. The St. Prokop Parish in Chicago is rated the strongest and supposedly the richest in the country.

No State supports a greater number of Catholic centers (churches, missions, stations, either wholly Čech, or mixed, that is, Čech-Irish, Čech-Polish, etc.) than Texas — 68. Wisconsin ranks next with 57 centers. Then follow: Nebraska, 48; Minnesota, 28; Iowa, 21; Kansas, 16; Illinois, 14 (of which 10 congregations are situated in Chicago); South Dakota, 12; North Dakota, 9; Michigan, 7; Missouri, 6; Ohio, 6 (all 6 in Cleveland); New York, 6 (2 in New York City); Oklahoma, 5; Maryland, 4; Massachusetts, 2; Pennsylvania, 2; Indiana, 2; Virginia, 2; and 1 each in New Jersey, Oregon, Colorado, Washington.[1]

The first Catholic house of worship was built in St. Louis, in the autumn of 1854. It was dedicated to St. John Nepomuk. Father Lipovský of Lipovice was the first priest.[2]

Under Father Joseph Hessoun, who took charge of the St. John Nepomuk Chapel about 1865, St. Louis grew to be the center and stronghold of Catholicism. To the present day the older immigrants harbor a peculiar affection for St. Louis even though

---

[1] The *Katolík*, for 1917, pp. 197–206.

[2] The Reverend Henry Lipovský, scion of a noble family, had an active career. He was assigned as a missionary to London, Rugby, and Cardiff; later he served in China as chaplain to British troops stationed there. He died in Prague in 1894, aged sixty-seven years.

the Chicago Benedictines wrested the scepter of leadership from it. In St. Louis Father Hessoun lived and labored for many years. He was the greatest prelate the American Čech Catholics have had.

Considering that in the mother country the Catholics constitute ninety-six per cent of the entire population and the Protestants less than three per cent,[1] the number of Čech-Protestant churches and congregations in the United States might seem to be disproportionately large. If the old country percentage were to hold good the Protestants should have four houses of worship instead of thirty-five which they really possess.

The Protestants, among whom the Presbyterians are very active, notably in the East, maintain 160 centers as follows: Presbyterians, 55 centers; Union of the Bohemian-Moravian Brethren in North America, 30; Baptists, 28; Methodists, 21; Congregationalists, 19; Independent Reformed, 5; Reformed Congregationalists, 2.

Several congregations are mixed; in Pennsylvania they are Čech-Slovak. About one hundred pastors have charge of the spiritual welfare of the evangelical parishioners. The Jan Hus Presbyterian Church in New York, Dr. Vincent Pisek, pastor, with 1057 children attending the Sunday School, leads the list.[2]

[1] According to the official Austrian statistics.
[2] The *Sion*, National Almanac for the year 1917. Schematism of the Čech-Slavic Evangelical Churches in America.
Reading: The Reverends William Šiller, Václav Průcha, and

MONSIGNOR JOSEPH HESSOUN

THE CHURCHES

Trying as the beginnings of the Catholics have been, they cannot be compared with the difficulties which beset the old-time Protestants. When the life story of the Reverend Francis Kún is told the emotions are moved as when reading a chapter from Sienkiewicz's novel *Quo Vadis*, depicting the hardships of the early Christians. Lack of churches and priests were the main drawback of the Catholics. Then, too, the clergy had to contend with religious indifference and in many instances the open hostility of the people. The Protestants of two generations ago had neither houses of worship, nor ministers, nor — religionists. So long was the evangelical faith discriminated against in Austria that at the time the ban against it was removed, by the Patent of Tolerance, there were scarcely any Protestants left in Bohemia and Moravia. There was not one regularly ordained minister in either country to attend to the spiritual needs of the scattered few who survived the anti-Reformation. Pastors (known to the church history as "Tolerance Pastors") had to be literally borrowed from neighboring Hungary to help.

Before the Union Theological Seminary in New York and the Slavic Theological Department in Oberlin College trained the first pastors of Čech

R. M. De Castello: *Memorial of Čech Evangelical Churches in the United States;* containing the description of all Čech congregations of Presbyterians, Independents, Reformed, Congregationalists, Methodists, and Baptists as they existed in 1900. 290 pp. Chicago, 1900. *Souvenir of Slavic Baptists in America.* 34 pp. Chicago, 1909.

nationality, the entire burden of missionary work devolved upon non-Čechs. In New York it was a Magyar, the Reverend Gustave Alexy, who sought out, instructed, and organized Čech Protestants. That was in 1874. The theological training of the first Čech minister in New York, Dr. Vincent Pisek, was not completed until 1883. The Reverend H. A. Schauffler, a member of the noted family of American divines of that name, did apostolary work among the Čechs in Cleveland. Having learned the language, Dr. Schauffler came to be recognized as their leading religious adviser and the champion of their wants before American co-religionists (Congregationalists). The Bethlehem Chapel in Cleveland, dedicated in 1885, was the result of Dr. Schauffler's untiring effort; the Slavic Theological Department in Oberlin College is likewise conceded to have been his idea and his achievement.[1]

Dr. Schauffler figures prominently in the religious revival of Chicago Čechs. At a Conference of the Board of Commissioners for Foreign Missions held in that city in 1883, Dr. Schauffler argued something like this: "What have you done for your 38,000 Čechs? Nothing. Chicago has the largest settlement of Čechs of any city in the land. Their newspapers advocate free thought and there are other reasons why evangelical endeavor should be

[1] (e) *The Slavic Department of Oberlin College.* Under the supervision of the Slavic Committee of Theological Seminary. 21 pp. Oberlin, 1916.

VINCENT PISEK, D.D.

furthered among them." A few weeks after the hold-
ing of this conference, Dr. Schauffler had the satisfaction of reporting to his friends that his appeal
had not been a fruitless one; that the Reverend
E. A. Adams, his colleague in Prague, would give
up his post in the Čech capital and would devote himself wholly to missionary work among
the Chicago Čechs.

Proficient in the Čech language like Dr. Schauffler, Dr. Adams won in time the respect and affection of the Chicago community. Even the liberals
learned to esteem this amiable, tolerant Yankee
churchman. In the autumn of 1884 Dr. Adams delivered his prefatory sermon before a congregation
consisting of some sixteen persons; in 1890 that
same congregation, with the help of American
friends, was able to build the Bethlehem Chapel at
a cost of $35,000.

A few words of tribute should be paid to the
pioneer evangelist, the Reverend Kún, who founded
the mother church at Ely, Iowa. Descended from
a family of preachers,— his grandfather had been
one of the Tolerance Pastors called from Hungary
to Bohemia and Moravia to care for Protestants
there and his father also had been a minister of the
gospel,— Kún's relation to the early Protestants
was precisely the same as that of Father Hessoun's
to the Catholics: he was an admired leader, and an
unselfish friend. Of his stern resolve and his devo-
tion to what he considered his duty to co-religion-

ists, we can form a faint conception when we remember that he often braved a trip of sixty miles through roadless country to visit his people. That was before and during the Civil War. He preached in English, Čech, or German, as circumstances required. To the United States Kún emigrated in 1856. Before coming he was warned that "the prospects for a Čech pastor were not encouraging." Kún was wont to make an annual tour to parishioners in Iowa, Minnesota, Dakota, Kansas. Ten houses of worship were built and as many congregations organized along his customary route. The worthy man died at Ely in 1894 in his sixty-ninth year.

The first evangelical service in Čech was held in Texas. The pastor conducting it was the Reverend Joseph Zvolánek, a colleague in Moravia of the Reverend Kún; the year was 1855 and the place, Fayetteville. However, it is not Fayetteville, but Wesley, in Washington County, which claims precedence as having the oldest evangelical congregation in Texas. The organization of the parish at Wesley dates to 1864. Among the pastors at Wesley is mentioned no less conspicuous a person than F. B. Zdrůbek, who had charge of the parish in 1872.[1]

The Protestants maintain 43 centers in Texas; 23 in Pennsylvania (mostly Slovak); Nebraska, 14; Illinois (Chicago), 12; Ohio (Cleveland), 11; Iowa,

[1] *Memorial of Čech Evangelical Churches in the United States*, p. 130.

JAN HUS CHURCH AND NEIGHBORHOOD HOUSE, NEW YORK

THE CHURCHES

10; Minnesota, 10; Wisconsin, 5; Kansas, 5; New York, 5; South Dakota, 4; Oklahoma, 3; Maryland (Baltimore), 2; Missouri (St. Louis), 2; Virginia, 2; 1 each in New Jersey, Delaware, Michigan, Tennessee.[1]

[1] The *Sion.* National Almanac for 1917, pp. 115–25. As to Baptists: *Souvenir* (book) published to commemorate the first convention of Baptists of Slavic nationality held in Chicago, 1909. Preface by the Reverend V. Králíček.

CHAPTER XVIII
FRATERNAL AND OTHER SOCIETIES

THERE are no dependable figures relative to the number of various Čech fraternal organizations in the United States. All is guesswork in this regard. Generally it is thought that the number of lodges and clubs is not below 2500. The Chicago community is credited with no less than 500. In 1915 the Chicagoans were represented in the Building Association League of Illinois with 227 Building and Loan Associations.[1]

Two distinct classes are recognizable: benevolent or confraternal organizations which pay a benefit in case of sickness or death, and non-benefit associations. Of the non-benefit class the most interesting are the Sokols (gymnastic),[2] the amateur theatrical clubs, and the choral societies. No community of any consequence is without at least one of the three. The Čech loves song and the choral society offers him an opportunity to sing; so long as the profes-

[1] *The Directory and Almanac of the Bohemian Population of Chicago*, p. 44. 1915.

[2] J. R. Jičínský: *The Memorial of the National Union Sokol* (Národní Jednota Sokolská) *in the United States*. In commemoration of its twenty-fifth anniversary. 224 pp. Chicago, 1904; J. R. Jičínský, editor: *Tracing the History of the American Sokols*. 43 pp. Chicago, 1865–1908; Henry Ort: *The First All-Sokol Convention*, held in Chicago, August 26–29, 1909. 132 pp. Chicago, 1909. Josef Scheiner: *The Sokol Excursion to America in 1909*. 108 pp. Prague, 1910; Josef Oswald: *The Excursion of Čech Sokols to America*. 1909. Příbram.

sional stage in America will not grant *entrée* to the dramas and the comedies of his native playwrights, he will have amateurs act on the amateur stage his kings, his heroes, his peasants, his maids. And what Čech youth would not enrol as a Sokol and give ready assent to the truism that only a healthy body can give lodgement to a sound mind?

The parent society, there is no doubt, originated in New York. Havlíček's *Slovan*, of May 7, 1851, contains this direct reference to it: "As an interesting piece of news for our readers we here give a brief extract of a letter of March 3, received by us from a Mr. T. who emigrated five years ago to New York." The writer, Mr. T., proceeds to tell how the Čech residents of New York had organized a club the year before (1850) giving it the name, Čech Society. Nationals who contemplate going to America are advised to write to the club if they desire trustworthy information about the country.

Who was T.? Presumably none other than the army deserter, Tůma, who fled from the garrison at Mainz either in 1847 or 1848, and who opened a saloon (casino) in New York.

From the diary of Vojta Náprstek we learn that the club alluded to by T. bore the name "Čech Society." Václav Pohl was president; Andrew Hubáček, vice-president; F. V. Červený, treasurer; Joseph Čilinský, secretary; Vojta Náprstek, librarian. The Čech Society met in the hotel (saloon) of Colonel Charles Burgthal (erroneously spelled

Burgthaler), 14 City Hall Place. This ramshackle building has been torn down to make room for the present Municipal Building. Colonel Burgthal was no colonel at all, but a non-commissioned officer in the Austrian army. He received his chevrons of colonel, not from the Austrian army command, but from the admiring patrons of his tavern. The fact that his wife was of Čech birth made the colonel's resort homelike to the countrymen of his wife.

Before the end of the year forty-two men had enrolled as members. Vojta Náprstek, at his own request, took charge of the society's library. Apropos, books were Náprstek's hobby; it is said that among the treasured volumes he had brought in his gripsack from Europe were the works of Voltaire, Fourier and Saint-Simon. An insatiable reader and a modernist in the fullest sense of the word, Náprstek was never happier than when he could lend his books to book-lovers.

Of the members of the Čech Society, none rose to greater prominence than Francis Korbel and Vojta Náprstek. By a singular twist of fortune the Government, which in 1848 tried to apprehend Korbel as a revolutionist, appointed him in 1894 Austrian Consul in San Francisco. Having retired from active business long ago, Korbel is living quietly in the Čech capital, from which he was forced to flee in 1848–49.

A picturesque member was Joseph Křikava.

FRATERNAL AND OTHER SOCIETIES

After various unsuccessful ventures — he tried photography and farming — Křikava opened a wine-shop at 50 Avenue B, which became the favorite haunt of the old-timers. "Grandfather Křikava," as his boon companions called him, died in New York in 1888. Václav Pohl claimed to have fought in 1848 behind the barricades in the short-lived revolution in Prague. A radical of the Havlíček type, Pohl converted many a pioneer to his way of thinking. By trade he was a cabinet-maker and a wood-carver, although he tried his luck at many trades.[1]

Andrew Hubáček [2] was related to the well-known family of that name. August Hubáček's saloon in East Fifth Street, New York, was for years the center of Čech social life. Great was the renown of the Hubáček name in New York. One of the Hubáčeks who settled in Rochester is reputed to have planted in that city the Bohemian prune tree.

F. V. Červený was of respected stock. The Červenýs of Králové Hradec, in Bohemia, have been far-famed since 1842 as makers of musical instruments. F. V. Červený, too, was apprenticed to this craft and worked at it in a shop at 16 John Street,

---

[1] Almanac *Amerikán*, 1890. Pohl died in Kewannee, Wisconsin, in 1893.

[2] *Wilson's City Directory of the City of New York for 1850–51* contains the name of Joseph Hubáček, capmaker, 73 First Avenue; the same directory for 1852–53 has Andrew Hubaczek, engraver, 86 East Broadway.

THE ČECHS IN AMERICA

New York City.[1] Like Náprstek, Červený removed early from New York to Milwaukee. There he died at the age of eighty-one.

Accounts vary as to the official name of the Čech Society. On the title-page of a volume which Náprstek donated to the society's library, there is this inscription: To the Čech-Slavic Union in New York (Česko-Slovanské Jednotě v New Yorku věnuje V. N. $18\frac{5}{9}52$).[2] Tůma thinks the title was Čech Society (Česká Společnost). A. Hubáček is certain the full title was the First Čech Slavic Society in America (První Česko-Slovanský Spolek v Americe).[3] Lastly, Anton Kotzian contends it was the Čech Linden Tree (Česká Lípa).

The oldest existing fraternal organization (established in March, 1854, in St. Louis) is the Čech Slavic Benevolent Society, known by its initials, Č.S.P.S. In miniature the history of the Č.S.P.S. is the history of Čech America — rather of the half of it which inclines toward liberal thinking — for the Č.S.P.S. fraternity stands for liberalism. Its potentiality first began to be felt after the eighties.

Before that time the influence it exercised on Čech affairs was unimportant, unless the Č.S.P.S. is to

[1] Doggett & Rode: *New York Directory for 1851-52.*

[2] The initials V. N. are undoubtedly in the handwriting of Vojta Náprstek, though they may be those of Václav Nebeský (1818-82), Klácel's literary friend and associate.

[3] Reminiscences of A. Hubáček (of San Francisco), *Pokrok Západu,* August 1, 1894.

JAN HUS MONUMENT, BOHEMIA, LONG ISLAND

BETHLEHEM CHAPEL, LOOMIS STREET, CHICAGO

be given credit for things done not by itself as an organization, but by its members.

Affiliated with the Č.S.P.S. is the Union of Čech Women (Jednota Českých Dám). The Western Čech Fraternal Union is an offshoot of the Č.S.P.S. Owing to conflict of interests between the East and the West, which the convention, held in St. Paul, Minnesota, in 1896, failed to reconcile, a number of opposition delegates met in a conference in Omaha the year following the St. Paul convention and organized there a wholly independent body, giving it the name Western Čech Fraternal Union. John Rosický, the Omaha editor, led the opposition. Fortunately the secessionists have affirmed their adherence to the ideals of liberalism which have ever been the distinguishing feature of the parent society.

To stand well in the opinion of his American neighbor was (and for that matter still is) the supreme concern of the immigrant. When a newspaper made a slurring remark about his nationality or, what hurt his sensibility still deeper, ignored or underrated him at this or that public function, grumbling was general. On the other hand, all rejoiced and felt proud when the race name, Bohemian, Čech, had been linked to some noteworthy act or when a Čech here or in Europe had been featured in the press.

Societies have been organized and newspapers established with the sole aim of "interpreting to

THE ČECHS IN AMERICA

Americans Čech ideals; of defending the honor of the Čech name in America." The National Union (Národní Jednota), the Čech American National Committee (Česko-Americký Národní Výbor), the National Sentinel (Národní Stráž), the National Council (Národní Rada), the Slavic Alliance (Národní Sdružení), the Čech American Press Bureau (Česko-Americká Tisková Kancelář) were some of the societies dedicated to this object. Every one of them performed some good service, removed some prejudice, added in some way to bringing knowledge of the Čech to Americans.

No society started out with brighter prospects of success than the Čech American National Committee. Backed by the Č.S.P.S., which fathered it (1891), supported by the entire liberal press, it bid fair to become the institution of all Čech factions. According to a programme outlined by L. J. Palda, its president, the Čech American National Committee proposed to open a press bureau in Prague to the end that American newspapers might be supplied with impartial news relative to Bohemia and the Čechs; to publish a monthly magazine in the English language; to publish in English or assist in the publication of the history of Bohemia; to found a library of English language works dealing with Čech and other Slav countries; to gather statistical and other data bearing on Čech immigration to the United States; to foster closer cultural and commercial relations between Bohemia and the United

States; to urge upon Čech immigrants the vital importance of American citizenship and of the knowledge of English, preserving, as far as practicable, the Čech tongue, so that Americans of Čech ancestry might be able to read, in the language of their fathers, the story of the sufferings of the Čech race and through this lesson prize more highly the blessings of liberty enjoyed by them in America. Robert H. Vickers's *History of Bohemia*, the first story of the nation in English, was published. *The Bohemian Voice* was issued as the "organ of the Bohemian National Committee" (with Thomas Čapek as editor). The other tasks the Committee could not realize at all, or only partially. The following Čechs and Slovaks were members of the Committee: L. J. Palda, Charles Jonáš, John Rosický, F. B. Zdrůbek, Bohumil Šimek, Anton Klobasa, J. V. Teibel, J. H. Štěpán, Václav Šnajdr, V. W. Woytišek, J. V. Matějka, Joseph Wirth, I. J. Gallia, Hynek Opic, F. Choura.[1]

The Society for the Promotion of Higher Education (Matice Vyššího Vzdělání), established in 1902, was planned chiefly by two men. Bohumil Šimek was its intellectual organizer. The practical promoter, the man who financed it, was W. F. Severa, manufacturer of proprietary medicines in Cedar Rapids. Severa's substantial endowment gift made the Matice not only realizable, but what

---

[1] *Minutes* of the Second Meeting of the National Commitee, held in Chicago, the 24th, 25th, and 26th November, 1892, 28 pp.

is more essential, he laid an enduring foundation thereto. An auxiliary of the Society for the Promotion of Higher Education is the Federation of Komenský's Educational Clubs. Everywhere in the Middle West where there is a college, and students of Čech birth or extraction attending it, there is apt to be a Komenský Club.

The Čech American Press Bureau (originating in Chicago in 1909) owed its existence to the generosity of Francis Korbel and rendered, aside from its purely reportorial function, meritorious service on two distinct occasions. It invited to America Count Lützow, pioneer in English Bohemica. Lützow delivered a series of talks in colleges, before audiences composed of youth who will mould the public opinion of to-morrow. No man was better qualified than Lützow to lecture on Bohemia before cultured Americans. His renown as an author and his thorough mastery of the language — Lützow was English on his mother's side — gave additional interest to his authoritative presentation of the subject. The Press Bureau coöperated with Burton Holmes in making motion pictures in Bohemia and in giving illustrated lectures in principal American cities.

Following a bad precedent and grouping them into Catholic and non-Catholic, the principal fraternal organizations, which pay full or only nominal sick and death benefits, are:

BIRTHPLACE OF THE Č.S.P.S.

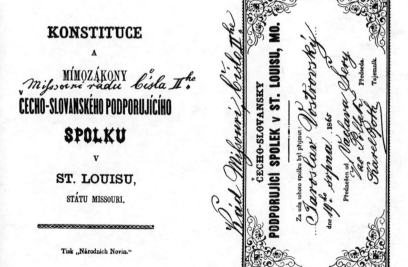

BY-LAWS AND TRAVELING PASS OF THE
Č.S.P.S. BROTHERHOOD, ISSUED IN 1865

FRATERNAL AND OTHER SOCIETIES

CATHOLIC ORGANIZATIONS [1]

Members

Čech Roman Catholic First Central Union in the United States (Česká Římsko-Katolická První Ústřední Jednota ve Sp. St. Amerických).............................. 5,188

Central Union of Women in the United States (Ústřední Jednota Žen ve Sp. St. Amerických)................... 9,580

Catholic Workingman (Katolický Dělník)............... 3,931

Čech Roman Catholic Central Union in Wisconsin (Česká Římsko-Katolická Jednota ve Státu Wisconsin)........ 900

Catholic Union in Texas (Katolická Jednota Texaská)..... 2,186

Western Čech Catholic Union (Západní Česká Katolická Jednota)... 3,703

Čech Roman Catholic Union of Women in Texas (Česká Římsko-Katolická Jednota Žen ve Státu Texas)........ 2.070

Čech Roman Catholic Benevolent Union under the patronage of St. John Nepomuk in Ohio (Česká Římsko-Katolická Podporující Jednota pod záštitou sv. Jana Nepomuckého ve Státu Ohio)............................. 2,200

Čech Roman Catholic Union of Women in Cleveland, Ohio (Česká Římsko-Katolická Jednota Žen v Cleveland, O.)... 1,500

Catholic Union Sokol (Katolická Jednota Sokol)......... 1,650

Total....................................... 32,908

NON-CATHOLIC ORGANIZATIONS [2]

Čech Slavic Benevolent Society (Česko-Slovanský Podporující Spolek, Č.S.P.S.). Official report, February, 1919.... 23,680

Western Čech Fraternal Union (Západní Česko-Bratrská Jednota, Z.Č.B.J.). Official report, November, 1918..... 21,149

Union of Čech Women (Jednota Českých Dám, J.Č.D.). Official report, February, 1918....................... 23,000

[1] For these figures the author is indebted to the Reverend Valentine Kohlbeck, editor of the Chicago *Národ* and *Katolík*. He writes (December 4, 1918): "These figures are official and, therefore, accurate. Quite a number of our people belong to other organizations, such as the Catholic Order of Foresters, Knights of Columbus, etc. These organizations are not Bohemian, although many of the societies (lodges) are entirely composed of Bohemians."

[2] For these figures the author's thanks are due to B. O. Vašků, editor of the *Č.S.B.P.J. Orgán*.

THE ČECHS IN AMERICA

CHAPTER XIX
THE PART THE AMERICAN ČECHS TOOK IN THE WAR OF LIBERATION

AT the time he was taking leave of his compatriots in America, President Masaryk (Farewell Address, November 11, 1918) declared that in the history of liberation the American Čechs and Slovaks are assured honorable mention.

The American Čechs played a double rôle in the drama which ended in the humbling in the dust of the Hapsburgs and the final disruption of the Dual Monarchy. In the first place they financed the external revolutionary movement. They are considered the richest, as they are admittedly the strongest, branch of the race outside the motherland. Secondly, it was expected of them that they would present the cause of the Čechoslovaks before the country and would endeavor to win for it American public opinion.

That it was Masaryk who had the rare insight and foresight to get away from Austria while it was yet time was regarded as a happy augury. On the occasion of his two previous visits Masaryk had made a host of friends here. The liberal and, notably, the intellectual element held him in high esteem. Masaryk is sincere in all his actions, and as Carlyle expresses it, "sincerity, a deep, great, genuine sincerity, is the first characteristic of all men in any way heroic." He enjoyed full confidence of the leaders at home. Vienna feared him, for it found that he was unassailable. Shortly before the war the readers of a Prague journal took a test vote on the question: if Bohemia were a republic, who would be elected its president? Significantly, Masaryk received the majority of the votes.

The external revolution against Austria was set in motion the moment Masaryk reached Swiss soil. For obvious reasons the first few months the propaganda he and his confrères planned had to be carried on in secrecy. Prague was known to swarm with spies and informers and no one must be unnecessarily compromised or sacrificed.

On July 6, 1915, the day of the quincentenary of the burning of Bohemia's national hero and martyr, Hus, Ernest Denis lectured on the essence of Hussitism in the Hall of the Reformation at Geneva, Switzerland. On this day Masaryk, in a few curt sentences which he delivered without any attempt at oratory, laid down the nation's platform: "Every Čech must now elect whether or not he is in favor of reformation or anti-reformation; must now say whether or not he is in favor of the Čech idea or the Austrian idea. Austria is the mouthpiece in Europe of anti-reformation and reaction."

Months before the Hus celebration in Switzerland, where Masaryk first publicly arraigned Austria, the American Čechs were busy at work. In

September, 1914, the New Yorkers formed the American Committee for the Liberation of the Čech People. An organization nation-wide in scope was formed in Chicago as a result of a conference held in that city, January 2–3, 1915. After June 6, 1915, this society was officially designated as the Bohemian National Alliance (České Národní Sdružení). Rapidly the Alliance spread a network of branches throughout the country; by the time the war ended, these branches numbered some 350. Dr. L. J. Fisher, a Chicago physician, now in the service of the Czechoslovak Government in Prague, was elected president, remaining at the head of the Alliance almost until the end of the war. Upon his departure for the front in France, Dr. Joseph F. Pecival assumed presidency. Joseph Tvrzický was chosen executive secretary and manager of the Press Bureau. Since 1916 Vojta Beneš acted as organizer. The important office of treasurer was entrusted to James F. Štěpina, president of the American State Bank. For a time Dr. J. E. S. Vojan functioned as secretary, J. J. Zmrhal and Dr. J. F. Smetanka attending to English language correspondence. When the United States declared war on the Central Powers, the Alliance promptly readjusted its programme to meet the new conditions incident to the war. Heretofore the Alliance had labored for Čechoslovak freedom. From that time on its branches became the sentinels of wholesome, loyal Americanism, efficient agencies for the sale of

Liberty Bonds, rallying points for volunteering and for war activities in general. That the Čechoslovaks bought as many Liberty Bonds as the official figures disclose they did, is due, in a large measure, to the efforts of the Alliance and its branches and to the Slovak League. The women kept an even pace with the men. Their sewing and knitting "Bees" turned out sweaters and comfort kits for the soldiers in France, Italy, and Russia. Many of the societies of the "Bees" became in war-time auxiliaries of the American Red Cross. Libuše S. Motak of New York, prominent in relief work, has been appointed since Representative for the United States of the Czechoslovak Red Cross.

If cannon is the *ultima ratio regum*, the last argument of kings, money is an indispensable weapon of the up-to-date revolutionary. Precisely how large a fund was raised by the American Čechs and Slovaks has not yet been made public; when official figures are available we may be surprised to find that the total runs not into the hundreds of thousands but into millions. The money was gathered by means of self-taxation, donations, bazaars,—not without hard work, scheming, and pinching. Three centuries of subjection, political and economic, have pushed the Čechoslovaks into the employee class; wealthy men are the exception. How to raise millions from workmen was a problem.

Not a dollar was asked for or accepted from any foreign source. Those were Masaryk's orders.

REV. OLDŘICH ZLÁMAL

ČECHS IN WAR OF LIBERATION

"This is our revolution, and we must pay for it with our own money." The first bazaar of consequence was held in New York in the winter of 1916. It yielded $22,250. This was thought an extraordinary achievement. The bazaar given in Cleveland in March, 1917, netted $25,000 and one closely following it in Chicago, $40,000. The comparatively small Omaha community surprised all by making $65,109.20 in September, 1918. A few weeks later the Texas Čechs got together at a bazaar fête in Taylor another $50,000 or $60,000. The bazaar at Cedar Rapids (Iowa) turned in $25,000. The Thanksgiving Day offering in 1918, which was nation-wide, totaled $320,000. To this Chicago gave over $100,000, Cleveland $40,000. All the money was not spent for political purposes. Large sums went to relieve distress on the other side. For instance, one million francs were cabled to the Čechoslovak Minister of Foreign Affairs in Paris for the purchase of food.

In order to reach and stir up the masses it was necessary to hold meetings without number. Meetings are the salt, the ferment of all questions requiring public discussion. Meetings sustain the spirit of the waverer, they dispel the doubts of the pessimist. Press publicity was another, though more subtle, lever of the agitator. Both agencies were employed as needs required or means permitted. Speakers visited every community of fellow countrymen from Canada to Texas. The majority of these speakers were, of course, Americans. Before he accepted service in the Military Intelligence Division of the United States Army, Captain Emanuel V. Voska of New York held in his hands the threads of the propaganda in the East.

Lecturers and propagandists came from Europe, too. F. Kopecký, a plain-spoken artisan from London, brought tidings from the small colony of Čechs there. Personal contact with the Čechoslovaks in Russia was established through Captain Ferdinand Písecký, who reached America in 1917. Under the auspices of the Alliance Captain Písecký toured the principal Čech and Slovak settlements. Four officers, Lieutenants Miloslav Niederle, Antonín Holý, Joseph Horvath, and Oldřich Spaniel, arrived in the winter of 1917–18. Although they came from France — rather from the Čechoslovak Army in France — all four were war veterans from Russia. The object of their journey was military; they were after recruits for war service in France. Soldiers who came here on missions connected with the war, military, political, and diplomatic were: General Milan R. Štefanik, Colonel Vladimír Hurban, Captains Zdenko Fierlinger, Jaromír Špaček, and V. Houska, Major John Šípek, Lieutenants F. Danielovský and Charles Zmrhal.

It is not known that many a Teuton plot to foment strikes, to set warehouses and docks on fire, to blow up munition-carrying ships was bared and many an evil-doer apprehended and sent to prison on evidence furnished to the Government by loyal Čechoslovaks. To run down the malefactors and checkmate their nefarious activity, Čechoslovak agents were scattered throughout the industrial centers in the East, to warn the Slavic workmen not to strike unless they wanted to do the bidding of the Kaiser and his paid agents.

Newspapers and magazines were established in foreign lands. At home the press was muzzled; the censor would not permit it to speak out the nation's will, the nation's hope. Since Prague was forced to keep mute, exiles living in Russia, France, Switzerland, England, and the United States, must speak. And they did speak. The Čechoslovak prisoners of war started a paper in Russia, which they called the *Čechoslovák*. It printed articles in Čech, Slovak, and Russian. Professor Ernest Denis, of the Sorbonne, brought out in Paris, May, 1915, *La Nation Tchèque*. A few months later appeared the *Československá Samostatnost* (Čechoslovak Independence), also in the French capital. *The New Europe*, with Masaryk among its collaborators, came out in London, October, 1916. The Alliance started publishing the *Bohemian Review* in Chicago in February, 1917; since November, 1918, it has appeared under the corrected title, *Czechoslovak Review*. Leaflets, pamphlets, and books printed in French, English, Russian, Italian, and Čech were turned out unstintingly and sent to college libraries, clubs, to men of affairs, men influential in politics and literature. Suffice it to give the titles of some of these books and leaflets: *Bohemia under Hapsburg Misrule* (Čapek); *Bohemian Question, Heart of Europe* (Pergler); *Voice of an Oppressed People, Problem of Small Nations* (Masaryk); *Future of Bohemia* (Seton-Watson); *Bohemia: her Story and her Claims* (Marchant); *Case of Bohemia, Czechoslovaks, an Oppressed Nationality* (Namier); *Bohemia* (Beneš and Zmrhal); *Bohemia's Claim for Freedom* (Procházka); *Bohemia's Case for Independence* (E. Beneš); *Czechoslovaks, a new Belligerent Nation* (Hazen); *Austrian Terrorism in Bohemia,* etc. The Slav Press Bureau was opened in New York; this formed the nucleus out of which grew the Czechoslovak Information Bureau now existing in Washington. Unobtrusive work was done outside the organization, too. For instance, the author of this volume made it a practice to send, during the war, propagandist letters to men prominent in public life in the United States and England.

The alarming news cabled to America of the massacres of rebellious soldiers, of executions of civilians, of trials for treason (Dr. Charles Kramář, the first Premier, and Dr. Alois Rašín, the first Minister of Finance were sentenced to death; President Masaryk's daughter, Dr. Alice G. Masaryk, was thrown into prison), of confiscations by the Government of properties of those found guilty of treason or desertion, or espionage, or opposing the armed power of the State, nerved the workers, if anything, to greater effort. More indignation meetings, more appeals for protection to the State Department, more pamphlets, more intensive agitation, more cables to agents and couriers in Europe.[1]

Then there was the minor detail work. Artistic stamps and post-cards were put into circulation, buttons and badges and diplomas were sold for the benefit of the campaign fund. Vojtěch Preissig, of the Wentworth Institute in Boston, designed masterful war posters. Most of such interesting trifles as badges, buttons, post-cards, came from the workshops of the members of the Čechoslovak Arts Club of New York. This Club decorated in an artistic manner the show windows of prominent business houses on Fifth Avenue with Čechoslovak colors, views and portraits, maps, posters, and printed matter. A most valuable exhibit from an educational point of view proved to be a huge port-

[1] Some of the news items cabled here were, fortunately, mere inventions of the war reporter. The St. Petersburg correspondent of the *New York Herald*, cabled on August 20, 1914, the particulars of a revolutionary outbreak in Prague which never took place: "The Kieff correspondent of the *Novoe Vremya* sends details of an uprising in Bohemia, when Czech Polish troops shot down their German officers, shouting, 'Down with William! Down with Austria! Long live Russia!' Prague for a whole day was in the hands of the mutineers. The next day the Austrians, who had been reinforced, reëntered the city and took fearful reprisals. Every Čech caught in the street was killed. The river Moldavia, it is declared, ran red with Čech blood. The finest monuments in the city were destroyed and shops were pillaged. A new uprising occurred two days later, followed by fresh reprisals. Among the victims was Dr. Kramarzh, M. Klofatch, a professor Masaryk, who was executed in the citadel. A similar fate is believed to have overtaken the Russian consul, Mr. Zhukovsky."

able map of Central Europe. This map showed the racial boundaries of the reborn state and marked the strategic positions of the Čechoslovak troops astride the Trans-Siberian railroad in Russia. The map was placed in front of the Public Library on Fifth Avenue and Forty-second Street. Thousands of New Yorkers passing by daily were compelled to take notice of the map. Who are the Čechoslovaks? Are they a faction of the Bolsheviks? Are they related to the Bohemians? What connection, if any, is there between the Bohemians living on the upper east side of New York and the Bohemians in Greenwich Village? Many a grown-up New Yorker learned his primer in Čechoslovak history by studying the map. From New York the map traveled to inland cities, to repeat there the errand of education it performed so admirably on Fifth Avenue.

At first it was confidently expected that the liberation of the race from thralldom would come from the east. The Russians were blood-brothers; they freed the Serbs and the Bulgarians, and they would redeem the Čechoslovaks next. Hence the propagandists concentrated their efforts on Russia. The Russian front collapsing, however, owing to Bolshevik betrayal, the center of activity was shifted to Paris. Two trusted lieutenants of Masaryk took charge of matters in the French capital, Dr. Edward Beneš (first Minister of Foreign Affairs) and the late General Milan R. Štefanik (first Minister of War).

ČECHOSLOVAK WAR POSTERS

Designed by Vojta Preissig, Wentworth Institute, Boston

An important conference was held in Cleveland in October, 1915, between the leaders of the Alliance and the Slovak League. Complete accord was reached and the two race groups, Čechs and Slovaks, agreed to work hand in hand, in pursuance of one aim under one supreme leadership.

February 5, 1917, a meeting was arranged in Chicago between the Catholic Party and the representatives of the Alliance. The Catholics expressed themselves as willing to share in the work of the Alliance and the Slovak League, but, standing fast on the ground of belief, how could they collaborate with the other side which held to unbelief? The Reverend Oldřich Zlámal, a priest from Cleveland, took a dissenting viewpoint. "The Čech of Catholic faith," he pleaded in the *Farník* (The Parishioner), "without in any way jeopardizing his religion and church interests, has no good reason why he should sympathize with the present-day Austria." One version, said to be the true one, of why the Catholic Party wavered so long was, that the Right Reverend Joseph M. Koudelka of Wisconsin, a Bishop of Čech nationality, in the first months of the war appended his signature to a public declaration, which sought to exculpate Austria and Germany for bringing on the war. Whatever the motive of the abstention, the Reverend Father Zlámal and other brave and patriotic priests prevailed in the end and the Catholic Party joined the Alliance. Thus at last all the factions, the liberals, the socialists,

275

and the Catholics, were fraternally united and pledged to work for the liberation of the Fatherland.

Masaryk reached the Pacific Coast on his way from Russia, in April, 1918. His arrival lent new zest to the drive which the propagandists were making to win American public opinion. Impressive receptions were given in his honor, in Chicago, New York, Baltimore, Cleveland; speeches were delivered before packed audiences in Carnegie Hall and elsewhere; interviews to newspapermen were granted. The publicity campaign took a sharp curve upward. Slowly but surely, Čechs and Slovaks were worming themselves into the headlines of the American press.

Meantime Austrian statesmen still pretended to believe that there was no such thing as a Bohemian or a Čechoslovak question; if there was, that it was one of internal Austro-Hungarian politics with which the Governments of Vienna and Budapest would concern themselves when the proper time came. But the principle of self-determination of nations — that government must rest upon the consent of the governed — was by this time rapidly gaining converts in America. The statesmen of Austria and Hungary knew that the principle of self-determination would mark the doom of the Hapsburg Empire.

June 30, 1918, President Poincaré of France journeyed to the war zone to make a formal presen-

VLADIMÍR A. GERINGER
United States Trade Commissioner to the Čechoslovak Republic
Publisher of the Chicago "Svornost"

tation of the Čechoslovak flag to the soldiers of that nationality. On that occasion M. Pichon, the Foreign Secretary, speaking for the government of the Republic, "deemed it equitable and necessary to proclaim the rights of the Czechoslovak nation to independence."

Recognition by the British Government is dated August 13, 1918. "In consideration of their efforts to achieve independence, Great Britain regards the Czechoslovaks as an allied nation and . . . recognizes the right of the Czechoslovak National Council as the supreme organ of Czechoslovak national interests and as the present trustee of the future Czechoslovak government. . . ."

September 2, 1918, the United States Government through Secretary Lansing declared that "the Government of the United States recognizes that a state of belligerency exists between the Czechoslovaks thus organized (that is, prosecuting their purposes for independence) and the German and Austro-Hungarian Empires. . . . It also recognizes the Czechoslovaks."

The Declaration of Independence, severing forever the ties binding Czechoslovakia to Austria-Hungary, bears date October 18, 1918, in Paris, and is signed by Thomas G. Masaryk, Prime Minister and Minister of Finance; Milan R. Štefanik, Minister of National Defense; and Edward Beneš, Minister of Foreign Affairs and of the Interior.

November 2, 1918, delegates representing all

political parties met in Geneva, Switzerland, and after adopting the draft of a constitution for the Čechoslovak Republic, patterned after that of the United States, elected unanimously as its first President, Thomas Garrigue Masaryk.

A full and impartial account of the Liberation Movement has not yet been written. The events are too recent and the persons concerned too close to enable the historian to form a critical estimate of the degree of credit due.

THE END

APPENDIX

APPENDIX[1]

THE theme of Čech emigration to the United States has been considered from every conceivable viewpoint, not only by American Čechs, but by visitors from the mother country as well. The conclusion of writers from overseas not unfrequently discloses a lack of preparation, if not an utter non-comprehension of American realities; moreover, much of the Americana printed abroad is light reading, calculated not so much to inform as to amuse the reader.

Dr. Joseph Štolba: *In North America*. 181 pp. Prague. 1876.

The earliest visitor from abroad, however, was not Dr. Štolba, but two Protestant ministers, Ludvík B. Kašpar and Heřman z Tardy. The first-named, Kašpar, prepared for his superiors a summary of the journey in *A Report of a Pilgrimage to America in the Summer of 1869*.

Ladimír Klácel, in the initial numbers of the *Hlas Jednoty Svobodomyslných* (no. 1 is dated February 19, 1872), collected data on pioneer immigration.

Joseph V. Sládek, poet and Shakespearean scholar, wrote for the Prague *Osvěta* and *Lumír* of his American experiences. "On a Čech Farm in Texas," by Sládek, appeared in *Lumír* in 1884. Sládek was among the first to translate the American Constitution into Čech.

For the information of the emigrant, Joseph Pastor published in Hamburg, in 1884, a monthly journal, *Čech Settlements in America*.

John Palacký, son of the historian Francis Palacký, compiled the *United States of America*. 142 pp. Prague. 1884. Palacký's work deals wholly with statistics; Charles Jonáš assisted this author, who knew America by hearsay only, never having visited here.

John Wagner: *The Čech Settlers in North America*. 63 pp. Prague. 1887. Unreliable and gossipy.

Thomas Čapek: *Monuments of Čech Immigration to America*. First ed. 1889; second ed., revised, 112 pp. Omaha. 1907.

Anton Peter Houšť: *The Čech Catholic Settlements in America*. St. Louis. 1890.

---

[1] All the sources quoted or referred to in the text or in the footnotes are in the Čech language except those marked (e) English and (g) German.

APPENDIX

R. W. Turner: (e) "Emigration from Bohemia," U.S. Consular Reports. 1890.

Charles Jonáš: (e) "Bohemian and Hungarian Emigration to the United States," U.S. Consular Reports. 1890.

Joseph Čermák: *The History of America*, after Benson J. Lossing and other sources; contains the lives and experiences of Čech soldiers who fought in the Civil War. Chicago. 1910.

Thomas Čapek: (e) "The Bohemians in America," *The Chautauquan*, October, 1891.

Joseph Kořenský: *Journey around the World in 1893–94*. Refers to New York Čechs in v. I, pp. 43–50. Prague.

John Wagner: *Transoceanic Gossip.* 155 pp. Prague. 1898. The same comment is pertinent to this book as to the author's other work.

Reverends William Šiller, Václav Průcha, and R. M. de Castello: *Memorial of the Čech Evangelical Churches in the United States.* 290 pp. Chicago. 1900.

Dr. Vladimír Novák: *Journeying through the United States of America.* 51 pp. Prague. 1900.

Josephine Humpal-Zeman: (e) *Bohemian Settlements in America.* Industrial Commission Reports, 1901.

J. Buzek: (g) "Das Auswanderungs-problem und die Regelung des Auswanderungswesen in Oesterreich," *Zeitschrift für Volkswirtschaft, Socialpolitik und Verwaltung*, v. 10. Wien. 1901.

J. J. Vlach: (e)"Our Bohemian Population," Proceedings of the State Historical Society of Wisconsin, pp. 159–62. Madison. 1902.

E. A. Steiner: (e) "Character of the Bohemians in the United States," *Outlook*, April 25, 1903.

Dr. George Guth: *My Vacation in America. Feuilletons and Causeries from a Trip to the St. Louis Exposition.* 137 pp. Prague. 1904.

Josephine Humpal-Zeman: (e) "Bohemia: a Stir of its Social Conscience," *The Commons*, July, 1904.

Václav Švarc: (e) "The Culture which the Slav offers America," *The Charities*, July 1, 1905.

Francis Saller: *America.* 47 pp. Prague. 1905. This travelogue by Saller reads like a tale from the Thousand and One Nights fabulous stories.

Dr. John Auerhan: "The Čechs in America," *Pokroková Revue.* Prague, v. 7, no. 16, April, 1906, pp. 420–28; no. 17, pp. 481–86. Dr. Auerhan is another commentator, who knows America by hearsay only.

John Rosický: *America as it is.* Omaha.

APPENDIX

E. G. Balch: (e) "The Story of a Bohemian Pioneer," *The Chautauquan*, February, 1906.

E. A. Steiner: (e) *On the Trail of the Immigrant*. New York. 1906.

Marie Ziegler: *Artist's Impressions*. 68 pp. Prague. 1907. "A Press Agent's Impressions" would have been a more appropriate caption for this pamphlet abounding in magniloquent phrases of a journey through America.

J. F. Votruba: "Americanization and American Čechs," *Pražská Lidová Revue*, v. IV. Prague. 1908.

E. G. Balch: (e) "The Peasant Background of our Slavic Fellow Citizens," *The Charities*, August 6, 1910.

John Habenicht: *History of the Čechs in America*. 773 pp. St. Louis. 1910.

E. G. Balch: (e) *Our Slavic Fellow Citizens*. 536 pp. New York. 1910.

R. H. Schauffler: (e) "The Bohemian," *Outlook*, March, 1911.

Thomas Čapek: *Fifty Years of Čech Letters* (Journalism and Literature) in America. From January 1, 1860, when the first Čech language newspaper was published in America, to January 1, 1910. With supplements to the beginning of 1911. 280 pp. New York. 1911.

"Emigration to America," *The Moravská Orlice*. Brno, Moravia, January 16, 1911.

Anton Pimper: "The Čech Americans and their Cultural Problem," *The Samostatnost*. Prague, July 20, 1911.

J. E. S. Vojan: *Čech American Epistles*. 192 pp. Chicago. 1911.

Dr. Francis Drtina: *Cultural Relations of American Čechs with their Motherland*. A speech delivered in the presence of American Čechs in the Měšťanská Beseda, Prague, July 4, 1912.

Dr. Francis Drtina: "The American Čechs," *The České Slovo*. Prague, March 1, 1912.

Dr. Frank Soukup: *America;* a series of pictures from American life. 363 pp. Prague. 1912.

Directory of Čechs in the United States. 104 pp. Compiled by E. St. Vráz with the collaboration, as to Chicago statistics, of J. Kramer Tvrzický.

Dr. John Auerhan, John Hejret, and A. Svojsík: *The Čech Emigration*. Reprint from *Osvěta*. Prague. 1912.

Dr. Emanuel Grégr: "A Discussion of Economic Subjects with American Čechs," in the Měšťanská Beseda, Prague. Reported in the Prague *Herold*, June 30, 1912.

Count Francis Lützow: (g) *American Impressions*, gleaned on a lecture tour on Bohemia, given in several institutions of learning. Prague. 1912.

APPENDIX

Francis Herites: *American and Other Sketches from my Journeys.* 252 pp. Prague. 1913.

Dr. Anton Boháč: Random chapters from Slavic statistics. "The Emigration of Slavs to America," *The Slovanský Přehled*, v. 15. 433 pp. Prague. 1913.

E. A. Steiner: (e) "Among the Bohemians," *From Alien to Citizen*, pp. 169–76. New York. 1914.

Šárka B. Hrbkova: (e) *The Bohemians in Nebraska.* Nebraska State Historical Society. 48 pp. Lincoln. 1914.

Gustav Haberman: *From my Life.* 299 pp. Prague. 1914.

Anton Pimper: *Emigration Problem.* 80 pp. Prague.

Dr. Navrátil: *Čech Physicians in America.* 25 pp. Prague. 1914.

Francis J. Swehla: (e) "The Bohemians in Central Kansas," Kansas Historical Society Collections, pp. 469–512. Topeka. 1915.

B. S(h)imek: (e) *The Bohemians in Johnson County.* Iowa. 10 pp.

Archibald McClure: (e) "Leadership of the New America, Racial and Religious," *Bohemians*, pp. 47–60. New York. 1916.

Karel Pelant: *The Real America*, v. 1. 135 pp. Moravská Ostrava, Moravia. 1919.

INDEX

INDEX

Adams, E. A., 251
Albieri, Paul, viii, 44, 206
Alexy, Gustave, 250
Americanization of children, 102; of names, 115
Anarchism, 143; revolutionary propaganda, 145; no creative thinkers, 146
Auerhan, John, 282, 283

Babka, John J., 90
Balatka, Hans, 39, 229
Balch, Emily G., v, 283
Bárta, Alois, 244
Bartošek, Theodore, 239
Bém, Franta, 79, 106, 107
Beneš, Edward, 140, 272, 274, 277
Beneš, Vojta, 119, 215, 244, 267, 272
Bílek, Thomas V., 8, 13
Bittner, Bartoš, viii, 133, 176, 181, 202, 204, 205, 211
Boháč, Anton, 284
Bohemia, conditions in, about 1848, 53
Bohemia Manor in Maryland, 11
Bohemian Voice, 261
Bohuněk, Rudolf, 235
Bolton, Robert, 12
Borecký, John, viii, 36, 38, 54, 79, 80, 121, 188, 189, 190, 229
Brož, John Stephen, 47, 209
Building and loan associations in Cleveland, 75; in Chicago, 76
Bujárková, F. S., 220
Buňata, Joseph, 138, 139, 219

Burian, Carl, 233
Business men; Jews carriers of Slavic names, 76
Buzek, J., 27, 282

Čapek, Anna V., 220, 221
Čapek, Catherine M., 90
Čapek, John V., 41, 85, 133, 182; talented humorist, 200
Čapek (Chapek), Joseph H., 225
Čapek, Norbert F., 64
Čapek, Peter, 230
Čapek, Thomas, vi, xi, 48, 171, 186, 187, 220, 221, 261, 272, 281, 282, 283
Čapek, Thomas, Jr., 220
Castello, R. M. de, 282
Catholics build first church, 247; St. Louis center, 247; St. Prokop's parish, 247; early trials, 249; societies, 263
Čechs, idealists, self-reliant, literate, xi
Čech-American National Committee, 260
Čech Colony (Česká Osada), 170
Čech Press Bureau, 239
Čech Humoristic Quartet, 232
Čech Singing Quartet, 233
Čech Society, 255, 256, 258
Čermák, Joseph, 157, 158, 159, 202, 203, 282
Červený, F. V., 255, 257
Charvát, Otakar, 161, 219, 220
Children are American, 102
Chládek, Adolph, 87
Choral Societies, 254
Chotek, Hugo, 42, 43

INDEX

INDEX

INDEX

INDEX

INDEX

INDEX

293

INDEX